ENGAGING WRITING

Paragraphs and Essays

Mary Fitzpatrick

College of Marin

longman.com

ENGAGING WRITING: Paragraphs and Essays

Pearson Education, 10 Bank Street, White Plains, NY 10606

Executive editor: Laura Le Dréan
Production supervisor: Christine Edmonds
Senior production editor: Kathleen Silloway
Senior manufacturing buyer: Dave Dickey
Photo research: Dana Klinek
Cover design: Pat Wosczyk
Cover image: Marjory Dressler Photo Graphics
Text design: Lisa Ghiozzi
Text composition: Laserwords
Text font: Minion 11.5/14; Univers 10/13
Text art: Burmar Technical Corp.
Text credits: see page xxi
Photo credits: see page xxii

Library of Congress Cataloging-in-Publication Data

Fitzpatrick, Mary
   Engaging writing : paragraphs and essays / by Mary Fitzpatrick.
      p. cm.
  ISBN 0-13-140889-5
  1.   English language—Paragraphs—Problems, exercises, etc. 2.
English language—Rhetoric—Problems, exercises, etc. 3.   Report
writing—Problems, exercises, etc. I. Title.
PE1439.F57 2005
808'.042--dc22

                          2004030305

ISBN: 0-13-140889-5

LONGMAN ON THE **WEB**

Longman.com offers online resources for teachers and students. Access our Companion Websites, our online catalog, and our local offices around the world.

Visit us at **longman.com**.

Printed in the United States of America
6 7 8 9 10–VHG–10 09 08 07

CONTENTS

Chapter 9   From School to Work: Writing an Argumentative Essay   231

Appendices

To the Instructor

Engaging Writing: Paragraphs and Essays came out of the need to have a textbook that would

- engage students with topics that interest them and practical exercises that improve their writing
- provide realistic models for students to use as benchmarks to judge their own work
- support students' writing process by modeling prewriting and teaching revision
- provide students with the analytical skills they need for academic success.

Engaging Writing meets these goals and in so doing provides a robust course of study for the high-intermediate to advanced writer. The primary audience is the academically oriented second language learner. However, the chapter themes and principles of academic writing presented are universal in scope, making *Engaging Writing* an effective text in any setting where academic English composition is taught. Key features include

- *Flexibility*. Instructors may select those chapters in the book that best suit their students' needs. Teachers whose students have limited writing experience may start with Chapter 1 (the descriptive paragraph) or 2 (the narrative paragraph), while those whose students have some background might begin with Chapter 3 (the expository paragraph) or 4 (the logical division paragraph and essay).
- *Thematic chapters*. From the initial prereading activities to the final exercises, each chapter develops a theme. All models and exercises in the chapter, including vocabulary exercises, are linked to the general context. In this way, students learn words, gather information, and develop ideas they can use in their assignment as they work through the chapter.
- *Rhetorical presentation*. Each chapter focuses on one mode (description, narration, example, logical division, cause and effect, comparison/contrast, classification, definition, or argument). The chapters introduce patterns of organization appropriate to each mode. As students proceed through the chapters, they gain confidence in their abilities to analyze and structure material.
- *Scope of the rhetorical instruction*. Students learn aspects of writing that are not usually included in books at this level, such as how to combine rhetorical modes, how to make their writing cohesive, how to qualify opinions and general statements, and how to use—and not use—repetition. Students who complete this text will be well prepared for more advanced writing classes.

- *Instruction linked to revision.* In the Composition Focus and Language Focus sections of every chapter, students learn the principles of rhetoric and sentence skills, and at the same time learn how to revise. As a result, students write better final drafts, have knowledge they can apply to future writing assignments, and understand that revision is an essential part of the writing process.

- *Communicative activities built into the text.* Exercises and activities give students opportunities to communicate about writing, to write together, and to share their writing, all of which enhance their sense that they that they are part of a community of writers. When students understand that they have an audience for their ideas, they are motivated to write.

- *Useful appendices.* The appendices provide a convenient supplement to the chapters. Appendix IA offers a review of grammar and Appendix IB a review of mechanics. The exercises in these appendices focus on editing and thus complement those in the chapters, which teach productive writing skills. Appendix IC contains an introduction to MLA and APA citation styles and summarizing and complements the lessons on paraphrasing in Chapters 7 and 8. Appendix II contains Peer Review forms for students to use as they complete their compositions and conclude each chapter.

The Teacher's Manual has suggestions for using the text, the answer key for the Student Book, and supplemental exercises with answer key. In addition, it contains thematic topics for freewriting, which students may do as they work through a chapter.

Engaging Writing fully integrates instruction with the students' writing process. Each part of a chapter is designed to meet the students' needs at a specific stage as they prewrite, draft, revise, and complete an assignment.

READING FOR WRITING

READING FOR WRITING

Before You Read

With a partner or a small group, read the following paragraph and discuss the questions that follow.

Culture is a broad term. It includes all the customs, values, and beliefs of a group of people. *Ethnic identity* is an even broader term. It is the sense of connection a person feels to a particular group and can be based on shared customs, race, language, religion, or homeland.

1. Are children usually aware of their culture or ethnic identity?

2. How do children learn about their culture or ethnic identity?

3. What gives children either positive or negative feelings about their culture or ethnic identity?

To Be an American, Black, Catholic, and Creole
by Alfred J. Guillaume, Jr.

1 I am a 50-year old American. I am black, Roman Catholic, and Creole. This is how I describe myself 50 years in the making. As a young boy growing up in the South, I was made to believe that I was different. Images of America did not mirror me. The segregated° South wanted me to believe that I was inferior. The Catholic Church taught me that all of God's people were equal. My French Creole heritage gave me a special bond to Native Americans°, to Europeans, and to Africans. This is the composite portrait of who I am. I like who I am and can imagine being no other.

2 I'm an American. I was born in New Orleans, Louisiana, whose elegance and exoticism° make it America's most European city and also its most Caribbean. Natives call it the Big Easy. From its founding, New Orleans has been a place that represents good times—the enjoyment of music, food, and celebration.

3 I'm an African American. Just within my lifetime, people of African ancestry have been called colored, Negro, black, and various derogatory° terms that I completely reject. I am proud to have been born black. My people paid a heavy price through toil and suffering to make America. Their unparalleled° creative contributions shaped American culture.

segregated: divided according to race

Native Americans: the original inhabitants of the Americas, Indians

exoticism: foreignness

derogatory: insulting

unparalleled: unequaled

Before You Read This informal exercise or activity opens each chapter, giving cues about ideas and issues that run through the reading.

Reading Students encounter a variety of texts and topics. Each opening reading introduces students to the general theme and the rhetorical focus of the chapter.

Understanding the Reading The follow-up discussion questions not only promote students' deeper involvement with the content and issues of the reading but also require them to use a full range of critical-thinking skills and to take note of the strategies professional writers use.

Vocabulary Expansion Students learn and practice selected vocabulary related to the chapter theme. As they proceed through the text, they learn about broad features of the lexicon, such as word families, and specific features, such as participial adjectives and compound nouns. Short exercises encourage dictionary usage and serve as a warm-up to the chapter writing assignment.

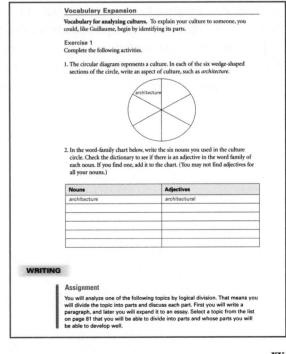

Vocabulary Expansion

Vocabulary for analyzing cultures. To explain your culture to someone, you could, like Guillaume, begin by identifying its parts.

Exercise 1
Complete the following activities.

1. The circular diagram represents a culture. In each of the six wedge-shaped sections of the circle, write an aspect of culture, such as *architecture*.

architecture

2. In the word-family chart below, write the six nouns you used in the culture circle. Check the dictionary to see if there is an adjective in the word family of each noun. If you find one, add it to the chart. (You may not find adjectives for all your nouns.)

Nouns	Adjectives
architecture	architectural

WRITING

Assignment
You will analyze one of the following topics by logical division. That means you will divide the topic into parts and discuss each part. First you will write a paragraph, and later you will expand it to an essay. Select a topic from the list on page 81 that you will be able to divide into parts and whose parts you will be able to develop well.

WRITING

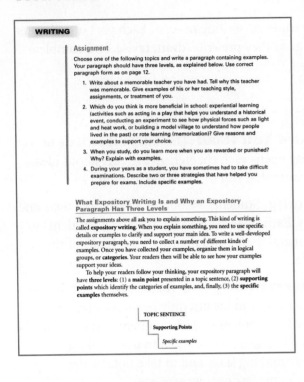

Assignment Students choose one of several topics related to the chapter theme. While all the topics in a chapter require the use of a single rhetorical mode, they vary enough to accommodate multiple interests and ability levels.

Prewriting The Prewriting section provides techniques and tips to help students come up with and organize their ideas and material. In each chapter, a "case study" shows students how to prepare, step-by-step, to write a first draft. Over the course of the chapters, students acquire a substantial tool kit of prewriting strategies. They also learn that even though writing assignments vary, every task requires brainstorming, focusing, and organizing.

STEP **1** | Draft a **topic sentence**.

Dion drafted this topic sentence.

On Fiji Day we have a wonderful time in Sula at public events, in casual matches on the volleyball courts and soccer fields, and at home.

STEP **2** | Develop each part of your topic by making a **brainstorming list** for it. If you have two parts, make two lists; if you have three parts, make three lists, and so on.

Dion decided to divide Fiji Day celebrations according to place. Because he had three locations to discuss, he made three lists.

At Public Events
government officials' speeches
singing competition between church choirs

On the Volleyball Courts and Soccer Fields
young people gather and form casual teams
after they play, they sit on the grass and chat
winners tease the losers, but there is no serious competition

At Home
relatives help prepare the meal which includes palusami, a mixture of chicken or beef, onion, and tomato wrapped in a taro leaf and cooked in coconut milk
the head of the household makes yaqona, our traditional drink, and offers it to the guests in coconut shell cups

STEP **3** | Make an **outline**. Your outline must have three levels: **topic sentence, supporting points**, and **development**.

Dion marked his topic sentence (*TS*), his supporting points (*SP*), and finally his development (*DEV*).

On Fiji Day we have a wonderful time in Sula at the public events, on the volleyball courts and soccer fields, and at home. (TS)

I. The public events give a feeling of national pride and provide some fine traditional Fijian entertainment. (SP)
  A. Public speeches are delivered by elected officials. (DEV)
  B. Awards are presented for the young people's essay contest. (DEV)
  C. There is a singing competition between church choirs. (DEV)

II. Soccer and volleyball games give us a chance to meet and play together with friends. (SP)
  A. Winners tease the losers, but there is no serious competition. (DEV)
  B. Players stay to chat after the game. (DEV)

REVISING

First Draft

Now you are ready to write the first draft of your paragraph. Following your outline, begin with your topic sentence, add supporting points and development, and finish with a concluding sentence. After writing, put your draft away for a while before you return to it. In the Revising section of this chapter, you will expand your paragraph into a simple essay.

REVISING

Composition Focus

Before you expand your paragraph to an essay, check it to [make sure it] communicates effectively. Follow the directions in the follo[wing Review and] Revise box.

Review and Revise 1: First-Draft Paragraph
Review your paragraph. Ask yourself if it has the three [parts a] paragraph should have: a clear topic sentence that pres[ents the main] idea, supporting points, and development. Review you[r topic] sentence to see whether it informs the reader that you [are going to] divide your topic into parts. If your topic sentence or y[our paragraph] needs improvement, revise it now.

Expanding a paragraph to an essay. We read paragraphs a[nd essays differently.] We read a paragraph of ten or twelve sentences and kee[p the main idea in mind.] However, when paragraphs become longer than that, we fi[nd it hard to focus] on the whole paragraph at once.

Therefore, when you have too much supporting inform[ation in one paragraph,] you need to break it down into smaller paragraphs. In orde[r to change your] paragraph composition to an essay, you will change your co[mposition in the] following ways:

1. **Topic Sentence ⟶ Thesis Statement**

   The topic sentence of your paragraph will become th[e thesis statement of] your essay.

2. **Supporting Points ⟶ Body Paragraphs**

   The supporting points will become the topic senten[ces of your body] paragraphs.

---

sandwich and a soda, while a newcomer would select a traditional meal of rice, vegetables, and bean curd.

As Shanghai's population has grown, it has become apparent that there are two social groups in the city. The residents of Shanghai identify themselves as either long-term residents or as newcomers by the way they speak, dress, and eat.

To the writer: _____
_____
_____
_____

Review and Revise 6: Development of Body Paragraphs
If your body paragraphs lack examples or explanation, add some now. Try to use various types of development (examples as well as explanations, which include the meaning of words, reasons, processes, or description) in your essay.

Language Focus

Adjective clauses. An adjective clause is a dependent clause that modifies a noun. Adjective clauses begin with the relative pronouns *who, whom, which, that, whose, where,* and *when.* Adjective clauses provide a way to combine short sentences and show relationships between ideas. Look at the following examples.

1a. King Sejong ruled Korea during a time of peace and prosperity. He was responsible for the invention of the Korean alphabet.

<small>RELATIVE PRONOUN</small>
1b. King Sejong, *who ruled Korea during a time of peace and prosperity,* was responsible for the invention of the Korean alphabet.

2a. The Korean alphabet has fourteen consonants and ten vowels. It is relatively easy to learn.

<small>RELATIVE PRONOUN</small>
2b. The Korean alphabet, *which has fourteen consonants and ten vowels,* is relatively easy to learn.

For more on adjective clauses, see Appendix IA, page 261.

In the examples above, notice that the relative pronouns *who* and *which* follow the nouns that they modify. In example 1b, *who* refers to *King Sejong,* and in example 2b, *which* refers to *Korean alphabet.*

Composition Focus
This section teaches the structural and stylistic aspects of the chapter mode.

Language Focus
Here students learn sentence skills appropriate to their level and to the chapter mode.

PEER REVIEW AND FINAL DRAFT

Students exchange papers with their classmates and fill out the assignment's Peer Review form, which is located in Appendix II. This activity not only reviews the main teaching points of the chapter but also reminds students that they are writing for an audience. After receiving feedback from their peers, students make final changes and proofread before handing their papers in to their instructors.

PEER REVIEW FORM
Chapter 4—*Culture, Identity, and Homeland*   **Simple Division Essay**

Writer: _____   Reader: _____

Read a classmate's essay and answer each of these questions.

1. What is the writer's thesis? Write it here. _____

   Does the thesis statement make clear that the writer will analyze the topic by logical division? ☐ Yes ☐ No

   Does the thesis reveal the basis of division (time, place, aspects, etc.)? ☐ Yes ☐ No

   What is the basis of division? _____

2. Do the thesis statement and the topic sentences of the body paragraphs clearly name the parts of the topic? ☐ Yes ☐ No

   If not, explain. _____

3. Does the essay have cohesion? ☐ Yes ☐ No

   If so, what repeated words, synonyms, or transition words did the writer use to link the thesis statement to the topic sentences of the body paragraphs? _____

4. Do any of the body paragraphs need more development (examples or explanation)? ☐ Yes ☐ No

   If yes, which one(s)? _____

   If you have any questions that will help the writer expand the body paragraphs, write them here.
   _____
   _____
   _____

5. Did the writer use adjective clauses to include additional information in the sentences? ☐ Yes ☐ No

   If not, can you suggest which sentence(s) the writer could add an adjective clause to? Write the first three words of that sentence or those sentences. _____
   _____

About the Author

Mary Fitzpatrick teaches composition at the College of Marin in California. She has also taught with the San Francisco Community College District and the Academy of Art College in San Francisco. Her specialty is teaching writing to English Language Learners.

Reviewers

Pearson Longman is grateful to the following individuals who reviewed the manuscript:

Carolyn Baughan-Roper, Illinois State University, Normal, IL; **Leslie Biaggi**, Miami-Dade College, Miami, FL; **Joyce Cain**, University of California–Irvine, Irvine, CA; **Sharon Cavusgil**, Georgia State University, Atlantia, GA; **Evelina Dimitrova-Galaczi**, American Language Program and Teachers College, Columbia University, New York, NY; **Anthony Halderman**, Cuesta College, San Luis Obispo, CA; **Janet Harclerode**, Santa Monica College, Santa Monica, CA; **Melanie Holland**, Mt. Hood Community College, Gresham, OR; **Steve Horowitz**, Central Washington University, Ellensburg, WA; **Greg Jewell**, Drexel University, Philadelphia, PA; **Gwendolyn Kane**, Rutgers University, Piscataway, NJ; **Vivian Leskes**, Holyoke Community College, Holyoke, MA; **Thomas Leverett**, Southern Illinois University, Carbondale, IL; **Craig Machado**, Norwalk Community College, Norwalk, CT; **Judy Marasco**, Santa Monica College, Santa Monica, CA; **Molly McGrath**, Hunter College, New York, NY; **Jennifer Murphy**, Georgia State University, Atlanta, GA; **Myo Kyaw Myint**, Mission College, Santa Clara, CA; **David Ross**, Houston Community College, Houston, TX; **Alice Savage**, North Harris Community College, Houston, TX; **Mille Stoff**, Miami-Dade Community College, Miami, FL; **Steven Storla**, Houston Community College, Houston, TX; **Elizabeth Wiegandt**, Miami-Dade Community College, Kendall Campus, Miami, FL.

CREDITS

Text Credits

Pages 4–6: Approximately 450 words (pp. 145–147) from *The Diary of a Young Girl: The Definitive Edition* by Anne Frank, edited by Otto H. Frank and Mirjam Pressler, translated by Susan Massotty (Viking, 1997), copyright © The Anne Frank Fonds, Basle, Switzerland, 1991. English translation copyright © Doubleday, a division of Bantam Doubleday Dell Publishing Group Inc, 1995.

Pages 26–29: Excerpt from *Annie John* by Jamaica Kincaid. Copyright © 1985 by Jamaica Kincaid. Reprinted in United States by permission of Farrar, Straus and Giroux, LLC.

Extract from *Annie John* by Jamaica Kincaid published by Vintage. Used internationally by permission of the Random House Group Limited.

Pages 48–52: Adapted from David G. Myers, "Memory," *Psychology* (New York, Worth, 2000), 317.

Pages 76–79: Adapted from Alfred J. Guillaume, Jr., "To Be an American, Black, Catholic, and Creole," *Among US: Essays on Identity, Belonging, and Intercultural Competence*. Myron W. Lustig and Jolene Koester, eds. (New York: Longman, 2000).

Pages 103–105: Adapted from Bruce Clark and John Wallace, "Economic Disparity in the World," *Global Connections: Canadian and World Issues* (Ontario: Pearson, 2002), 200–206. Reprinted with permission by Pearson Education Canada Inc.

Pages 136–139: Adapted from Sumiko Iwao, "The New Lifestyles of Japanese Women," delivered in Lima, Peru, September 1996. The Japanese Ministry of Foreign Affairs, http://www.mofa.go.jp/j_info/japan/opinion/iwao.html

Pages 167–170: Adapted from David I. Levine, with Paul S. Adler and Barbara Goldoftas, "NUMMI: A Case Study," in *Reinventing the Workplace: How Business and Employees Can Both Win* (Washington, D.C.: The Brookings Institution, 1995).

Pages 201–203: Adapted with permission from *Exploratorium Magazine*, Spring 1983, 7:1 © Exploratorium, www.exploratorium.edu

Pages 232–234: "The Sorcery of Apprenticeship." Updated and adapted from Wilfried Prewo, "The Sorcery of Apprenticeship," editorial, *The Wall Street Journal*, 17 February 1993: 10.

Pages 235–236: Adapted from Damien Jackson, "McDonald's or IBM?" San Francisco, The Independent Press Association (2002), *Rethinking Schools*, Winter 2002/2003, 26 July 2004. http://www.rethinkingschools.org/

Pages 326–327: "The Rainforest in Your Cup." Adapted from Curtis Runyan, "The Rainforest in Your Cup," *World Resources Institute*, January 2004. http://pubs.wri.org/pubs_content_text.cfm?ContentID=2368

Pages 329–330: "The Ecological Capital of Brazil." Daniel B. Botkin and Edward A. Keller, "The Ecological Capital of Brazil," in *Environmental Science: Earth as a Living Planet*. Copyright © John Wiley & Sons, 2003. Reprinted with permission of John Wiley & Sons, Inc.

Pages 330–331: "The Death of the World's Coral Reefs." Adapted from Joshua Reichert, "The Death of the World's Coral Reefs," editorial, *The San Francisco Chronicle*, 20 July 2001: A25.

Photo Credits

Page 3, © Jeffrey Coolidge/Corbis; **page 5,** AP/Wide World Photos; **page 25,** © Kevin Schafer/Corbis; **page 47,** © Pete Saloutos/Corbis; **page 75,** © Bob Daemmrich/The Image Works; **page 101,** © Kevin R. Morris/Corbis; **page 135,** Larry Dale Gordon/The Image Bank/Getty Images; **page 166,** Holly Harris/Taxi/Getty Images; **page 168,** © Touhig Sion/Corbis Sygma; **page 199:** (top left) Nancy R. Cohen/Photodisc Green/Getty Images, (bottom right) Antonio M. Rosario/Photographer's Choice/Getty Images, (top right) Christian Hoehn/Stone/Getty Images, (bottom left) © Peter Guttman/Corbis; **page 231,** © Comstock Images.

ACKNOWLEDGMENTS

I would like to express my sincere thanks to all the people at Pearson/Longman who helped make this book possible. First and foremost, I am very grateful to Laura LeDréan, Executive Editor, whose invaluable insight and expertise guided this project from its beginning to publication. I would also like to thank Senior Production Editor Kathleen Silloway and Development Editor Molly Sackler for their expert contributions, Dana Klinek and Julia Carmona for photo research, and Laura McCormick and Shana McGuire for help with permissions.

I want to thank Ann Hogue for the suggestion that I try to write a book and for generously offering her time and expertise to help me get started. I also owe a great debt of gratitude to Carmel Underwood of the Higher Colleges of Technology at the Abu Dhabi Women's College for her many thoughtful suggestions and for piloting the manuscript in her classes, and I want to thank Linda Gilette of City College of San Francisco for piloting and critiquing the early chapters. I also owe a great deal to all the reviewers whose professional criticism I relied upon in the development of the manuscript. Finally, I want to express my appreciation to my fellow teachers and to all my students over the years, whose motivation and creativity always inspire me.

—MARY FITZPATRICK

Welcome! You are about to begin a new writing course. As you use this book, you will read about new topics, explore ideas, and do a lot of writing. Your writing will improve as you proceed step by step toward writing for academic success. Let's get started by talking about what the title of this book means. Look at the dictionary definition of the verb *engage*.

> **en·gage** /ɪnˈgeɪdʒ/ *v* to attract and keep someone's attention

With a partner or a small group, discuss the following questions.

1. When you talk to people, how do you engage them?

   _____
   _____
   _____
   _____

2. When you write a composition, how do you engage readers?

   _____
   _____
   _____
   _____

When you talk to people, you can smile, make eye contact, ask them if they understand, and watch their faces for signs of interest. When you write, however, you don't have as many ways to be sure that you are engaging your readers. As a writer, you have to think about the people who will read what you have written. You have to guess what they need to know. You need to be clear and organized so they can follow you. You need to explain things to them and give them examples so that they can experience the things you have seen and heard.

Now look at the dictionary definition of *engage* followed by the preposition *in*.

> **engage in** *v* to take part or become involved in an activity

As you use the chapters of this book, you will engage in reading, discussion, thinking, writing, revising, and editing. Learning to write well takes a lot of effort and engagement. To begin, look at the writing assignment below.

Assignment

As you proceed through the chapters of *Engaging Writing* and write your compositions, your teacher and classmates will be your audience. That is, they will be the readers of the papers you write. Write a letter introducing yourself to your teacher and classmates. Tell them about yourself—where you are from originally, where the members of your family are, what your interests are, why you are studying writing, what goals you have for the future, and anything else you can think of that will help them get to know who you are.

CHAPTER 1

Possessions

◆ Writing a Descriptive Paragraph

We sometimes keep our possessions for many years because they are our link to the past. They can remind us of events and people from our lives that have helped shape who we are today.

This chapter will help you

- use prewriting techniques to prepare to write a descriptive paragraph.
- write and develop a topic sentence.
- support the topic sentence with sensory details and specific words.
- use adjectives and noun modifiers to make details more specific.
- use coordinating conjunctions to connect ideas.

READING FOR WRITING

Before You Read

With a partner or a small group, discuss the following questions.

1. A diary is a personal record of a writer's life experience and is usually private. Why do people keep diaries? How is diary writing different from the writing you do for school? Have you ever kept a diary? If so, would you want it published? Explain why or why not.

2. The selection you are about to read is from the diary of a fourteen-year-old girl. The girl and her family, who were Jewish, had decided to hide in a secret apartment in a warehouse building, which they called the "Annex," to avoid being sent to a concentration camp during World War II. Imagine yourself as a fourteen-year-old moving into a secret hiding place, never going outside, remaining only with the members of your family and one other family for an indefinite period of time. Would this be difficult for you? What are three ways that you would find it a hardship?

From *The Diary of a Young Girl*

by Anne Frank

Thursday, 11 November, 1943

Dearest Kitty,

1   I have a good title for this chapter:

Ode° to My Fountain Pen
In Memoriam°

ode: a long, formal poem

in memoriam: in memory of

nib: point

My fountain pen was always one of my most priceless possessions; I value it highly, especially because it had a thick nib°, and I can only write neatly with thick nibs. It has led a long and interesting fountain-pen life, which I will summarize below.

2   When I was nine, my fountain pen (packed in cotton) arrived as a "sample of no commercial value" all the way from Aachen°, where my grandmother (the kindly donor) used to live. I lay in bed with the flu, while the February winds howled° around the apartment house. This splendid° fountain pen came in a red leather case, and I showed it to my girlfriends the first chance I got. Me, Anne Frank, the proud owner of a fountain pen.

Aachen: a city in Germany

howl: to cry like a wolf

splendid: wonderful

3 When I was ten, I was allowed to take the pen to school, and to my surprise, the teacher even let me write with it. When I was eleven, however, my treasure had to be tucked away again, because my sixth-grade teacher allowed us to use only school pens and inkpots. When I was twelve, I started at the Jewish Lyceum° and my fountain pen was given a new case in honor of the occasion. Not only did it have room for a pencil, it also had a zipper, which was much more impressive. When I was thirteen, the fountain pen went with me to the Annex°, and together we've raced through countless diaries and compositions. I'd turned fourteen, and my fountain pen was enjoying the last year of its life with me when . . .

The building where Anne Frank hid with her family and wrote her diary.

4 It was just after five on Friday afternoon. I came out of my room and was about to sit down at the table to write when I was roughly pushed to one side to make room for Margot and Father, who wanted to practice their Latin. The fountain pen remained unused on the table, while its owner, sighing, was forced to make do° with a very tiny corner of the table, where she began rubbing beans. That's how we remove mold° from the beans and restore them to their original state. At a quarter to six I swept the floor, dumped the dirt into a newspaper, along with the rotten beans, and tossed it into the stove. A giant flame shot up, and I thought it was wonderful that the stove, which had been gasping its last breath, had made such a miraculous° recovery.

5 All was quiet again. The Latin students had left, and I sat down at the table again to pick up where I'd left off. But no matter where I looked, my fountain pen was nowhere in sight. I took another look. Margot looked, Mother looked, Father looked, Dussel° looked. But it had vanished.

6 "Maybe it fell in the stove, along with the beans," Margot suggested.

7 "No, it couldn't have!" I replied.

8 But that evening, when my fountain pen still hadn't turned up, we all assumed it had been burned, especially because as celluloid° is highly inflammable°. Our darkest fears were confirmed the next day when Father

---

lyceum: school specializing in the classics

annex: an addition to a building

make do: (informal) manage

mold: a fuzzy growth on food that is not fresh

miraculous: amazing

Dussel: one of the people who shared the Annex with the Frank family

celluloid: a type of plastic

inflammable: (same as *flammable*) burnable

conjecture: to guess, to draw a conclusion
consolation: comfort
cremate: to burn a body after death

went to empty the stove and discovered the clip, used to fasten it to a pocket, among the ashes. Not a trace of the gold nib was left. "It must have melted into stone," Father conjectured°.

9 I am left with one consolation°, small though it may be: my fountain pen was cremated°, just as I would like to be some day!

Yours, Anne

concentration camp: prison where people are held during war
typhus: a serious disease carried by certain insects

About the Author

Anne Frank received a diary as a gift for her thirteenth birthday in 1942 and wrote her thoughts and experiences in it for two years. The diary tells about Anne's life before and after going into hiding. When Anne and her family were discovered and taken to concentration camps°, Anne's diary was left behind. Anne died of typhus° in a camp in 1945, but her diary was later found and published. In the diary Anne had written, "I want this diary itself to be my friend, and I shall call my friend Kitty."

Understanding the Reading

With a partner or a small group, discuss the following questions.

1. What happened to Anne Frank's fountain pen? Why did Anne write about her pen in her diary?

2. Anne protected her fountain pen by keeping it in a small container. How does she describe the two different cases that held her pen?

3. Underline the words and phrases Anne used to describe her pen. Can you imagine how it must have looked and felt in the hand? Do you wish she had included more description? Write two or three questions asking for additional information about the pen.

4. What did you think when you read the title and the last line of this diary entry?

5. *Drawing Conclusions.* We often look back on the events in our lives to determine why things happened. For example, when Anne could not find her pen, she **concluded** that she had accidentally put it in the stove. When her father could not find the gold nib among the ashes, he concluded, "It must have melted into stone." As readers and writers, we also draw conclusions. By paying attention to **details** (small pieces of information) in what we read, we are able to draw conclusions about authors and their cultures or lifestyles.

   a. While reading this selection, did you draw any conclusions about Anne Frank as a person? What kind of young woman was she? Look at the following list of details from the story and draw your own conclusions.

Conclusions about Anne Frank as a Person	
Details	**Conclusions**
1. Anne's favorite possession was a fountain pen.	1. She probably liked to write.
2. Anne took good care of her pen and used it for many years.	2.
3. Anne said that she could only write neatly with a thick nib.	3.
4. Anne wanted to be alone at the table to write; she said her father and sister "roughly" pushed her to one side when they came to the table to study Latin.	4.

b. People don't always draw the same conclusions. Compare your conclusions with a partner's. Are they different?

c. While reading Anne Frank's diary entry, did you draw any conclusions about her culture or her family's lifestyle? Complete the chart.

Conclusions about Anne Frank's Culture or Lifestyle	
Details	**Conclusions**
1. One teacher "even let" Anne write with her fountain pen; another teacher allowed the students to use only school pens and inkpots.	1. Her teachers were probably strict.
2. Anne's parents sent their children to a school where the classics were taught and her father studied Latin with Anne's sister.	2.
3. Living in hiding, the family had to eat moldy beans. To make the beans palatable, Anne had to spend time rubbing the mold off.	3.

d. Think about the conclusions you have drawn about Anne Frank as a person and about her culture or lifestyle. Then discuss the following question: Why did she consider her fountain pen to be "one of [her] most priceless possessions"?

As you explore writing topics in this book, you will reflect on your own life experiences and draw conclusions about them. Some of the conclusions you draw will become the topics of your compositions.

Vocabulary Expansion

Dictionary use and word families. As you write, you will discover that you need to expand your vocabulary. When you consult your dictionary, you will find that it can give you the meaning not just of one word but also of related groups of words, or word families. Look at the two word families below.

price (noun)   an amount of money that must be paid in order to buy something

priceless (adjective)   so valuable that you cannot give a price

pricey (adjective)   an informal way to say *expensive*

value (noun)   the amount of money that something is worth; the amount of meaning or importance a person attaches to something

valuable (adjective)   worth a lot of money

Sometimes there are important differences between similar words. For example, there are times when it is appropriate to talk about the *price* of a possession (*I bought this T-shirt for the low price of $10.00*) and other times when it is appropriate to talk about its personal *value* (*This T-shirt is of great value to me because I bought it on my trip to Paris*).

Exercise 1

A. Use your dictionary to complete the word-family chart. When you see a gray space, you do not need to find a word to fit there.

	Nouns	Verbs	Adjectives
1.	*possession*	possess	
2.			treasured
3.		inherit	inherited
4.			cherished
5.	importance		
6.			impressive
7.		signify	
8.	meaning		
9.	value		

For more on nouns, verbs, and adjectives, see Appendix IA, pages 267, 290, and 297.

B. Read the first sentence in each pair. Find the underlined word in the chart. Then use a word from its family in the next sentence.

1. Keiko <u>cherishes</u> her camera.

   Keiko's camera is her most _____ cherished _____ possession.

2. My antique watch is the only thing I own that is of real <u>value</u>.
   My antique watch is the only _____ thing that I own.

3. Liu received a painting as part of his <u>inheritance</u> from his father.
   Liu _____ a painting from his father.

4. My mother's greatest <u>treasure</u> is her diamond ring.
   My mother _____ her diamond ring.

5. Jose's basketball trophies <u>mean</u> a lot to him.
   Jose's basketball trophies are very _____ to him.

6. Chen's sports car makes a big <u>impression</u> on his friends.
   Chen's sports car _____ his friends.

7. Gerald's most unusual <u>possession</u> is an old comic book.
   The most unusual thing that Gerald _____ is an old comic book.

8. Sasha's visa is very <u>important</u> to her.
   Sasha's visa is of great _____ to her.

9. Ali's certificate from a school of international business is <u>significant</u> to him because he studied hard for two years to earn it.
   Ali's certificate from a school of international business _____ two years of hard study.

You may use some of the words from this exercise in your first writing assignment.

WRITING

Assignment

Write a one-paragraph composition about one of your possessions. Describe what it looks like, how you got it, what experiences you have had with it, and how it makes you feel. Your audience is your teacher and classmates, and so you have to think about how to describe your possession with details so that they can imagine it easily.

Prewriting

To write well, you must do a lot of thinking, and you must begin reflecting on the topic before you begin to write. We call the thinking we do before writing **prewriting**. Prewriting means gathering ideas (**brainstorming**) and discovering what about the topic is really important to you (**focusing**).

There are a number of techniques you can use to brainstorm and focus. The following steps show some prewriting techniques that will be useful for writing a descriptive paragraph. As you read through the steps, you will see how Marina, a student from Russia, prepared to write a paragraph about one of her possessions.

STEP 1 To select a topic, make a **brainstorming list** of your possessions. From the items on the list, choose the one that you would like to write about and that you think you can describe.

Marina made the following list. She chose to write about a set of nesting dolls from Russia for three reasons: She thought she would enjoy describing it, it had belonged to her grandmother and therefore was very special to her, and she thought readers would find it interesting.

CD player
coffee urn I inherited from my grandmother
award for public speaking I earned in high school
leather jacket
driver's license
✓ nesting dolls from Russia
guitar

STEP 2 Make a list of **focused questions** and answers about the possession to collect further information.

Marina wrote the following questions and answers.

<u>What</u> are nesting dolls?
—They are a traditional Russian toy.

<u>When</u> did I receive my set of nesting dolls?
—I got them from my grandmother when I was a child.

<u>How many</u> dolls are in my set?
—It's a set of five dolls.

<u>What</u> do they represent?
—They represent a family—a large, healthy peasant mother with all her children inside her.

<u>How</u> did I play with them when I was small?
—I used to take them apart and put them together.

STEP 3 With your prewriting notes completed, **discuss your topic** with some of your classmates.

Marina learned that her classmates thought the topic of nesting dolls was interesting, but they did not know much about it. Marina realized that she would have to describe her possession very thoroughly. After writing several drafts, Marina wrote the following draft.

Nesting Dolls

My favorite possession is a traditional set of nesting dolls called "*matrioshka*" that I played with as a child in Russia. Each *matrioshka* is an egg-shaped hollow wooden figure that comes apart in the middle. *Matrioshka* come in a set and are of different sizes so that they can nest one inside the other. Each doll in a set is painted in a distinctive manner, usually representing a member of a family. My set has five figures. The largest and most elaborate is the peasant mother who wears a scarf, skirt, and apron covered with hand-painted flowers. Inside her is a little boy, two girls, and a baby. Like the mother, each family member is painted in bright yellow, white, red, and blue. Each one holds something in his or her hand: The mother has a spoon; the son holds a whistle; one little girl has a flower and the other a handkerchief; the baby clutches a rattle. The inside of each figure still smells of the wood from which it was made and shows how precisely it was shaped. The two halves of each figure fit perfectly together. When I was little, I spent hours taking them apart and fitting them together, just as my grandmother and mother did when they were children. Now my *matrioshka* set waits patiently on my shelf for the day when I will have a daughter to play with it.

Exercise 2

Underline the words, phrases, or sentences in Marina's draft that you think are the most descriptive. Then compare your answers with a partner's. Discuss why the parts you underlined are effective as description.

For your own composition, follow the sequence of prewriting steps Marina used.

First Draft

As you write the **first draft** of your paragraph, remember that a draft is not a perfect, polished paper. It is your first attempt to say what you can or want to say. Your only goal in writing a first draft is to get as many of your ideas as possible on paper. You will refine and correct your work later when you revise.

Here and on the next page are some guidelines on paragraph form that you should follow as you write the first draft of your assignment.

Paragraph Form
- Number each draft.

- Center your title on the first line; that is, write it in the middle. Always use a capital letter for the first word in the title. Use capital letters for all other words except for articles and prepositions.

- Indent the first line of the paragraph five spaces.
- Double-space.
- Start the rest of your lines at the margin line on the left.
- Each of your lines should end at about the same place on the right.

Look at the following example.

Number each draft.

Write the title in the center of the top line.

Indent the first line of the paragraph.

Write to the right of the margin.

Double-space.

DRAFT#2

My Cell Phone

One possession I bought recently is changing my life. With my new cell phone, my business has doubled. I keep my four-ounce phone in my pocket all the time while I am on the road or working at a job site, and I can receive calls from clients and answer their questions without delay. I can even send e-mails when someone needs a printed statement. The phone contains a directory, an appointment calendar, and a calculator, so I am never fumbling with pen and paper. The service charge is reasonable—it costs less than my lunches—so I'd recommend it to anyone whose business keeps him on the go.

REVISING

All writers revise, or rewrite, to improve their writing. Even experienced writers cannot produce good writing in just one attempt; sometimes it takes many drafts. Students usually need to write about three drafts in order to produce a piece of writing that is complete, clear, and correct.

Tips for Revising

- After you've written your draft, set it aside for a few hours or days. When you pick it up again, you will be better able to see it as others see it. This helps you determine what information to include and what connections to strengthen.
- Look at your draft often. Don't be afraid to cross words out or add new ideas. The more often you read and revise your work, the better it will be.
- Keep the paper you are working on in a special folder. Taking special care of your work can help you become a more successful writer because it makes you feel proud of your work. Always have this folder with you in class; you will revise your composition as you learn more about writing.

The lessons and exercises in the Composition Focus and Language Focus sections below will help you revise. You will be using the information in the lessons and Review and Revise boxes to develop your sentences and your composition as a whole, so keep your draft nearby.

Composition Focus

The paragraph. One difference between writing and talking is that the reader is not face-to-face with the writer to ask the writer questions. Therefore, when you write, you must be clear and focused. You must make a point in a direct way and support it with sufficient details.

The basic unit in writing is the **paragraph**, which consists of two parts: the **main point** or topic sentence and **the support**.

The topic sentence. We usually make our main point in the first sentence of a paragraph, which is called a **topic sentence**. It is the most general sentence in a paragraph. Its purpose is to help the reader focus on the main point and to prepare the reader for the information that follows. The other sentences in the paragraph are the support. The supporting sentences provide the details and evidence the reader needs to understand the main point. Look at the following topic sentence and supporting sentences below.

Topic sentence

When I was eight years old, I received the most wonderful birthday gift—a pair of soccer shoes.

Support

I adored the shoes because I cared more about soccer than anything else when I was a boy. I practiced every day with my teammates, and I never missed a game.

The most important reason that the shoes were wonderful is that my cousin Karl gave them to me, and he had been a great soccer player. Karl came to all my games and cheered me on. He showed me how to pass and score.

The shoes were unusual. They had flaps over the laces with red cougars sewn on them. Everyone noticed them.

Exercise 3

Read these two student paragraphs. Notice how their topic sentences prepare you for the information that follows. Underline the topic sentence in each paragraph.

1.
My Car

My Mazda RX-7 has been one of my highly valued possessions ever since I purchased it last fall. I like it first of all for its exterior. It has dark black paint decorated with very narrow red stripes on its sides. It also has alloy wheels. Furthermore, its covered headlights and sliding sunroof provide a feeling of speed. Secondly, my car has a very well-designed interior with a dark red dash and matching carpets and leather seats. The dash design is clean and highly functional. I purchased a new stereo, and with four speakers I can really enjoy my music loud and clear. My car has only two seats and it's not very roomy inside, but the seats are comfortable. The rear third door provides very easy access to the trunk. Finally, an extraordinary rotary engine, which not many cars have, delivers excellent acceleration, power, and smoothness. The car's amazing handling gives me confidence and lets me enjoy driving. My Mazda RX-7 is a lot of fun because of its sporty design, well-done interior, remarkable handling, and great performance.
—Marek Dohnal

2.
My Digital Camera

I have a special toy, a digital camera, which has several useful features. First of all, it has a ten-times zoom function, which lets me take pictures of things that are far away. I used this when my son wanted me to take a picture of a panda bear in a zoo in China which was about twenty meters from where I stood. Second, there is a viewfinder on the back of the camera, which I use to frame pictures I want to take and to review pictures I have taken. Using the viewfinder, I can edit shots that don't turn out well. It helped me get good results when I photographed my cousin's wedding. The main reason that I love this digital camera is that I can connect it to my computer and download my pictures. I use e-mail to send messages and photographs to my parents in China and my brother in Toronto. I was able to send my parents pictures of my son on vacation in Disneyland and of my brother and me on our trip to Niagara Falls. I'm glad I bought this camera; it has given me good results and helped me share my experiences with members of my family.   —Eagle Leung

Here is Marek's topic sentence with his supporting points.

My Mazda RX-7 has been one of my highly valued possessions ever since I purchased it last fall.

- how the exterior looks
- what the interior has
- how it performs and handles

Here is Eagle's topic sentence with his supporting points.

I have a special toy, a digital camera, which has several useful features.

- ten-times zoom function
- viewfinder and editing
- computer hookup and e-mail

Notice that the supporting points present three reasons that the possessions are highly valued.

Exercise 4

Read each list of supporting points and write a topic sentence for it. Use the vocabulary from Exercise 1 on page 8.

1. _____

    _____

    - when and why I got my leather jacket
    - what it looks like and how it feels
    - when and where I wear it and why it makes me feel elegant and sophisticated

2. _____

    _____

    - how my tiny boat is a copy of a traditional Thai boat
    - how I got this boat as a gift from a coworker and friend
    - how the boat represents the province of Nan, where I spent a year working with youth groups

3. _____

_____

- the photograph of my grandfather is the only picture I have of any of my grandparents
- it shows his home on a Greek island, so it indicates what kind of life he led
- I think I look like my grandfather in this picture, and I hope to be a good father to my family as he was

4. _____

_____

- how I got a copy of Gandhi's autobiography as a birthday gift
- why Gandhi's nonviolence was unique
- how Gandhi understood race relations
- how Gandhi was a source of inspiration for me when I was studying political science

---

Review and Revise 1: The Topic Sentence
Check the first sentence in your paragraph and make sure it presents your main point and prepares the reader for what is to follow. If your topic sentence does not identify your main point clearly, rewrite it now.

The support. Supporting ideas provide the details that readers need to understand the main point. The supporting ideas must relate logically to the topic sentence, and a reader should be able to find them easily. We sometimes introduce supporting ideas with words like *First* and *Second* to help readers identify the ideas. Even without these words, though, readers can recognize the supporting ideas by their logical relationship to the topic sentence.

Exercise 5

Read the following two paragraphs. Put <u>one line</u> under the topic sentence and <u>two lines</u> under the supporting points.

1. **My Wallet**

I have a very old wallet that my friends tell me I should throw away, but I won't part with it for several reasons. First of all, my name is sewn on the side of it. When my father bought me the wallet for my twelfth birthday, he asked the leather worker to stitch my name, Horacio, on it with red thread. Second, I believe that this wallet is meant to stay with me. Once I went fishing, and I dropped the wallet off the pier into the water. I thought it would sink and I'd never see it again. But it floated, and a guy with a net rescued it for me. Ever since then, I've felt that I could not lose or give up this wallet. Finally, the wallet is a style of leatherwork that is only done in the region in Mexico where I come from. I left my home six years ago and haven't been back since, but because I have my wallet, there's something from home always next to me.

2.   **My Lucky Ring**

I own a ring that I regard as very precious because it belonged to my grandmother. It is a medium-sized ruby set on a 24-karat gold band, and the simple but elegant design reminds me of my grandmother's temperance. She always knew what to say and do even in difficult social situations, and she never drew excess attention to herself. When other members of the family behaved recklessly or angrily, my grandmother remained calm and controlled. In addition, the red glow of the ruby reminds me of my grandmother's generous heart. She took care of my sisters and me when we were small, and she tried to give us everything we wanted. She saved her money to buy us books and clothes. Finally, because my grandmother always wore this ring, I feel close to her when I have it on. I wear it when I have to make a decision or face a new challenge. At those times, I feel that the ring helps me act as wisely and generously as my grandmother did.

You have probably noticed that each of these model paragraphs has three supporting points, and you may be wondering if all compositions must have three points. When you write, you should include as many supporting points as you think are suitable; that may be two, three, four, or even more. However, three is the most common number of supporting points because it is a convenient number to work with—neither too small nor too large.

Review and Revise 2: Support
Read over your draft and decide how many supporting points it contains. If your paragraph doesn't have as many supporting points as you think it should, add one or more supporting points now. If it has too many supporting points, delete one or more now.

Language Focus

Sensory detail. The best way to get a reader interested in your writing is to describe how something looks, sounds, smells, tastes, or feels. This is called **sensory detail**. For example, in "Nesting Dolls" on page 11, Marina described how *matrioshka* look (*egg-shaped hollow wooden figure*), how they smell (*the inside . . . still smells of* *the wood from which it was made*), and how they feel (*the two halves of each figure fit perfectly together*).

Exercise 6

A. Which of the following descriptive paragraphs contains more sensory detail and helps you imagine the object better?

1.   The telephone is well designed. The two parts, receiver and cradle, fit together well. It is comfortable to hold and easy to use. I like the large buttons. I can see them in the dark. I even enjoy the sound of it. It doesn't make a loud noise.

2.   The telephone is well designed. [1]The surface of the telephone is a soft silvery gray, and its organic shape reminds me of a whale. [2]The receiver fits perfectly in its cradle and is just the right size for my hand as well. [3]The surface has a slight texture, so it doesn't feel sticky when my hand is sweaty. [4]The buttons on the underside of the receiver are large and illuminated so that I can dial a number even in the dark. [5]Its ring is not sharp and high like that of most phones, but more like the loud purring of a cat.

B. Which of the five senses—sight, hearing, touch, smell, and taste—does each supporting sentence in paragraph 2 appeal to? Write the sense or senses on the lines.

Sentence 1: _____   Sentence 4: _____

Sentence 2: _____   Sentence 5: _____

Sentence 3: _____

Exercise 7

Reread Anne Frank's diary entry on pages 4–6. Write *sight, hearing, touch, smell,* and *taste* in the margin where she used sensory details. What type of sensory details did she use most? Compare your answers with a partner's.

Exercise 8

With a partner or a small group, select three objects in your classroom. Complete the following chart with notes about how these objects look and feel. If they have a sound, taste, or smell, write about that too. Then share each description with your classmates without naming the objects you are describing. Have them guess what the object is.

Objects	Sight	Feel (Touch)	Sound	Taste	Smell
a sweater	gray pullover-style; looks handmade	soft wool; the texture is pleasant to handle			smells like wool

Review and Revise 3: Sensory Detail
Check your first draft. Underline examples of sensory information like the ones you wrote in Exercise 8. If you don't have enough sensory details, add some more.

Specific information. As writers, we need to remember that readers often have no previous knowledge of what we are describing. Readers depend on us to include specific information in our writing so they can understand what we are trying to say. In addition, specific information stimulates readers' imaginations, which makes reading more enjoyable.

When we write first drafts, we tend to use common, basic words that represent broad **categories**, or groups, of things. For example, we might write *clock* to mean a tiny red plastic travel alarm clock, a heavy carved oak grandfather clock, or a simple aluminum rectangle with two slender bronze hands. If we don't use specific words, readers have no idea what kind of clock we mean.

To satisfy readers' need for information, we need to learn to think about how specific our information is. Look at the levels of specificity represented in the following exercise.

Exercise 9

With a partner, complete the ladders of specificity for the following words. Use a dictionary if necessary.

1. building _____

       house _____

          small house _____

            small green cottage _____

2. _____

       car _____

       _____

       _____

3. _____

       toy _____

       _____

       _____

4. _____

       dictionary _____

       _____

       _____

5. _____

       painting _____

       _____

       _____

6. _____

       chair _____

       _____

       _____

Exercise 10

A. Read the first draft Elena wrote about her backpack. The underlined words and phrases do not have enough specific information. Write questions in the margins near those words asking for more information.

My Backpack

1. What kind of store did you buy it in?

    I have a wonderful backpack, which I bought in a <u>store</u> in <u>my hometown</u>. It was one of the first times I had gone shopping alone and spent my own money. The clerks were patient with me as I examined every backpack in stock and tried <u>a great many</u> on. I finally chose <u>one</u>. It was <u>the right shape and size</u> and, though not the most expensive, it was <u>well made</u>. I chose it because it was <u>different from all the rest</u>. That was five years ago, and I still really enjoy it. I <u>use it</u> almost every day.

B. Make up answers to your questions. Then rewrite Elena's paragraph using the details from your answers.

C. Share your revision of Elena's paragraph with your classmates.

> **Review and Revise 4: Adding Specific Information**
> Make your first draft about your possession more specific. Underline the words that are not specific enough and revise.

Adding detail with adjectives and noun modifiers. To make your writing specific, add adjectives and noun modifiers to your sentences. Compare the following phrases.

a cup	(article + noun)
a blue cup	(article + adjective + noun)
a blue coffee cup	(article + adjective + noun modifier + noun)

For more on the order of adjectives and noun modifiers, see Appendix IA, page 267. A noun modifier is a noun used to modify (to limit or restrict the meaning of) another noun. *Coffee* is a noun, but when it is used to modify *cup*, it is a noun modifier. Notice that noun modifiers, unlike nouns, are never plural.

INCORRECT: This is a keys chain.

CORRECT: This is a key chain.

CORRECT: This is a chain for keys.

A noun modifier that contains a number has a hyphen: *a four-room apartment* and *a five-story apartment building.*

Exercise 11

With a partner, read the phrases. Then label the adjectives *adj.*, the noun modifiers *n.m.*, and the nouns *n*. Use a dictionary if necessary, but note that the dictionary will identify a noun modifier as a noun.

   (adj.) (n.m.) (n.)
1. a brown leather case

   ( ) ( )( ) ( )
2. a rusty old iron gate

    ( ) ( ) ( )
3. an unusual gold watch

   ( )( ) ( )
4. a tin army cup

   ( ) ( ) ( ) ( )
5. a long black graduation gown

Exercise 12

Rewrite these phrases with noun modifiers.

1. a <u>bracelet</u> made of <u>jade</u>   a _____<u>jade</u>_____ _____<u>bracelet</u>_____

2. an <u>opener</u> that is for <u>letters</u>   a _____ _____

3. an <u>heirloom</u> that belongs to a <u>family</u>   a _____ _____

4. a <u>house</u> that is <u>two stories</u>   a _____ - _____ _____

5. a <u>suit</u> with <u>three pieces</u>   a _____ - _____ _____

6. a <u>boy</u> who is <u>six years old</u>   a _____ - _____ - _____ _____

Review and Revise 5: Adding Adjectives and Noun Modifiers
Look for adjectives and noun modifiers in your paragraph. Mark them
adj. and *n.m.* Add additional adjectives and noun modifiers to make
your first draft more descriptive.

Connecting ideas with coordinating conjunctions. The connecting words called
conjunctions help writers combine short sentences and show relationships
between ideas. Three coordinating conjunctions are *and, but*, and *so*. They all do
the same job—connect independent clauses—but they have different meanings.
Look at the examples below.

1. I have a good-looking car, **and** it drives very smoothly.

2. I have a good-looking car, **but** it has mechanical problems.

Why did the writer use *and* in sentence 1 and *but* in sentence 2? We use *and* to
add information that is expected and *but* to add contrasting or unexpected
information. If a car is good-looking, we expect it to perform well and not to have
mechanical problems.

Look at this example with *so*.

3. I own a car, **so** I have to pay for insurance.

So introduces a result. *I have to pay for insurance* is the result of owning the car.

Exercise 13

Read each pair of sentences. Choose a coordinating conjunction that links them in a logical way, and write each new sentence on another piece of paper. Be sure to put a comma before every coordinating conjunction.

1. This camera takes excellent photographs. It's easy to use.

   This camera takes excellent photographs, and it's easy to use.

2. I believe my jade ring brings me good luck. I wear it all the time.

3. The doll my grandmother made is not pretty. I love it.

4. I bought this guitar with my first paycheck. It's a reminder of my satisfaction at making my own money.

For more on independent clauses and coordinating conjunctions, see Appendix IA, page 282.

5. I have kept the shirt I wore the day I got married. I will never wear it again.

6. This plaque reminds me of how my team won the debating contest. I will always treasure it.

Review and Revise 6: Connecting Ideas with Coordinating Conjunctions

Check your paragraph to see if you can combine any sentences with coordinating conjunctions. Connecting sentences with coordinating conjunctions helps readers better understand the relationships between your ideas.

PEER REVIEW AND FINAL DRAFT

Exchange papers with one or two classmates. Read each other's papers carefully. Turn to page 332 in Appendix II, and fill out the Peer Review form.

After considering your classmates' suggestions, prepare a final draft of your composition. Before handing your paper in to your teacher, proofread it carefully to make sure that you have used capital letters at the beginning of your sentences and periods at the end, and check your spelling.

CHAPTER REVIEW

Look back at what you have accomplished in Chapter 1. Check (✓) what you have learned and what you have used as you have written and revised your composition.

Chapter 1 Topics	I understand this	I have used this
brainstorming with a list and questions (page 10)		
using correct paragraph form (pages 10–11)		
writing a topic sentence to present the main point of a paragraph and help prepare the reader for what will come (page 13)		
recognizing supporting points (pages 13–14)		
describing with sensory details and specific words and phrases (pages 17–20)		
recognizing adjectives and noun modifiers (page 21)		
using the coordinating conjunctions *and, but,* and *so* to link ideas (page 22)		

CHAPTER 2

◆ **Writing a Narrative Paragraph**

We have many decisions to make in life. When we face a decision, we gather all the evidence we can, but we still don't really know how things will turn out. Therefore, it takes courage and conviction to make a major decision that may change the course of our lives.

This chapter will help you

- write a narrative paragraph that focuses on a main point.
- develop the paragraph by including background information and specific details.
- maintain paragraph unity.
- include dialogue.
- write a paragraph conclusion.
- use time signals and correct verb tense in narration.

READING FOR WRITING

Before You Read

The story you are going to read is about a young woman who travels from Antigua to England. With a partner or a small group, discuss the following questions.

1. On a map, find Antigua in the Caribbean, and then find England. Imagine that you left your home in Antigua and traveled by ship to England. Antigua, a former colony of England, is a small tropical island with a population largely of African descent. What changes would you experience on this voyage and upon reaching England?

2. What changes usually occur in a teenager's life? How does a teenager's view of his or her parents change as he or she matures?

A Walk to the Jetty°

by Jamaica Kincaid

jetty: a structure in the water used to protect a harbor

1 "My name is Annie John." These were the first words that came to my mind as I woke up on the morning of the last day I spent in Antigua, and they stayed there, lined up one behind the other, marching up and down, for I don't know how long. At noon on that day, a ship on which I was to be a passenger would sail to Barbados, and there I would board another ship, which would sail to England, where I would study to become a nurse. My name was the last thing I saw the night before, just as I was falling asleep; it was written in big, black letters all over my trunk, sometimes followed by my address in Antigua, sometimes followed by my address as it would be in England. I did not want to go to England, I did not want to be a nurse, but I would have chosen going off to live in a cavern° and keeping house for seven unruly° men rather than go on with my life as it stood. I never wanted to lie in this bed again, my legs hanging out way past the foot of it, tossing and turning° on my mattress, with its cotton stuffing all lumped just where it wasn't a good place to be lumped. . . .

cavern: a large cave

unruly: hard to control

toss and turn: to move restlessly during sleep

2 Lying there in the half-dark of my room, I could see my shelf, with my books—some of them prizes I had won in school, some of them gifts from my mother—and with photographs of people I was supposed to love forever no matter what, and with my old thermos°, which was given to me for my eighth birthday, and some shells I had gathered at different times I spent at the sea. In one corner stood my washstand and its beautiful basin of white enamel with blooming red hibiscus° painted at the bottom and an urn° that matched. In another were my old school shoes and my Sunday shoes. In still

thermos: a bottle that keeps hot drinks hot and cold drinks cold

hibiscus: a large tropical flower

urn: a water pitcher

bureau: furniture for holding clothes

another corner, a bureau° held my old clothes. I knew everything in this room, inside out and outside in. I had lived in this room for thirteen of my seventeen years. I could see in my mind's eye even the day my father was adding it to the house. Everywhere I looked stood something that had meant a lot to me, that had given me pleasure at some point, or could remind me of a time that was a happy time. But as I was lying there my heart could have burst open with joy at the thought of never having to see any of it again.

3   If someone had asked me for a little summing up of my life at that moment as I lay in bed, I would have said, "My name is Annie John. I was born on the fifteenth of September, seventeen years ago, at Holberton Hospital, at five o'clock in the morning. At the time I was born, the moon was going down at one end of the sky and the sun was coming up at the other. My mother's name is Annie also. My father's name is Alexander, and he is thirty-five years older than my mother. Two of his children are four and six years older than she is. Looking at how sickly he has become and looking at the way my mother now has to run up and down for him, gathering the herbs and barks° that he boils in water, which he drinks instead of the medicine the doctor has ordered for him, I plan not only never to marry an old man but certainly never to marry at all. The house we live in my father built with his own hands. The bed I am lying in my father built with his own hands. If I get up and sit on a chair, it is a chair my father built with his own hands. When my mother uses a large wooden spoon to stir the porridge° we sometimes eat as part of our breakfast, it will be a spoon that my father has carved with his own hands. The sheets on my bed my mother made with her own hands. The curtains at my window my mother made with her own hands. The nightie I am wearing, with scalloped neck and hem and sleeves, my mother made with her own hands. When I look at things in a certain way, I suppose I should say that the two of them made me with their own hands. For most of my life, when the three of us went anywhere together I stood between the two of them or sat between the two of them. But then I got too big, and there I was, shoulder to shoulder with them more or less, and it became not very comfortable to walk down the street together. And so now there they are together and here I am apart. I don't see them now the way I used to, and I don't love them now the way I used to. The bitter thing about it is that they are just the same and it is I who have changed, so all the things I used to be and all the things I used to feel are as false as the teeth in my father's head. Why, I wonder, didn't I see the hypocrite° in my mother when, over the years, she said that she loved me and could hardly live without me, while at the same time, proposing separation after separation, including this one, which, unbeknownst to her°, I have arranged to be permanent? So now I, too, have hypocrisy. . . ."

bark: the outer covering of a tree

porridge: hot cereal

hypocrite: a person who expresses ideas or shows feelings he or she does not really have

unbeknownst to her: without her knowing

antroba: eggplant

souse: pigs' feet

in due time: eventually

absurd: ridiculous

dislodge: to remove

stevedore: a dock worker

barge: a flat-bottomed boat that is towed

shrivel up: to shrink

stab: to cut as if with a pointed weapon

4   At breakfast, I was seated in my usual spot, with my mother at one end of the table, my father at the other, and me in the middle, so that as they talked to me or to each other I would shift my head to the left or to the right and get a good look at them. We were having a Sunday breakfast, a breakfast as if we had just come back from Sunday morning services: salt fish and antroba° and souse° and hard-boiled eggs, and even special Sunday bread from Mr. Daniel, our baker. . . . My parents were in a festive mood, saying what a wonderful time I would have in my new life, what a wonderful opportunity this was for me, and what a lucky person I was. They were eating away as they talked, my father's false teeth making that clop-clop sound like a horse on a walk as he talked, my mother's mouth going up and down like a donkey's as she chewed each mouthful thirty-two times. . . . I was looking at them with a smile on my face but disgust in my heart when my mother said, "Of course, you are a young lady now, and we won't be surprised if in due time° you write to say that one day soon you are to be married."

5   Without thinking, I said with bad feeling that I didn't hide very well, "How absurd°!"

6   My parents immediately stopped eating and looked at me as if they had not seen me before. My father was the first to go back to his food. My mother continued to look. I don't know what went through her mind, but I could see her using her tongue to dislodge° food stuck in the far corners of her mouth. . . .

7   At ten o'clock on the dot, I was dressed and we set off for the jetty. . . . Starting out, as if for old time's sake and without giving it a thought, we lined up in the old way: I walking between my mother and my father. I loomed way above my father and could see the top of his head. We must have made a strange sight: a grown girl all dressed up in the middle of a morning, in the middle of the week, walking in step in the middle between her two parents. . . .

8   My mother and my father—I was leaving them forever. My home on an island—I was leaving it forever. What to make of everything? I felt a familiar hollow space inside. I felt I was being held down against my will. I felt I was burning up from head to toe. I felt that someone was tearing me up into pieces and soon I would be able to see all the little pieces as they floated out into nothing in the deep blue sea. . . . Across from the jetty was a wharf, and some stevedores° were loading and unloading barges°. I don't know why seeing that struck me so, but suddenly a wave of strong feeling came over me, and my heart swelled with a great gladness as the words "I shall never see this again" spilled out inside me. But then, just as quickly, my heart shriveled up° and the words "I shall never see this again" stabbed° at me. I don't know what stopped me from falling in a heap at my parents' feet. . . .

9   The good-byes had to be quick, the captain said. My mother introduced herself to him and then introduced me. She told him to keep an eye on me, for I had never gone this far away from home on my own. . . . My father kissed me good-bye and told me to be good and to write home often. . . . My mother said, "Well," and then she threw her arms around me. Big tears streamed down her face, and it must have been that—for I could not bear to see my mother cry—which started me crying too. She then tightened her arms around me and held me to her close, so that I felt that I couldn't breathe. With that, my tears dried up and I was suddenly on my guard°. "What does she want now?" I said to myself. Still holding me close to her, she said, in a voice that raked across my skin, "It doesn't matter what you do or where you go, I'll always be your mother and this will always be your home. . . ."

on one's guard: alert and self-protective

About the Author

Jamaica Kincaid, who was born Elaine Potter Richardson in St. Johns, Antigua, immigrated to New York at the age of seventeen. There she worked as an au pair° and attended college before beginning her career as a writer. When she returned to her homeland almost twenty years later, she was a staff writer for *The New Yorker* magazine and had published a novel called *Annie John.* "A Walk to the Jetty" is adapted from the last chapter in *Annie John.*

au pair: babysitter

Understanding the Reading

With a partner or a small group, discuss the following questions.

1. On her last morning in Antigua, why did Annie John spend a long time lying in bed looking at all her possessions?

2. Kincaid uses a lot of details to describe both Annie's surroundings and her inner emotional world. Which details tell you that Annie felt she had outgrown her family and her home?

3. A writer carefully chooses which information to include and which information to leave out. For example, Kincaid does not report everything that Annie and her parents said to each other the morning of Annie's departure. Why do you think she uses so little dialogue? Can you think of any other information that is not included in this excerpt?

4. What is hypocrisy? Why did Annie accuse her mother of hypocrisy? Does that seem fair? Explain.

5. Do you think Annie understood her parents? Do you think Annie's parents understood her? Use information from the reading to support your answers.

6. Do you think this description of Annie John contains general truths about teenagers? Explain.

7. Annie felt very ambivalent (had conflicting emotions) about leaving her home. Find the part or parts of the reading that reveal her ambivalence.

8. Do you think it is normal to feel ambivalent about major events in one's life? Explain why.

9. Annie said she did not want to go to England or be a nurse. Do you think sometimes it is better to do something, even something you don't want to do, than nothing at all? Explain.

Vocabulary Expansion

Adverbs of manner. Adverbs of manner, such as *quickly* or *slowly*, tell how events happen or how people behave. These adverbs are especially useful in narrations because they make verb phrases more specific.

Adverbs of manner are formed by adding **-ly** to adjectives. These adverbs are usually placed at the end of a sentence, as in the following example.

Katrina examined the package of instant soup *curiously*.

Exercise 1

A. Read the list of adverbs of manner, and discuss what each one means.

aggressively	enthusiastically	skillfully
apologetically	firmly	successfully
appreciatively	hopefully	superbly
beautifully	optimistically	swiftly
disappointedly	quietly	sympathetically
effectively	regretfully	wonderfully

B. With a partner, fill in each blank with an appropriate adverb of manner.

It was the final soccer game of the season, and the Jaguars and Cobras were tied for first place. The score was zero to zero, there were two minutes left in the game, and both teams had been playing almost (1) _____perfectly_____. On the Jaguars' side, José passed the ball to Tomás, but the defense forced Tomás to kick the ball just outside of the goal. The Cobras responded (2) _____. They got the ball and took it down the field (3) _____. Within seconds, the Cobras' mid-fielder scored a goal, and the game was over.

"I shouldn't have missed that shot," Tomás said to José (4) _____.

"That was too bad," José answered (5) _____, but don't worry about it. They were a tough team, and you played the rest of the game (6) _____."

"You did, too," Tomás said (7) _____."

"It's OK. We'll beat them next season," José answered (8) _____.

Read the completed story with the adverbs you added aloud to your class or a small group of classmates. Listen to other students read the story as well. Notice how different adverbs of manner can change the meaning of the story.

WRITING

Assignment

Choose one of the following topics and write a one-paragraph composition. Use correct paragraph form as shown on page 12.

1. Have you ever made a decision to change the direction of your life—such as leaving home, taking a job, enrolling in a school or a program, or joining the military? Tell how you made that decision or how it felt to go through with that decision.

2. Our lives change not only because of decisions we make but also because of events that are beyond our control. Have you ever had a significant experience that changed you? Describe the experience and its effects on you.

Prewriting

In Chapter 1, you learned that you need to brainstorm and focus to prepare to write. You made a list and wrote focused questions in your prewriting.

In this chapter, you will learn a new brainstorming technique, **freewriting**. Freewriting is writing about a topic for a fixed period of time without worrying about grammar, spelling, or organization. The purpose of freewriting is to explore a topic and gather ideas. When you freewrite, you may write more than you need, but afterward, you can select the parts of your freewriting that are useful and delete the rest.

The steps below will lead you from freewriting to focusing on the point you want to make in this narrative paragraph. As you read through the steps, you will see how Cornelia, a student from Colombia, prepared to write on topic 1—a decision that changed the direction of her life.

STEP 1 **Freewrite** for fifteen minutes about the topic you have chosen.

You will see Cornelia's freewriting in Step 3.

STEP 2 Review your freewriting, and ask yourself what **point you want to make** with this story. Write a **draft topic sentence** about the point you want to make.

Cornelia shared her freewriting with a classmate, and after they discussed it, she wrote the following sentence.

The point I want to make with this story is that leaving home was a hard, but important, decision.

STEP 3 **Cross out** the parts of your freewriting that do not support the point you want to make.

Cornelia reviewed her freewriting and crossed out the parts that did not support her point that leaving home was a hard, but important, decision.

When I was in college, I kept wondering what kind of work I would do after graduation. I talked to my sister several times, and she invited me to come see her in the capital, Bogotá. ~~I wanted to visit her and see some of my friends there.~~ Most of all, I really needed to learn what companies were there and how I could find a job there.

The last time I called my sister she said she really needed help. ~~She said she had been waiting to hear from me. She begged me to come and stay with her to look after my three-year-old niece because she and her husband were both working at that time.~~ When I told my parents I was planning to go, they got very upset. It was horrible having them both feeling so bad about me, but I packed my bags anyway and left.

I babysat for my niece, Luisa, every day. ~~I had no idea a three-year-old could be so much work. But she was a lot of fun, too. She used to say, "Aunt Cornelia, would you like to have tea with me?"~~ At night after Luisa had gone to bed, I finally had some free time to write letters. I sent my resume to all the big companies in Bogotá. I had been waiting to find a job for five and a half months when I finally got an interview with a telecommunications company. I did very well in the interview and I was hired. It was a very rewarding job. During my time there, I learned new skills, met a lot of people, and made some good friends. Leaving home was an excellent decision.

STEP 4 | Write **focused questions** to develop your ideas about your main point.

Cornelia realized that her freewriting didn't support her main point. It didn't explain *how* making the decision and carrying it out was hard but important. Using **focused questions** and answers helped her develop her main point.

> Why was it hard to leave home?
> —My parents opposed it, and I didn't want to make them unhappy.
>
> Why were my parents opposed to my leaving?
> —In my country, young women usually live with their parents until they marry.
>
> Why was my situation difficult after I got to Bogotá?
> —I had to cook, do housework, and look after my niece; on top of that, I couldn't find a job in my field right away.
>
> Why was this decision important in my life?
> —I got an interesting job in a great company, and it was a good start to my career.

Cornelia began with the main point and limited the ideas in her paragraph to information that supported that point.

After writing several more drafts, Cornelia wrote the following one-paragraph draft.

Leaving Home

Moving out of my parents' home when I was twenty-four years old was the most important decision I have ever made, but it wasn't an easy step to take. I knew there were no jobs in business administration in our small town, San Jacinto, and that I would eventually have to move to the capital, Bogotá, where my sister and her husband lived. One night as we ate our evening meal, I told my parents I wanted to go to Bogotá and stay with my sister. They glanced at one another and then looked down at their plates. I took a big drink of water as I waited for them to speak. When they finally looked up at me, I saw that Mom was brushing away a tear and Dad's forehead had more lines in it than I had ever seen. "But Cornelia," he said, "you're not married." I finished his sentence in my mind, "And girls from good families do not leave home until they're married." But my father seemed to know I had made up my mind. "Do what you think is best, Cornelia," he said, but neither of them really looked at me, so I wondered how upset they were. My doubts lingered even after I moved to my sister's place because it took me six months to find a good job. When I finally called home to say that I had landed a managerial position with a large telecommunications company, my parents seemed truly relieved, and nowadays they brag to their friends about their daughter Cornelia, the Global Network Managerial Assistant.

Exercise 2

With your classmates, discuss how Cornelia's draft is different from her freewriting on page 32.

1. How many paragraphs are there in each piece of writing?

2. Where is the main idea statement in each piece? Which position is better for the reader?

3. Which piece focuses mainly on a single experience? What is the effect of narrowing the focus and telling a story through a single incident?

4. Which piece contains more detail?

For your own composition, follow the sequence of prewriting steps Cornelia used.

First Draft

Write your first draft. Begin your one-paragraph composition with your main point, and limit the ideas in the paragraph to information that supports the main point. After writing, put the draft away for a while before you review it.

REVISING

Tips for Revising

• Always keep your drafts and brainstorming together while you are working on a paper. You will occasionally need to return to an earlier step to re-evaluate changes you have made.

• Reread your most recent draft frequently. Every time you review your paper, you will get a clearer idea of what is good in it and what needs to be revised.

Composition Focus

Narration. Both writing assignment topics in this chapter ask you to tell a story, that is, to write a **narration**. Good narrations like Jamaica Kincaid's "A Walk to the Jetty" are a pleasure to read because they have a sequence of events to follow, descriptive details, and characters whose feelings we can appreciate.

Chapter 1 emphasized that in descriptive compositions, specific words and phrases help support the main point and help the reader imagine what the writer is trying to describe. Specific information is effective in narration for the same reasons. The following sections show you how to include additional specific support in your narration.

Recognizing adequate development. Readers look for two kinds of development:

• *Background Information.* At the beginning of a composition, readers expect certain essential facts. When the composition tells a story, they want to know *where* and *when* the story took place. For example, in Cornelia's narration "Leaving Home," you learn in the first few lines that she was twenty-four years old, lived in San Jacinto, Colombia, and wanted to move to Bogotá.

- *Supporting Details.* In the body of the composition, readers expect to find details, especially sensory details, that support the writer's main point. For example, Cornelia provided visual details: *Mom was brushing away a tear and Dad's forehead had more lines in it than I had ever seen.* Specific sensory details like these keep readers interested, help them remember what they read, and enable them to understand the writer's point.

To understand the importance of development, read the two paragraphs below and then discuss them.

1. **My Illness**

Once I had a terrible sickness which had two bad effects on my life. First of all, I was studying at school. I was a good student, and I had many friends. When I got sick, my friends brought me the homework, but I could not even do it because I didn't feel well. I had to drop all my classes in school because I missed many lectures. The second thing that bothered me was my appearance. My face looked awful. I felt so embarrassed when anyone saw me. I felt depressed, so I would not go out, even when I got over the sickness. Finally, I got a special treatment, so I feel better now.

2. **My Illness**

When I was in my first semester of college in Lisbon, I got chicken pox, a childhood disease which affects adults quite severely. This illness had two terrible effects on me. First of all, I missed five weeks of lectures. My friends brought me their notes and the assignments, but because I had a fever, I could not concentrate on studying. I missed several tests and quizzes as well. As a result, I eventually had to drop all of my classes—biology, computer science, history, and math. A second bad effect of the chicken pox is that I got red, itchy bumps all over my face. There was almost no empty space on my face! When I got over the chicken pox, these horrible spots did not go away; they just turned darker. People who saw me would stare, so I did not want to leave my room. Finally, I went to a clinic and got laser treatments, but my face still shows some scars.

With a partner or a small group, discuss the following questions.

1. Which paragraph is better developed?

2. Does the better-developed paragraph give background information? Circle the background information. Tell what questions it answers.

3. Does the better-developed paragraph contain good supporting information? Are there sensory details? Underline the supporting details in the body of the paragraph.

You should have identified paragraph 2 as the better-developed paragraph. It contains **background information** to answer questions such as *What kind of sickness did you have?* and *When and where did it happen?* It also contains

supporting details to develop the idea that chicken pox had two terrible effects on the writer. We learn that the writer *missed several tests and quizzes* and consequently had to drop her college classes. She also had *red, itchy bumps* on her face that did not go away. Finally, the better-developed paragraph contains **more specific vocabulary**: For example, in paragraph 1, the writer says she got *a special treatment*, while in paragraph 2, she explains that she got *laser treatments* at a *clinic*.

Exercise 3

On the line, write *WD* if the sample paragraphs are well developed and *UD* if they are underdeveloped. In the well-developed paragraphs, circle the background information at the beginnings of the paragraphs. Underline the specific details in the bodies of the paragraphs.

1a. _____   **My Driving Test**

   I failed my driving test. It was a bad experience that I will never forget. I got in the car with the examiner, but I couldn't respond to any of her requests. She asked me to show her some things in the car, but for some reason, what she said didn't make any sense, and I couldn't remember where anything was. She asked me to start the car and leave the parking lot. I made two mistakes before I drove out of the parking lot. Then when we left the lot, she told me to do a number of things. I followed her directions and didn't have any problem until I got into a confusing situation. The driver in front of me was doing something strange, and I didn't know how to react. It was a very frightening moment. I waited for the examiner to tell me what to do, not knowing that she expected me to know how to deal with problems on the road. After that she told me to go back to the parking lot. When I got into the parking lot, she informed me that I had not passed the test, and she said I should take some more driving lessons before trying the test again.

1b. _____   **My Driving Test**

   Last month I failed my driving test after having spent a good deal of money on lessons and many hours practicing. When I got in the car with the examiner, she said, "Show me where the headlights and emergency lights are," but, for some reason, all the buttons and knobs looked unfamiliar to me, and I couldn't distinguish one from the other. When she asked me to start the car and exit the parking lot, I made a couple of big mistakes: First, I forgot to fasten my seat belt, and then I backed up without checking the rearview mirror. After we left the lot, she directed me to the main road. There I found myself in a confusing situation. I was in the inside lane, and the driver in front of me slowed down to a crawl. Thinking it was illegal to pass to the right, I waited for the examiner to tell me what to do, but she remained silent. "What should I do?" I asked. "Go around," she replied curtly. By this time, I was shaking. When we got back to the parking lot, the examiner informed me that I had failed and told me to take some more driving lessons before attempting the test again.

2a. _____   **A High School Dropout**

Young people who drop out of high school usually learn too late that it is a poor decision. My friend Kam was one of them. A year ago he quit school because he thought there were a lot of opportunities out there in the world. He thought he would work full time at the local variety store and make money to buy a car. He used to say to his friends, "Hey, I'm going to buy a red Corvette and take you guys to the beach every weekend." When Kam quit school, he got a job at Parson's Variety Store, but he had to work six days a week and never had weekends off, so he never saw his friends. After deductions, his weekly paycheck was only about $250, so he had to buy a beat-up old sedan instead of a fancy sports car. I saw Kam a week ago, and he said he realizes now that he will need a high school diploma to get ahead, so he's back in school—night school—and saying, "I wish I had never dropped out."

2b. _____   **A High School Dropout**

Young people who drop out of high school usually learn too late that it is a poor decision. My friend Kam was one of them. He quit school because he thought there were a lot of opportunities out there in the world. He thought he'd get a chance to make money and then be able to buy things. He thought he would have a lot of free time to spend with his friends. He saw a very rosy picture of life outside of school. However, Kam didn't find freedom or happiness when he dropped out of high school. He realized that he had fewer opportunities than people who had earned their high school diplomas. He discovered that he didn't earn as much money as he had thought he would and he couldn't buy the things he had expected to be able to buy. He found that he actually had less free time than he had had when he was in school and that his friends, who had remained in school, were not available when he was off work. Now he regrets his decision to drop out of high school.

With a partner, discuss what makes two of these paragraphs underdeveloped and what makes the other two better developed. Compare what you have circled and underlined with what your partner has circled and underlined. Consider also how the writer's use of dialogue affects two of the paragraphs.

> **Review and Revise 1: Adequate Development**
> Check the development in your paper. Decide whether your draft is well developed or underdeveloped. If it is underdeveloped, add background information and specific details.

Unity. Readers want writers to make a point and give specific evidence that supports it. They don't want unnecessary information that isn't related to the point. Therefore, as writers, you need to be selective about what to include. Limit the contents of your paragraphs to those details that support the point you are trying to make. When all your supporting information is clearly related to your point, your composition has **unity**.

Exercise 4

Read the topic sentence. Then check (✔) the sentences that support the point it makes.

Topic sentence: I joined the army because my father, a retired officer, wanted me to follow in his footsteps; however, I paid too great a price to please my father.

_____ 1. The training camp was at a high elevation, and it was very cold at night, yet the army only provided one thin blanket to each soldier.

_____ 2. I saved my paychecks while I was in the service, so I had some savings when I got out.

_____ 3. I had just had my appendix out, and I had not recovered from the surgery when I enlisted.

_____ 4. My best friend Miguel was in my unit.

_____ 5. The army issued new soldiers boots that didn't fit well, and I got blisters on my feet the first week.

_____ 6. At the end of the training, we had to jump out of a tower. I had heard many soldiers had injured themselves in the fall and been discharged. I almost wished for an injury, but I made the jump successfully and was thus committed to my two-year enlistment.

_____ 7. The scenery around the base was beautiful. I saw a lot of alpine flowers and birds I had never seen before.

_____ 8. Army food was terrible. The rice was brown and sticky, and the bread was always stale. Vegetables were overcooked, so they were mushy and tasteless. Everything was oversalted, and there was hardly any meat.

_____ 9. We had to get up at 5:00 A.M. and take cold showers every morning.

_____ 10. I had to walk between twenty and twenty-five kilometers over rough terrain every day carrying a heavy pack. As a result, every part of my body ached all night long.

> **Review and Revise 2: Unity**
> Check the appropriateness of the supporting details in your paper. If you find sentences that do not develop or add to the understanding of your main point, omit them. Make sure your paragraph has unity.

Developing a paragraph. Your most important task as a writer is finding details and putting them into words. The following exercise will give you additional practice developing ideas with specific support.

Exercise 5
With a partner or a small group, add detail to complete the following paragraphs.

1.   **A Difficult Beginning**

    My first day in the International English Program was stressful. On my way to class, I got lost. _____

_____

When I was given the results of my test and my class placements, I knew there was something wrong. _____

_____

_____

I felt uncomfortable in my reading class because of something my teacher asked me to do. _____

_____

_____

_____

At break time I felt very left out. _____

_____

_____

After that first day I was ready to quit. Fortunately, I didn't. As the days have gone by, school has gotten better and better.

2.   **A Thoughtful Friend**

My friend Keiko is one of the most considerate people I have ever known. I met her in the college cafeteria about a month ago. That day there weren't any empty tables, so I asked her if I could join her and the two friends she was with.

_____

_____

After we got to know each other that day in the cafeteria, Keiko and I started to study together regularly. We're both taking math classes, but Keiko is taking a much higher-level class than I am. _____

_____

_____

Keiko and I have talked to each other about our families a great deal. She knows that I get homesick on Saturday nights, so last Saturday night she did the kindest thing for me. _____

_____

_____

I have been very grateful to have a friend like Keiko. Knowing her has made being away at college so much easier for me.

Read your completed paragraphs aloud to your classmates. Listen to other students read their paragraphs, and notice the various ways an idea can be developed. Pay attention to the degree of specificity in each added sentence.

Dialogue. One tool that writers use to develop narrative paragraphs is dialogue. The actual words of people in a story usually catch readers' interest, and they can do more: Dialogue helps readers understand the characters in the story and can guide them to a better understanding of the writer's main point.

When you write dialogue, make sure that it reveals something about the characters in the story or supports your main point. For example, compare the two examples below. Which one do you think reveals more about Keiko (the subject of "A Thoughtful Friend" above).

1. "Hi, my name is Keiko. What's your name?"

2. "I saw you were alone, and I thought you might be new here. It's such a big school, and it's hard to meet people. My name is Keiko, and these are my friends Yuan Ling and Carolina."

The second example tells us much more about Keiko: We learn what she was thinking as she spoke. We also see that she has empathy for people who are alone in a new environment. These lines of dialogue support the main idea of the paragraph, that Keiko is a considerate person.

Review and Revise 3: Dialogue
Reread your draft. If you don't have any dialogue in it, ask yourself whether you could add some. If you have some dialogue, ask yourself if it supports the main point you want to make in your narration. Finally, check your punctuation.

To review punctuation for direct quotations, see Appendix IB, page 317.

Paragraph conclusions. The last sentence (or sentences) of a paragraph should signal to the reader that the writer is finished. We can send this signal in a number of ways. In narrative paragraphs, we often present a lesson that can be learned or a conclusion that can be drawn from the story. For example, in "A Difficult Beginning" on page 39, after the writer has told us how hard his first day of school was, he concludes by bringing his narration to the present and telling us how he feels about school today.

> After that first day I was ready to quit. Fortunately, I didn't. As the days have gone by, school has gotten better and better.

Similarly, the writer of "A Thoughtful Friend" on page 40 concludes with her opinion about her friend, an opinion that is based on the experiences she has narrated in the paragraph.

> I have been very grateful to have a friend like Keiko. Knowing her has made being away at college so much easier for me.

Exercise 6

1. With a partner, discuss the concluding sentences in the model paragraphs in this chapter: "My Illness" (2, page 35), "My Driving Test" (1b, page 37), and "A High School Dropout" (2a, page 37). Which concluding sentences best signal the end of the paragraph? Which show a conclusion drawn or lesson learned from the events of the story? Which show a shift from past to present tense? Share your ideas with your teacher and classmates.

2. With your partner, choose one of the model paragraphs mentioned above. Write a different concluding sentence for it. Then, as your teacher directs, read the paragraph with the new concluding sentence aloud to your classmates.

> **Review and Revise 4: Paragraph Conclusions**
> Review your draft and make sure your last sentence signals the reader that the composition is finished. Consider whether you want to change the last sentence to include a lesson you have learned or conclusion you have drawn.

Language Focus

In narrations, we rely on various signals to understand the story. On page 30, you learned that adverbs of manner tell *how* events took place or *how* people behaved in a story. But we also need to know *when* events in the story took place. For that we rely on **time signals** and **verb tenses**.

Time signals. When you read a story, you keep track of the events by placing them on a mental time line—what happened first, second, next, and after that. You also want to know how much time passed between the events in the story. To do this, you rely on the time signals the writer has used, which can be **words**, **phrases**, or **clauses**. Here are some examples of each.

Words (adverbs)	Phrases (adverbial phrases)	Clauses (adverbial clauses)
then	at first	as we walked into the classroom
finally	for quite a while	before the teacher spoke
often	every morning at 8:00	when I finished my composition

To learn about the difference between phrases and clauses, see Appendix IA, page 298.

What is the difference between a phrase and a clause? Discuss the difference with your classmates and teacher.

Exercise 7

A. Read the narration and <u>underline</u> the words, phrases, and clauses that are used as time signals. Label them *W* (for word), *P* (for phrase), and *C* (for clause).

A Difficult Job

Working as an air-conditioner installer in Hong Kong was the most difficult job I have ever had. I installed window air conditioners in fifty-story buildings. <u>After just two ^Pdays of training</u>, I began installing three to six air conditioners a day. During an installation, I first drilled through the window frame to install the brackets which would hold the air conditioner. After I installed the brackets, I had to put the air conditioner through the window and fit it into the brackets. That was the most difficult and dangerous part of the job because the air conditioners weighed over 100 pounds. Sometimes I had to put half of my body outside the window to hold the air conditioner in place while I screwed it into the brackets. It was very dangerous work, but installing air conditioners paid more than other jobs that were available to me at that time. I did this for about seven months while I saved a little money. A year later I used this money and went to Japan to study. Air-conditioner installation was my worst job, but I don't regret it now because my earnings paid for me to continue my studies.

B. Compare your answers with a partner's. Where do you find most of the time signals—at the beginning, in the middle, or at the end of sentences? Why?

C. There are two time lines in this paragraph. One time line describes the writer's seven-month-long experience as an air-conditioner installer. What is the shorter time line contained within this story?

Time clauses. Time clauses are useful when writing narrations because they show time relationships. They also allow you to add variety to your sentences. Time clauses begin with subordinating conjunctions of time, such as *while* or *until*, as in the following examples.

> *While Gil was sleeping,* his wife Sue was working in the kitchen.

> He woke up *when he heard the doorbell ring.*

> Sue had closed the door *before he reached the bottom of the stairs.*

> *After she examined the envelope,* she opened the letter.

> She did not look at Gil *until she had finished reading it carefully.*

For more on adverb clauses, see Appendix IA, page 270.

Review and Revise 5: Time Signals
Underline the time signals in your narration. Make sure that you have provided enough time signals to help the reader form an accurate mental time line of the events in your story. Ask yourself if you have used a variety of time signals—words, phrases, and clauses. If you can add to or improve your time signals, do so now.

Tenses and time frames. English has twelve verb tenses that fit into three time frames—past, present, and future.

Present Time Frame	Past Time Frame	Future Time Frame
simple present	simple past	simple future
present progressive	past progressive	future progressive
present perfect	past perfect	future perfect
present perfect progressive	past perfect progressive	future perfect progressive

For examples of the 12 tenses, see Appendix IA, page 304.

When you write a narration, you usually tell the story in the past time frame—that is, the simple past, past progressive, past perfect, and past perfect progressive tenses. However, you can use the present or future time frame in a story if you need to. For example, the introduction to your narration might be a general statement in the simple present tense. The conclusion might be a statement about either the present or the future.

Exercise 8

Read the following narration. It has three time frames and several tense shifts. With a partner, <u>underline</u> the verbs and name their tenses. Draw a vertical line (|) where the writer changed the time frame. Finally, write the time frames in the margin.

<u>**Time Frame**</u>

present

My Best Job

simple present

[1]I am a coin-laundry technician, and it is the best job I've ever had. | [2]I started to work for Baker Coin Laundries five years ago as a technician's assistant. [3]For eighteen months I went out in the truck every day with Jim, a very experienced repairman and a nice guy. [4]Jim showed me how to take the machines apart, find the problem, install new parts, and reassemble the machine. [5]He told me that there are different kinds of customers. [6]The appreciative ones give the repairmen little gifts and always say thank you, the impatient ones expect the repair to be done quickly, and the nervous ones don't trust repairmen. [7]After I had been accompanying Jim every day for about a year and a half, the boss asked if I was ready to do repairs on my own. [8]He told Jim to let me fix the machines by myself and to watch me. [9]One day Jim watched me do a very tough repair on an old dryer for which we had no replacement parts. [10]I carefully took out all the bearings in the motor,

cleaned them, and repacked them in grease. [11]When I was done, the machine ran so quietly that all one heard was a soft humming sound. [12]Jim was impressed. [13]He told the boss that I was capable of fixing any washer or dryer. [14]Ever since then, I've been on my own. [15]I drive my truck all over my territory. [16]I've gotten to know all my customers, and many of them are my friends. [17]I love this job, and I will keep it as long as I can.

With your teacher and classmates, discuss the writer's reasons for using the various time frames and tenses in this paragraph.

Review and Revise 6: Verb Tenses
Check the verbs in your draft. If you have changed tenses in your draft, make sure you have a reason for the changes. Mark any changes in time frame in your paper with a vertical line (|). If you are unsure about some of your verbs, write a note to your teacher in the margin of your draft.

PEER REVIEW AND FINAL DRAFT

Now that your composition is nearly complete, it is time to share your writing with others. Exchange papers with one or two classmates. Turn to page 333 in Appendix II, and fill out the Peer Review form.

After considering your classmates' suggestions, prepare a final draft of your composition. Before handing your paper in to your teacher, proofread it carefully. Check your spelling and punctuation.

CHAPTER REVIEW

Look back at what you have accomplished in Chapter 2. On the following chart, check (✓) what you have learned and what you have used as you have written and revised your composition.

Chapter 2 Topics	I understand this	I have used this
using prewriting skills: freewriting, identifying a main point, using focused questions (pages 31–33)		
developing a narrative paragraph with background information and supporting details (pages 34–35)		
focusing on a main point and maintaining paragraph unity (page 38)		
using dialogue to develop a narration and reveal the personalities of the characters (pages 40–41)		
writing a paragraph conclusion (page 41)		
using time signals to guide the reader through the narrative (page 42)		
recognizing time frames in a story and choosing correct verb tenses (page 44)		

Memory and Learning

◆ Writing an Expository Paragraph

In Chapters 1 and 2, you used your memory to describe an important possession and a life experience. In Chapter 3, you will turn your attention to memory itself, the capacity that makes it possible for you to learn.

This chapter will help you

- organize ideas from general to specific and group details or examples into categories.
- develop a prewriting outline.
- write an expository paragraph with a topic sentence, supporting points, and supporting examples.
- use transitions to introduce examples.
- use subordinating conjunctions to join clauses.

READING FOR WRITING

Before You Read

Complete the following activities.

1. A Chinese proverb says, "Tell me, and I forget. Show me, and I remember. Let me do, and I understand." Can you think of specific learning experiences you have had when someone told you how to do something, showed you how to do something, or let you do something? Describe one of these learning experiences to a partner.

2. Think of one learning experience from your childhood. Then ask yourself why that memory has stayed with you: Is it associated with strong feelings? Did it have important outcomes? Spend fifteen minutes freewriting about this experience.

Memory

by David G. Myers

national anthem: patriotic song

pit someone against someone else: to put them in opposition

offense: a wrong; a cause for hurt feelings

momentary: brief

1   Be thankful for memory. We take it for granted, except when it malfunctions. But it's our memory, notes Rebecca Rupp (1998), that "allows us to recognize friends, neighbors, and acquaintances and call them by their names; to knit, type, drive, and play the piano; to speak English, Spanish, or Mandarin Chinese." It's our memory that enables us to sing our national anthem°, find our way home, and locate the food and water we need for survival. It's our shared memories that bind us together as Muslims, Buddhists, or Christians; as Brazilians, Saudis, Germans, or Koreans. And it is our memories that occasionally pit us against those° whose offenses° we cannot forget.

2   In large part, you are what you remember. Without memory, there would be no savoring joyful moments past, no guilt or anger over painful recollections. You would instead live in an enduring present. Each moment would be fresh. But each person would be a stranger, every language foreign, every task—dressing, cooking, biking—a novel challenge. You would even be a stranger to yourself, lacking that continuous sense of self that extends from your distant past to your momentary° present.

3   Memories, unlike videotapes or photocopies, are personally constructed. And that is why two people can experience the same event and recall it differently. One student remembers that the homework assignment is to answer the questions; another student remembers it is to read over the questions. This is because our minds do not just record what we see and

hear; what we remember about an event has to do with what we expect to happen, what we have experienced in the past, and what happens to us after that event.

Effortful Learning and Repetition

4   With little or no effort, we remember a vast amount of things: trips we have taken, celebrations we have attended, what we ate for breakfast, where we put our shoes. Other types of information, however, we remember only with effort and attention. When learning novel kinds of information such as names, we can boost our memory through rehearsal, or conscious repetition. We also learn information better when our rehearsal is distributed over time, a phenomenon° called the spacing effect. In a nine-year experiment, Harry Bahrick and three of his family members (1993) practiced foreign language word translations for a given number of times, at intervals ranging from 14 to 56 days. Their consistent finding: The longer the space between practice sessions, the better their retention°. Spreading out learning—say, over a semester or a year—beats cramming°.

The Importance of Meaning

5   When we study new words in a foreign language, our minds encode° them various ways: We remember the spelling, the sound, and the meaning. What kind of encoding do you think yields° the best memory? Visual encoding of images? Acoustic encoding of sound? Semantic encoding of meaning? To find out, Fergus Craik and Endel Tulving (1975) flashed° a word at people. Then they asked a question that required the people to process the words either (1) visually (the appearance of the letters), (2) acoustically (the sound of the words), or (3) semantically (the meaning of the words). They used questions such as these:

1. Was the word written in capital letters or small letters?

2. Does the word rhyme with *crate*?

3. Can you use the word in a sentence like this?

     The girl put the _____ on the table.

Craik and Tulving's results showed that asking people to focus on the meaning of a new word helped them remember.

6   Other researchers have shown the benefits of rephrasing what we read and hear, that is, putting the new ideas in our own words. For example, you might read this sentence in your textbook, "As Wayne Wickelgren (1977) noted, 'The time you spend thinking about material you are reading and relating it to previously stored material is about the most useful thing you can do in learning any new subject matter.'" You could rephrase the sentence this way: *It is important to spend time thinking about what you study and*

---

phenomenon: something that one can observe

retention: ability to remember

cram: to study for a test very intensively for a very short time just before the test

encode: to record, remember

yield: to produce

flash: to show quickly

connecting it to what you already know, or you might say, *Wickelgren believes in the value of reflecting on what you read and associating it with what you already know.*

rate: to say how much
something is worth

arouse: to excite

7   Research has also shown that we have excellent recall for information we can relate to ourselves. If asked how well certain adjectives describe someone else, we will often forget them; if asked to rate° how well the adjectives describe ourselves, we remember the words well. Perhaps this is because relating adjectives to ourselves arouses° feelings, and feelings make memories stronger. Perhaps it is because when we associate information to ourselves, we connect it to many other pieces of information, and the more associations we have for the new information, the more likely we are to remember it.

Chunking

8   Chunking means organizing information into meaningful units, or chunks. Chunking information into meaningful units occurs so naturally that we take it for granted. To experience the importance of chunking, look at each of the three lines in the following box and then look away and try to write what you remember.

---

1. OM ⚲ NENT ‖ bPNLPK

2. WOTNOEEHTER

3. TWO ONE THREE

---

9   You no doubt found number three easiest to remember. Why? You recognize the groups of letters as meaningful chunks, or words. And you might remember the whole line as one chunk, say as someone's address. How did you do with number two? Did you try to break it into manageable chunks like WOT NO EEHTER? Maybe you tried to give it meaning by connecting it to a phrase like "What, no eat?" And how was number one? Impossible? Without meaning, chunking does not work.

10   Here's another exercise to try. Study the following list of words for a minute, then look away and write down as many as you can remember:

finger, stairway, hair, brain, basement,

knee, elbow, living room, doorway, arm, neck,

kitchen, shoulder, bedroom, window, eye, doorbell

11   You probably found yourself putting the words into categories. How many categories did you make, and what were the names of your

categories? Most people use the categories parts of the body and parts of a home. Using categories makes the task of memorizing much easier. When people have knowledge about the material they are trying to learn, they process information not only in categories, but also in hierarchies. A hierarchy contains two or more levels of categories.

body

   head

      brain

         cortex, hippocampus, amygdala

12   You may have recognized that the relationship between the items in this hierarchy can be expressed as *a part of*. (The head is *a part of* the body, the brain is *a part of* the head, and the cortex, hippocampus, and amygdala are *parts of* the brain—incidentally, they are parts of the brain essential to the processing and storing of memories.) In a hierarchy, the relationship between an item and the item above it is expressed as *a part or aspect of* or *a more specific example of* and sometimes as *a cause of* or *a result of*.

Learning Strategies

sought: past tense of *seek,* meaning *to look for*

13   Learning new information is a challenge, and students have always sought° ways to use their memories more effectively. Today scientific research has confirmed the effectiveness of the strategies learners have discovered. Here are some of the strategies that have been found to be effective.

1. ***Study repeatedly to boost long-term recall.*** Overlearn. To learn a name, say it to yourself after being introduced; wait a few seconds, and say it again; wait longer and say it again. Provide yourself with many separate study sessions by taking advantage of life's little intervals—riding on the bus, walking across campus, waiting for class to start.

2. ***Spend more time rehearsing or actively thinking about the material.*** Rehearsing means reviewing the material in your mind without rereading it or checking your notes. Actively thinking about the material includes comparing it to other things you have studied and asking questions about the material such as "Why did this event happen?" "Why is this true?" or "Why do people disagree on this point and what is my perspective?"

3. ***Make the material personally meaningful.*** Mindlessly repeating information is relatively ineffective. Put the information in your own words and relate it to what you already know or what you have experienced. If you can find a way to relate it to your own life, you will be very likely to remember it.

4. *Organize the information in meaningful categories and hierarchies.* A category or hierarchy is easier to remember than an unorganized list because it has a shape that you can recall visually and an organization that appeals to the logic of your mind.

14   Try to use these strategies when you need to learn new information. You will find that they really work.

Bahrick, Harry P., L. E. Bahrick, L. S. Bharick, and P. E. Bahrick. "Maintenance of Foreign Language Vocabulary and the Spacing Effect," *Psychological Science* 4 (1993): 316–321.

Craik, Fergus, and Endel Tulving. "Depth of Processing and the Retention of Words in Episodic Memory," *Journal of Experimental Psychology: General* 104 (1975): 268–294.

Rupp, Rebecca. *Committed to Memory: How We Remember and Why We Forget.* New York: Crown Publishers, Inc., 1998.

Wickelgren, Wayne. *Learning and Memory.* Englewood Cliffs, NJ; Prentice Hall, 1977.

About the Author

David G. Myers, Ph.D., is a professor of psychology at Hope College in Michigan. He is the author of four college textbooks in the fields of psychology and sociology, all of which have been translated into other languages. He has also written books on the relationship between psychology and religion. "Memory" is adapted from Myers' popular textbook *Psychology*.

Understanding the Reading

With a partner or a small group, discuss the following questions.

1. What would your life be like if you had no memory? Explain by giving examples from your own experience.

2. Why is it that sometimes two people who have experienced the same event remember it differently (paragraph 3)? Give an example from your own life that shows how people's memories of an experience differ.

3. What did Bahrick's research show about learning and memory (paragraph 4)? What did Craik and Tulving's study show (paragraph 5)? What have you noticed about your own memory when you have tried to learn new vocabulary in English or another language?

4. Why do you think rephrasing helps people remember what they read?

5. What strategies could language teachers use in the classroom to help students remember?

6. Several general learning strategies are recommended in paragraph 13. Do you think you need to use different learning strategies for different subjects? For example, when you study math or history, do you use the same strategies as when you try to learn a language? Explain with examples.

7. In academic writing, authors often present a general idea and follow it with an example. Notice these two sentences from the beginning of paragraph 7:

example <u>Research has also shown that we have excellent recall for information we can relate to ourselves</u>. If asked how well certain adjectives describe someone else, we will often forget them; if asked to rate how well the adjectives describe ourselves, we remember the words well.

Locate two more examples in the reading, and write *example* in the margin. Then find the general point each one illustrates and underline it. Share your findings with your teacher and classmates.

Vocabulary Expansion

Prefixes, roots, and suffixes. Words can have three parts: a **prefix** + a **root** + a **suffix**. The root is the core, or center, of a word. A prefix can be added to the beginning of a word, and a suffix can be added to the end. Prefixes and roots provide clues to the meaning of words. For example, the prefix *re-* means *again*. Some words that begin with this prefix are *review, revise,* and *repeat*. The root *mem-* means *memory*. Some words that have this root are *memory* and *memorize*.

You learned about word families in Chapter 1. The members of a word family such as *memory, memorize,* and *memorization* share a common root, *mem-*. We can distinguish the members of a word family from one another by their suffixes, or **word forms**. A word form tells us what part of speech a word is. Some common noun and verb word forms or suffixes are listed in the chart below.

For more on word forms, see Appendix IA, page 311.

Noun Suffixes	Verb Suffixes
-ance, -ence	-ate
-ness	-ize
-tion, -sion	
-y, -ity	

Exercise 1

Underline the correct word forms in the passage. Then identify each word form by writing *n.* (for noun) or *v.* (for verb) in the parentheses.

(*v.*)
Many students complain that they (1. forgetfulness/<u>forget</u>) too much of what they learn in school, but what they call forgetting is actually incomplete learning. For example, if a group of students listens to a lecture one day, they may not remember more than half of the contents of the lecture the next day unless they
( )
do one of the following: They (2. familiarity/familiarize) themselves with the
( )
contents of the lecture before hearing it, or they (3. reflection/reflect) upon or
( )
(4. discussion/discuss) the material after the lecture. If the students are given a test the day after the lecture, those who have previewed the material before the lecture or reviewed it afterward do better than those who have not made these efforts.

In addition to the efforts students can make to improve their own learning,
( )
teachers can do a great deal to (5. determination/determine) how well students
( )
(6. acquisition/acquire) knowledge. First of all, the amount and difficulty of the
( )
(7. information/inform) in a lecture will affect student learning. The more material
( )
a teacher decides to (8. inclusion/include) in a lecture and the more difficult that
( )
material is, the less students are likely to (9. recollection/recollect) it later. Second, the kind of material in the lecture will affect student learning. If the students can
( )
see a (10. relationship/relate) between the material and their own lives, their
( )
learning will be better. Finally, the (11. presentation/present) of the information in
( )
the lecture affects how much students learn. If teachers (12. organization/organize)
( )
the material very carefully and (13. emphasis/emphasize) their organizational plan,
( )
student (14. retention/retain) of the information is greater.

While learning is complicated, we know that students and teachers can do
( )
certain things to (15. facility/facilitate) it. Students can preview material before lectures and review it afterward. Teachers can adjust the amount and difficulty
( )
of the material to suit their students' needs, (16. connection/connect) the
( )
material to students' lives, and (17. delivery/deliver) lectures in a carefully organized way.

WRITING

Assignment

Choose one of the following topics and write a paragraph containing examples. Your paragraph should have three levels, as explained below. Use correct paragraph form as on page 12.

1. Write about a memorable teacher you have had. Tell why this teacher was memorable. Give examples of his or her teaching style, assignments, or treatment of you.

2. Which do you think is more beneficial in school: experiential learning (activities such as acting in a play that helps you understand a historical event, conducting an experiment to see how physical forces such as light and heat work, or building a model village to understand how people lived in the past) or rote learning (memorization)? Give reasons and examples to support your choice.

3. When you study, do you learn more when you are rewarded or punished? Why? Explain with examples.

4. During your years as a student, you have sometimes had to take difficult examinations. Describe two or three strategies that have helped you prepare for exams. Include specific examples.

What Expository Writing Is and Why an Expository Paragraph Has Three Levels

The assignments above all ask you to explain something. This kind of writing is called **expository writing**. When you explain something, you need to use specific details or examples to clarify and support your main idea. To write a well-developed expository paragraph, you need to collect a number of different kinds of examples. Once you have collected your examples, organize them in logical groups, or **categories**. Your readers then will be able to see how your examples support your ideas.

To help your readers follow your thinking, your expository paragraph will have **three levels**: (1) a **main point** presented in a topic sentence, (2) **supporting points** which identify the categories of examples, and, finally, (3) the **specific examples** themselves.

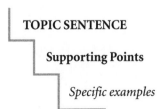

TOPIC SENTENCE

Supporting Points

Specific examples

An **outline** shows the structure of a three-level paragraph.

Main Idea (Topic Sentence)

   I. Supporting Point
     A. Details/Examples
     B. Details/Examples

  II. Supporting Point
     A. Details/Examples
     B. Details/Examples

 III. Supporting Point
     A. Details/Examples
     B. Details/Examples

Making an outline. The first step in writing an outline is grouping details and examples into categories, or logical groups.

Exercise 2

Read the topic sentence, categories, and examples. Then write a number next to each example to indicate its category.

A. **Topic sentence**: Many kinds of experiential learning are beneficial to students.

Category 1: Experiential learning in music

Category 2: Experiential learning in history

Category 3: Experiential learning in science

    __1__   1. Students can learn about rhythm by beating drumsticks on a table.

    _____   2. Students can pretend to be famous people in history; they can wear costumes and deliver speeches, acting the part of historical figures.

    _____   3. Students can learn about melody by changing the words of familiar songs.

    _____   4. Students can grow plants and record the effect of light and water on their growth.

     5. Students can visit parks to learn about the plants and animals.

     6. Students can visit historical buildings and art museums to learn how architecture and painting reflected political change in their country's past.

     7. Students can use computer programs that allow them to compose music.

     8. Students can write letters addressed to people of the past such as Christopher Columbus, asking questions and giving opinions about their adventures.

     9. Students can care for animals in their classrooms and observe their growth and behavior.

B. **Topic sentence**: I learn more when I am rewarded by my teachers.

Category 1: rewards in the form of grades

Category 2: rewards in the form of teacher's comments and gestures

     1. After I received 99 percent on a history test, I made a great effort to study history thoroughly because I wanted to receive more high grades.

     2. I remember my biology teacher's smile when she saw my first-year science project; with the next year's project, I tried to please her again.

     3. When I saw the "A" written on my English composition, I felt much more committed to writing well.

     4. When my dance teacher suggested that I perform before the whole school, I felt a surge of confidence that made me rehearse especially hard.

     5. I saw my computer programming teacher's nod of approval when I presented my solution to the class; after that, I became a more attentive student in class.

     6. I got straight As in geometry, so I was motivated to try a more advanced math class.

Exercise 3

Complete the two student outlines by writing the supporting points (category names) in the blanks.

1. **Topic sentence:** When my school is closed for vacation, I can continue learning English in several ways.

   I. _____
      A. read newspapers and magazines
      B. read signs on the streets and advertising on buses
      C. surf the Internet

   II. _____
      A. watch TV
      B. listen to the lyrics of my favorite songs
      C. go to parties where English is spoken
      D. play a sport with English speakers

   III. _____
      A. write e-mail to friends
      B. write down the words of popular songs I hear on the radio

2. **Topic sentence:** The way I prepare for final exams depends on the subject.

   I. _____
      A. I make index cards for each chapter in my history book and write a summary on each card.
      B. I discuss the important historical events with my father; we talk about their importance and why they occurred.

   II. _____
      A. I memorize the definitions of terms such as *real number* and *hypotenuse*.
      B. I do ten algebra or geometry problems each day. If I miss a problem, I look for additional problems of the same kind to get more practice.

Note that some outlines are written with complete sentences, and some outlines contain only words and phrases. Because an outline is a tool for organizing information, you can write it in any way that is useful to you.

Prewriting

In Chapters 1 and 2, you used various prewriting strategies, including listing, identifying the main idea, and writing focused questions. In this chapter, your prewriting will also include putting examples in categories and making an outline.

After you have chosen a topic, follow the prewriting steps below. As you read through the steps, you will see how Miguel, a student from Mexico, prepared to write about his high school physical education teacher, Mr. Jimenez.

STEP **1** | Make a **list** of details and examples. Then decide on the point you want to make in your paragraph, and draft a topic sentence.

You will see Miguel's list in step 2. After Miguel made a list, he discussed it with two of his classmates. Then he drafted the following topic sentence.

I remember Mr. Jimenez, my high school physical education teacher, because he taught me self-discipline.

STEP **2** | Study your list and choose **categories** for your examples. Number each example to identify its category. Cross out the information that does not fit in any category.

Miguel discovered that Mr. Jimenez taught him discipline in two ways—first, by demanding it of his students, and second, by modeling it himself. Miguel decided that his paragraph would be organized around these two supporting points. He crossed out the details that did not fit in these two categories.

(2) he wore nothing but white—white shirt, white shorts, white socks, white shoes, white visor cap

~~six feet tall~~

(1) made us do push-ups, sit-ups, chin-ups, and jumping jacks, and we had to run more laps than the soccer team

~~he walked very fast; if a student wanted to talk to him, he had to run to keep up~~

(1) made us wear a clean white uniform; no uniform, no practice; dirty uniform, lose points; he was never late for class

(1) students who were late had to run five extra laps

(1) I took a summer swim class with him, and I became a very strong swimmer because he made me do the butterfly stroke for twenty minutes every day.

(1) other classes played basketball, soccer, or field hockey; we only did calisthenics and ran laps

~~he talked to us about how to train for competitions~~

~~he had been in the Panamerican Games in 1979, in the marathon, and 5,000~~

~~and 15,000 meter races~~
~~he led the drive to build a stadium for our school~~
(2) he worked out with every P.E. class he taught and every team he coached all day, every day; he was assistant principal, and he used to get to work at 7:00 A.M. to do his office work

---

STEP **3** | Use the categories to make an **outline**.

Miguel's outline shows three levels of development: first the topic sentence (*TS*), then supporting points (*SP*), and finally examples (*EX*).

I remember Mr. Jimenez, my high school physical education teacher, because he taught me self-discipline. (TS)

    I. He demanded self-discipline of his students. (SP)
       A. He made us come to class on time; students who were late had to run five extra laps. (EX)
       B. He made us wear a clean white uniform. Students without uniforms missed practice, and those with dirty uniforms lost points. (EX)
       C. Other P.E. classes played games, but Mr. Jimenez made us do calisthenics and run laps; he made us do push-ups, sit-ups, chin-ups, and jumping jacks. (EX)

    II. He modeled self-discipline himself. (SP)
       A. He was never late for class. (EX)
       B. He dressed neatly in a white shirt, shorts, socks, shoes, and visor cap. (EX)
       C. He worked out with every P.E. class he taught and every team he coached all day, every day. (EX)
       D. He was assistant principal, and he used to get to work at 7:00 A.M. to do his office work before he began teaching. (EX)

With his outline complete, Miguel was ready to write. He wrote several drafts in which he deleted details and added others before completing the following draft.

A Memorable Teacher

More than any other teacher I ever had, I remember Mr. Jimenez because he taught me self-discipline. He was my high school physical education teacher for three years. When I found myself in his class in my sophomore year, I was dismayed because he was so strict, but as time went on, I grew to appreciate him. First, he taught us self-discipline because he demanded it of us. He made us come to class on time; students who were late had to run five extra laps.

He made us wear clean white uniforms; students without uniforms had to stand on the side during practice, and students with dirty uniforms lost points. While other P.E. classes were having fun playing basketball, soccer, or field hockey, those of us in Mr. Jimenez' class had to do push-ups, sit-ups, chin-ups, and jumping jacks, run up and down stairs, and do more laps around the soccer field than the soccer team. Second, he taught us self-discipline because he modeled it for us. He was never late for class. He dressed very neatly. He wore nothing but white—white shirt, white shorts, white socks, white shoes, white visor cap. He worked extremely hard. He was the assistant principal, and he used to get to work at 7:00 A.M. to do his office work, and then he worked out with every P.E. class he taught and every team he coached all day, every day. When I start to feel a little lazy, I think of Mr. Jimenez and how hard he made us work, and how physically fit and well trained we became as a result. Mr. Jimenez taught me a very important lesson: In order to accomplish things, we must have self-discipline.

Exercise 4

Find the three levels of development in Miguel's paragraph. Put one line under the first level (topic sentence), two lines under the second level (supporting points), and brackets [ ] around the third level (specific examples).

After selecting a topic from the list on page 55, follow the sequence of prewriting steps Miguel used.

First Draft

Once you have completed brainstorming and organizing your ideas into a workable outline, write your first draft. Begin with your topic sentence, and follow your outline as you develop the paragraph. After writing, put your draft away for a while before you reread it and revise.

REVISING

If you have followed all the steps listed in the Prewriting section, you should have a good first draft. Still, first drafts always need revision, so it is necessary to evaluate your draft point by point and work on it to improve it. As you work through the lessons in the Composition Focus and Language Focus sections of the chapter, look at the Review and Revise boxes, which will tell you specifically what to do to your draft.

Composition Focus

Effective topic sentences. In Chapter 1, you learned that a topic sentence is the most general sentence in a paragraph, and it announces the writer's main point. An effective topic sentence will engage your readers and make them want to read more because it raises a question. Not all topic sentences are effective, however. Which of the two sentences below, if used as topic sentences, would make you want to read more?

My biology teacher gave us weekly tests.

The method that my biology teacher used will always stay in my mind.

Most readers find the second sentence a more engaging topic sentence because it raises a question: *What method did this biology teacher use?* The first sentence does not raise any question at all.

In addition, an effective topic sentence is neither too general nor too specific. Some main idea statements are too broad for a paragraph; they need to be developed in an article, essay, or book. Others are too narrow; they don't allow room for development. Look at these sample sentences.

We can learn things in many ways.

We learned the names of the capitals of all the countries in the world.

The best way to study history is to discuss why events occurred and what consequences they led to.

The first sentence is too broad. It contains no specific words, only the very general terms *things* and *many ways*. It gives no sign of how the writer plans to develop it. The second sentence is too narrow. It is just a factual statement and so doesn't suggest a direction for development. The third sentence is a workable topic sentence because it has a limited topic, *the best way to study history,* and a controlling idea that suggests a plan of development, *to discuss why events occurred and what consequences they led to.*

Exercise 5

Read each sentence and decide if it is a potential topic sentence. Write *TB* (too broad), *TN* (too narrow), or *JR* (just right).

___JR___ 1. Classmates from different cultural backgrounds can teach each other about their customs and values.

_____ 2. During my years in school, I learned many things.

_____ 3. A student can use several tricks to memorize facts for examinations.

_____ 4. I learned how to play Beethoven's sonata number 5 on the piano.

_____ 5. Education is very important and a good thing to have.

_____ 6. Dropping out of school in eleventh grade was not a smart decision for Adam, my next-door neighbor.

_____ 7. When I finished high school, I could write about 7,000 Chinese characters.

_____ 8. I had a hard time passing my economics class, but I managed to do it because I joined a study group.

Compare your answers with a partner's. Discuss any answers you disagree about with your teacher and classmates.

> **Review and Revise 1: Effective Topic Sentences**
> Check the topic sentence of your paper. Make sure that it isn't too broad or too narrow. Ask yourself if your topic sentence will engage readers' interest and make them want to read more because it raises a question.

The topic and the controlling idea. A topic sentence has two parts: the topic and the controlling idea. Look at these examples.

┌──────TOPIC──────┐ ┌─────────CONTROLLING IDEA─────────┐
Humor in the class has several positive effects on students.

┌──────TOPIC──────┐ ┌──CONTROLLING IDEA──┐
My best friend taught me three valuable lessons.

The topic tells you the general subject of the paragraph. The controlling idea limits the topic. It tells you what comment the writer wants to make about that topic, what aspect of that topic the writer wants to focus on, or how the writer plans to analyze that topic. The controlling idea is usually, but not always, at the end of the topic sentence. Here is an example of a topic sentence with the controlling idea at the beginning.

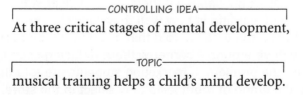

┌──────────CONTROLLING IDEA──────────┐
At three critical stages of mental development,

┌──────────────TOPIC──────────────┐
musical training helps a child's mind develop.

Exercise 6

Identify the parts of each topic sentence. Underline the topic with <u>one line</u> and the controlling idea with <u>two lines</u>.

1. <u>When I was in elementary school, my teachers rewarded us for our achievements</u> <u>in several ways</u>.

2. It is not easy to learn vocabulary because each new word represents several kinds of information.

3. Modern technology has affected my learning of English in two significant ways.

4. High school entrance exams should be eliminated because they ruin young people's lives.

5. When students arrive late for class, they affect their classmates negatively.

6. For three reasons, music was my favorite subject in high school.

7. From my experience in high school, I can classify teachers according to the pace of their classes.

8. Students learn much faster when they play an active role in class discussions for several reasons.

Compare your answers with your classmates'. As you identify the controlling ideas, tell what question the paragraph will answer.

Exercise 7

Read each paragraph, and write a topic sentence for each one.

1. _____

_____

For one thing, students learn more when they understand why they are studying certain material, or what their purpose is. For example, the other day my teacher taught conditional sentences with *would*. Before beginning the grammar lesson, she explained that without *would*, we couldn't discuss imaginary situations, such as what it would be like if there were peace in the world or what would happen if there were nuclear war. Another factor that affects student learning is how well they can relate new information to their lives. If physics students are told that a certain problem relates to what happens when they drive around a corner without reducing speed, they will better understand the problem. If marketing students are told that a certain concept relates to the brand of toothpaste they select in the store, they will tend to remember the concept. Finally, students learn best if they review—not just once, but repeatedly. For that reason, it is helpful if teachers make their exams cumulative. That means they should give exams that include not only the most recently studied material but also material from lessons studied earlier in the term. In sum, three factors—understanding the reason for study, relating study to one's life, and reviewing—all have a positive effect on student learning.

2. _____

_____

One strategy is to make use of all my mistakes. If my teacher writes a comment on my paper like, "You sometimes leave *it* off at the beginning of your sentences," then I check for the subject *it* in all my sentences. In addition, I have asked my roommates to correct my mistakes, and when they do, I try to write down what they tell me so that I can review it later. Another strategy I have found useful is to try to learn English in as many different situations as I can. I don't hear English just at school; I also hear it in my tennis class and my folk-dance class. In those situations I practice English with my classmates, and I also learn new verbs while I am performing the actions they describe. Finally, I think pronunciation is important, so I've developed two strategies to improve mine. One technique I have is to repeat out loud exactly what someone has said just after I've hung up the phone or left a store. At that moment, I can still hear the person's voice in my mind, and it is easier to copy their sounds. The other technique is to pronounce a word out loud when I look it up in the dictionary; that way I'm learning the pronunciation along with the part of speech and meaning. All these strategies take some effort, but with them, I'll become fluent in English much sooner.

3. _____

_____

A little stress can aid learning. A minimal amount of stress increases attention, and when people pay attention, they learn more. For instance, if students know that they will have a quiz every Friday, they pay closer attention in class. Too much stress, however, decreases a person's ability to pay attention. For example, if a teacher asks a student to do something he or she has never done, like giving an oral summary of a chapter, stress may prevent the student from remembering even the title of that chapter. Finally, a situation of prolonged stress, such as a period of military combat, has a negative effect on the mind's ability to learn and remember. Because stress affects learning, teachers and students must try to understand the various ways it works.

> **Review and Revise 2: The Topic and the Controlling Idea**
> Make sure your topic sentence has two parts: the topic and the controlling idea. If you are not sure, ask your teacher or a classmate. If your topic sentence doesn't have two parts, rewrite it.

The supporting points in the three-level paragraph. The supporting points are the second level in the three-level paragraph. The supporting points must be clearly stated in the paragraph because they connect the topic sentence and the examples.

Exercise 8

The topic sentences in each of the following paragraphs are underlined with <u>one line</u>. Read the paragraphs, find the supporting points, and underline them with <u>two lines</u>.

1. **Success in College**

<u>Several conditions can help make a student successful in college.</u> First, her life should be comfortable and stress free so that she can devote her attention to her studies. It is ideal if she does not have to work, does not have to look after others, and has a private place to study. Second, she needs to be responsible and organized. She must keep track of due dates for all her assignments. She must also have a place for the papers she receives from teachers and for her written work. Finally, she must have motivation to study. Several things can motivate her: She may want a career, or she may just love what she is studying. Whatever her source of motivation is, something must keep her engaged in her studies so that when she feels frustrated, she will keep going.

2. **Ways to Remember**

<u>People have developed strategies to help them memorize things.</u> One way to memorize is to use mental images. For example, if a person has to remember a group of unrelated words like *dog, apple,* and *tennis racket,* he can assign locations to them on a mental map; he can imagine the apple in his kitchen, the dog in front of his house, and the tennis racket by his front door. Another way to memorize the words is to create a story about the list like this: *I hit the dog with the tennis racket to make him stop eating the apple.* The more unusual or silly the story is, the easier it is to remember. A third way to remember the list is to take the first letters in each word on the list and create a word from them, an acronym. The acronym for *dog, apple,* and *tennis racket* would be DAT. A final technique is to use auditory memory: a person can find other words that sound like the words to be learned. To do this, he finds words that sound like dog (*log*), apple (*grapple*), and tennis racket (*Dennis Lambert*). Although these techniques require remembering additional information, people have found that they are effective. When it comes to remembering, associations or connections are the key.

Compare your answers with a partner's. Did you both find the same number of supporting points in each paragraph? Discuss your results with your teacher and classmates.

Review and Revise 3: Supporting Points
Check your paragraph for supporting points. If you do not have sentences that clearly state the supporting points in your paper, add them.

Specific examples. Good writing contains examples for several reasons. If your paragraph has a topic sentence and supporting points but no examples, your readers may say, "Why is that important?" or "I don't think that's true." Readers may not see the importance or truth in what they read without examples. In addition, examples give readers pleasure and help them remember what they read, especially when the examples contain good sensory details.

Exercise 9

This paragraph contains a topic sentence, supporting points, and examples. Put brackets [ ] around the examples.

Three Aspects of Memory

Psychologists who study memory tell us that our memories have three parts. First, there is our short-term memory, which holds on to sights, sounds, smells, tastes, and tactile experiences for only a minute or so. When we turn off the radio or TV, the last few words or bit of music echoes in our minds for a few moments. When we look up a phone number, we remember it just long enough to dial it. The second type of memory is working memory, which is where we use memory to think: We make comparisons, look for causes and effects, and predict what will happen in the future. When we consider buying a new shirt in a store, we use our working memory to compare it to our other clothes, look for reasons why we should or should not buy it and predict how we will feel if we buy it. Finally, long-term memory is what we keep for many years. It is where we store the words to a song learned in childhood, a telephone conversation that brought happy or sad news to us, the special outfit we wore on high school graduation day, and many more things that make up our storehouse of knowledge. We need all three kinds of memory to function well in life.

Compare your answers with a partner's. Did you both find the same number of examples in the paragraph? Discuss your results with your teacher and classmates.

Exercise 10

This student paragraph has a topic sentence and several supporting points, but it lacks specific examples. The parts that are not specific enough are underlined. Rewrite the paragraph on a piece of paper, adding specific examples.

NOT SPECIFIC: . . . so if the class does <u>one thing</u> on Monday . . .

MORE SPECIFIC: . . . so if the class reads *Tom Sawyer* on Monday . . .

MORE SPECIFIC: . . . so if the class writes a dialogue with the past perfect tense on Monday . . .

Effective Review in a Language Class

Review activities are an important part of a language class, but to be effective, these activities must be varied. Students want to use all their language skills—reading, writing, listening, and speaking, so if the class <u>does one thing</u> on Monday, it should <u>do another thing</u> on Wednesday. Whether reviewing or learning new material, most students enjoy working with partners and in small groups. In a group, one student can <u>do one part</u> while another <u>does a different part</u>. When students review, they prefer to learn something new at the same time. If a class learned <u>a certain skill</u> last week, this week it can review the old skill, and at the same time, learn <u>some new information</u>. When review activities are well designed, every student is interested in the lesson and every student's learning is enhanced.

Compare your rewritten paragraph with your classmates'. Notice the variety of examples. Discuss your results with your teacher and classmates.

Exercise 11

This paragraph has a topic sentence and supporting points but no examples. With a partner, rewrite the paragraph on a piece of paper and add *two or more* specific examples after each supporting point. If you cannot think of actual examples that are true, you can invent some "facts" for this exercise.

Learning Culture

Language and culture are connected, so students of English usually learn quite a bit about American culture. They know about movie stars and movies. They are familiar with current events in the United States. They even know a little about American history. For students of English, language learning and learning about culture go hand in hand.

After everyone has finished rewriting the paragraph, pass the revisions around the room and evaluate them for the number and quality of examples they contain. Rank the revisions from *1* to *4* according to the descriptions below.

1—does not have specific examples for each supporting point

2—has at least one example for each supporting point, but the examples are short and not very specific

3—has one or two examples for each supporting point, and the examples are quite specific

4—has two or more specific, memorable examples for each supporting point

Review the evaluations your classmates gave your paragraph. If your examples received a rank of *1* or *2*, rewrite them to make them more effective.

> **Review and Revise 4: Specific Examples**
> One of the most common problems writers have is lack of
> examples, or lack of specificity in examples. Ask someone—a
> classmate or a friend—to check your paper to see if you have
> enough examples and if your examples are specific enough. If you
> need to develop your examples, ask your classmate or friend to
> write questions to help you.

Transition words and phrases. A paragraph that contains several supporting points and a number of examples usually needs some signals, or **transitions**, that help readers follow its organization.

One type of transition signal indicates that an example is coming: *for example* or *for instance*. *For example* and *for instance* come at the beginning of a sentence and are followed by a comma. They are the same in meaning and use. *Such as* and *like* are transitions used in the middle of sentences. *Such as* and *like* are prepositions and are followed by nouns or noun phrases. They are also identical in meaning and use.

Transitions	
To Introduce Sentence-long Examples	**To Introduce Words or Phrases Used as Examples Within Sentences**
For example,	such as
For instance,	like

Exercise 12

A. Turn back to the three paragraphs in Exercise 7 on pages 64–65. Circle the transitions to introduce examples in each paragraph.

B. Read the paragraphs and fill in the blanks with the following transitions: *for example*, *for instance*, *such as*, and *like*.

1. Humans are not the only creatures with memories. Animals need memories to survive in nature. (a) _____, squirrels must remember where they buried their nuts so that they can eat in the winter, and salmon must remember the stream where they were born so that they can return to it to spawn. Birds must remember their

migratory routes in order to escape harsh arctic conditions and survive the winter months in warmer zones. Animals also show great ability to learn from human beings. (b) _____, dogs that are trained to aid blind and deaf people learn to perform tasks (c) _____ waiting until a traffic light turns green before crossing the street or running to the door to signal that the doorbell has rung. In fact, scientists have found that even simple creatures (d) _____ worms, sea slugs, and fruit flies can learn and remember. It seems that memory is fundamental to living things, for any creature that eats must remember what tastes good and where to find it, or it would not survive.

2. Some substances seem to enhance memory. (a) _____, scientific experiments have shown that consumption of sugar improves recall. Some herbs (b) _____ sage and ginseng are also memory enhancers. Then there are the recently developed smart drugs (c) _____ ampakines, which have been shown to have positive effects on the memories of laboratory animals and human volunteers.

A second type of transition indicates that ideas are in a sequence: *first, second, third* or *one, another. First, second, third*, and *finally* come at the beginning of a sentence followed by a comma. *One, another*, and *others* are not used with commas because they are adjectives (and sometimes pronouns).

Transitions to Signal a Sequence		
To Introduce Items in a Series	**To Point to Items from a Group or Category**	
first	one	some
second	another	others
also		
in addition		
third	the other	the others
final		
finally		

To review *one, another, some*, and *others*, see Appendix IA, page 295.

Exercise 13

A. Turn back to the paragraphs in Exercise 8 on page 66. In each paragraph, circle the transitions that are listed in the chart on page 70.

B. Read the two paragraphs below and fill in each blank with any of the transitions from the chart on page 70. Then compare your answers with your classmates'.

1.   **How the Young Can Teach the Old**

When we think of people teaching each other, we imagine older people teaching youth. Certainly this is the most common form of learning in society, but it is not the only way that learning takes place. Younger people have a lot of things to teach older people, too. (a) _____, culture changes all the time. New games, dances, songs, and fashions appear daily. Young people always learn these new trends before older people, so if an adult wants to find out what *hip-hop* or *extreme sports* is, he or she should ask someone under twenty-five. (b) _____, technology changes continually. Each new product that comes out requires that the public be educated to use it, and younger people seem to learn how much faster than older people. Therefore, if older people want to learn how to program a Palm Pilot or download music from the Internet, they should just ask someone born within the last quarter century to show them how. By learning from each other, both the older and the younger generations will lead richer lives.

2.   **How My Computer Has Helped Me**

My computer has changed the way I study. (a) _____ way it has helped me is with writing. I can revise on the computer very easily, so I do not need to redo an entire draft. I just make a copy of it and move sentences around and change vocabulary to explore different ways to express my ideas. Because revising on the computer is so easy, I now write much better papers, and when it's time to turn my work in, I am very proud of its clean, professional appearance. (b) _____ way that the computer has helped me with my studies is with research. I can check the library catalogue online to see if a book is in the library without leaving my home. I can locate many facts through various Web sites including online encyclopedias. (c) A _____ way the computer has helped me in school is that it has improved communication with my classmates. The students in my psychology class have a chat room where we ask each other questions or share our comments about what we have learned. These changes made possible by computer technology make my studying not only more productive but more fun.

Concluding sentences. Remember that a paragraph needs to have a final sentence that signals the writer is finished. In expository paragraphs, you can indicate the conclusion by repeating the main idea and perhaps even the supporting points. You can also draw a conclusion about the information in the paragraph, as the writer did in the last sentence of "How My Computer Has Helped Me."

> **Review and Revise 5: Transitions and Concluding Sentence**
> Check your paragraph. If your supporting points or examples need to be marked, add transitions. Also, check the concluding sentence in your paragraph. Make sure that it signals the reader that the paragraph is finished.

Language Focus

Subordinate clauses. In Chapter 1, you learned about the coordinating conjunctions *and, but,* and *so*; in Chapter 2, you learned about the subordinating conjunctions of time *after, before, until, when,* and *while*. There are also subordinating conjunctions of reason (*because*), surprising result (*although*), and condition (*if*). Here are some examples.

> Childhood experiences affect people throughout their lives <u>because those experiences are stored in memory</u>.

> <u>Although people don't remember all their childhood experiences</u>, those experiences can determine the way they think and act later in life.

> <u>If a person heard music as a child</u>, he or she will be able to learn a musical instrument more easily as an adult.

For more on subordinating conjunctions, see Appendix IA, page 270.

Note that when a subordinate clause comes at the beginning of a sentence, it is followed by a comma.

Exercise 14

A. The following composition contains no subordinate clauses. To make it more readable, combine the pairs of sentences in brackets [ ] using the subordinating conjunctions below. Use a comma when the subordinate clause is at the beginning of the sentence. Rewrite the composition on a piece of paper.

after	because	until	while
although	before	when	

A Reward from My Math Teacher

[(1) I reached high school. I had been very good at math.] [(2) But I had difficulties. I got in trigonometry class.] One day our teacher gave us a test in trigonometry. I had studied, but I had not understood the problems at all. As a result, I got only 25 percent. My classmates were shocked. [(3) I got a low score. I was humiliated.] Afterward, I started to study harder. [(4) I did not understand a particular problem. I asked for help right away from my teacher or classmates.] Three weeks later, there was another test. I got the second highest score. My teacher was very impressed. [(5) He told all my classmates that I was a model student. I had made the greatest effort and the most progress.] [(6) He gave me a beautiful mechanical pencil as a reward. I had not earned the highest score.] This had never happened in our school. A reward had never been given to the student with the second highest score. [(7) This event was so unusual. I will never forget it.]

B. Read aloud the rewritten paragraph in Exercise A, and notice how combining clauses adds variety and improves the paragraph.

C. Check your sentences for commas. How many sentences need commas? Compare your use of commas with a partner's.

Review and Revise 6: Subordinate Clauses
Look for subordinate clauses in your paper. If possible, combine some sentences with subordinating conjunctions. Using sentences with subordinate clauses improves your composition because subordinate clauses show relationships between ideas.

PEER REVIEW AND FINAL DRAFT

Now that you have revised your composition, it is time to share your writing with others. Exchange papers with one or two classmates. Turn to page 334 in Appendix II, and fill out the Peer Review form.

After considering your classmates' suggestions, prepare a final draft of your composition to hand in to your teacher. Before turning it in, check your spelling and punctuation, especially of subordinate clauses.

CHAPTER REVIEW

Look back at what you have accomplished in Chapter 3. Check (✔) what you have learned and what you have used as you have written and revised your composition.

Chapter 3 Topics	I understand this	I have used this
organizing ideas from general to specific, grouping examples in categories, and making an outline for a three-level paragraph (pages 55–58)		
writing a topic sentence with a controlling idea (p. 63)		
presenting supporting points in sentences that link the topic sentence and the examples (pages 65–66)		
using specific examples to make the main and supporting points believable (page 67)		
using transitions to guide the reader (pages 69–70)		
using subordinating conjunctions to link ideas (page 72)		

Culture, Identity, and Homeland

♦ **Writing a Division Paragraph**
♦ **Writing a Simple Division Essay**

Who are you? Very likely your answer to this question has several parts. Your response will probably include your name, where you were born, and what cultural or ethnic group you belong to. It may also include your ancestry, the history of your homeland, and your language, customs, and beliefs. In this chapter, you will reflect on and then write about a topic related to your cultural or ethnic identity.

This chapter will help you

- analyze a topic by logical division.
- expand a paragraph to a simple essay by developing supporting points as body paragraphs.
- use parallel structure in thesis statements.
- increase cohesion by using repeated words, synonyms, and transitions to create links between your thesis and the topic sentences of your body paragraphs.
- use adjective clauses to include additional information in your writing.

READING FOR WRITING

Before You Read

With a partner or a small group, read the following paragraph and discuss the questions that follow.

Culture is a broad term. It includes all the customs, values, and beliefs of a group of people. *Ethnic identity* is an even broader term. It is the sense of connection a person feels to a particular group and can be based on shared customs, race, language, religion, or homeland.

1. Are children usually aware of their culture or ethnic identity?

2. How do children learn about their culture or ethnic identity?

3. What gives children either positive or negative feelings about their culture or ethnic identity?

To Be an American, Black, Catholic, and Creole

by Alfred J. Guillaume, Jr.

segregated: divided according to race

Native Americans: the original inhabitants of the Americas, Indians

1   I am a 50-year old American. I am black, Roman Catholic, and Creole. This is how I describe myself 50 years in the making. As a young boy growing up in the South, I was made to believe that I was different. Images of America did not mirror me. The segregated° South wanted me to believe that I was inferior. The Catholic Church taught me that all of God's people were equal. My French Creole heritage gave me a special bond to Native Americans°, to Europeans, and to Africans. This is the composite portrait of who I am. I like who I am and can imagine being no other.

exoticism: foreignness

2   I'm an American. I was born in New Orleans, Louisiana, whose elegance and exoticism° make it America's most European city and also its most Caribbean. Natives call it the Big Easy. From its founding, New Orleans has been a place that represents good times—the enjoyment of music, food, and celebration.

derogatory: insulting

unparalleled: unequaled

3   I'm an African American. Just within my lifetime, people of African ancestry have been called colored, Negro, black, and various derogatory° terms that I completely reject. I am proud to have been born black. My people paid a heavy price through toil and suffering to make America. Their unparalleled° creative contributions shaped American culture.

Protestants: members of various Christian churches that separated from the Catholic Church

nun: a woman who joins a religious order

seminarian: a man studying to be a priest

4   I am Catholic. I thought everyone was Catholic until I went to school and learned that there were Protestants°. The nuns° taught my schoolmates and me to pray for them and for all other non-Catholics. My values were formed in large part by my religious faith. As a child I dreamed of becoming a priest. I left my parents at age 12 to study for the priesthood in New York. I made my first long journey on a train with five other seminarians° from my parish.

5   I am Creole. I trace my ancestry to Africa, to Europe, and to Native America. The word *Creole* is used to define Europeans who came to the Americas, but *Creole* also refers to blacks in the Americas, mixed-blood people whose ancestry can be traced to Africa as well as to Europe. This is my heritage: a blend of Africa, Europe, and Native America. The first languages of my maternal grandparents were French and Creole, a kind of pidgin° French. I regret that my siblings and I never learned to speak the language. We lived in the city and the language was spoken primarily in the rural areas. My mother understood the language but never spoke it to us. Speaking English correctly was important, particularly without the melodic° Creole accent so characteristic of natives of southern Louisiana. Yet even without the language, I speak with a regional accent. On my paternal side were the Houma Indians. Pictures of my great-great grandmother are prized family possessions.

pidgin: a language that is a mixture of two other languages

melodic: musical

6   I grew up in the segregated South. My parents shielded us from racism. Our upbringing, our religion, and our schooling protected us. We lived in a middle-class neighborhood, attended a Catholic elementary school run by a black order of nuns called the Holy Family Sisters, and went to Mass at a black Catholic church. We lived in a cocoon° in our black, Catholic, Creole world. Because of all the support Creole society provided, it seemed that segregation did not affect us. It was not until the sixties, during my teenage years, that I became fully aware of the dehumanizing° effects of segregation.

cocoon: a protective covering like the kind a caterpillar makes while it is becoming a butterfly

dehumanizing: having the effect of removing human dignity

7   Creole society could not totally isolate us from racial prejudice. I remember sitting with my maternal grandmother in the colored section of the bus, behind the "Colored Only" sign, when a white patron removed the sign and put it behind us, forcing us to stand and relinquish our seat to him. I remember the separate water fountains, the separate entrances to restaurants, the separate playgrounds, the separate schools and churches. In department stores and other businesses, blacks did menial work; the salespeople and bosses were white. I remember the day my dad took me with him to the post office, where he worked. At the desks and the service counters were only whites; I asked my dad to show me his office. I had no notion then that only whites had offices.

8   My first recollection that black meant being inferior occurred one morning as I walked to school. In the segregated South, only white children were bused to school. A young white boy, about my own age—eight or so— yelled out the window of the yellow school bus, "Hey, chocolate boy!" When I related this story to my maternal great aunt her response to me was, "Cher (My dear), you a pretty chocolate boy." Since then I have always taken a particular delight in being "chocolate."

9   Though the message of segregation was hatred and subjugation°, my parents taught my four siblings and me never to feel inferior to whites. We never heard a disparaging° word in our home about white people. Rather than thinking that whites were superior, we grew up thinking that we were special. We were Americans. And not only were we colored, we were Creole and Catholic. My father took particular delight in repeatedly saying that each of us was a jewel; we were five dazzling jewels, and each was different. My parents taught us to believe in ourselves above all else, and that we were never to forget where we came from.

subjugation: forcing people into an inferior position

disparaging: critical or disrespectful

10   What I've accomplished professionally I owe to discipline, a good education, and opportunity. Education was stressed in my family. My siblings and I knew from an early age that we would go to college. My parents taught us that everything was within our reach, because success depended on our hard work and persistence. My dad taught us never to give up, that the word "can't" is not in the dictionary. We were Guillaumes, he would say, and a Guillaume never gives up. He told us never to accept mediocrity°. He encouraged us in our schoolwork always to aim for an *A*. "It is far better to aim high and miss the mark," he would say, "than aim low and make it." We understood that to mean that if we studied for an *A* and failed, then our reward would be a *B* or no less than a *C*. But if we studied for a *D* and succeeded, the results would be disastrous. I consider myself blessed to have had parents who valued education and who understood the limitless potential education affords.

mediocrity: the condition of being no better than average

11   I am divorced with two sons, ages 19 and 11. I know that each is trying to find his place in a society that is increasingly multicultural but whose power base remains white. As young black men they struggle with the stereotypical° images of what being black means in America. This is particularly true for my older son, who learned bitterly what it meant to be black when, as a young boy of 11, he was stopped by campus police at a Midwest university and escorted off campus because he did not belong there. He was afraid to tell them that his father was the vice president. My younger son, to my knowledge, has not yet experienced racism at its ugliest. He remains open and accepting of others. He hates talk of black people and white people and proudly proclaims that all people are the same. For him, the important quality in a person is whether he or she is nice.

stereotypical: having to do with a possibly wrong or unfair idea of what a particular type of person is like *integrity:* the quality of being honest and of having high moral principles

12   I am raising my sons as my parents raised me. I teach them that it is less important that the world sees you as black, and it is more important that the world recognizes you as a person of strength and integrity°. As my father taught me, I teach them to be strong and independent, to be individuals. I tell them that they are jewels, that there are no others like them, that they have unique gifts of self, and that they should be willing to share their gifts of self with others. Color is not important; character is. They are special and they honor their father and their heritage.

About the Author

Alfred J. Guillaume, Jr., Ph.D., is the vice chancellor for academic affairs at Indiana University, South Bend. He has also held the position of provost and vice president for academic affairs at Humboldt State University and St. Louis University. "To Be an American, Black, Catholic, and Creole" is adapted from a longer essay by the same name.

Understanding the Reading

With a partner or a small group, discuss the following questions.

1. In the first paragraph of the essay, Guillaume tells us that he is going to give us a *composite portrait* of himself. What is a composite portrait, and why must Guillaume's be composite?

2. Guillaume develops the parts of his composite portrait with details and examples. Which ones do you remember (without looking back at the essay)? Why are they memorable?

3. Which parts of his composite identity (nationality, race, religion, and culture) does Guillaume emphasize most in this essay? Why do you think he does this?

4. What is a Creole? How do you think being Creole protected Guillaume and his family from racial discrimination?

5. What examples does Guillaume use to illustrate the fact that he experienced racial discrimination at an early age? How did he manage to retain his pride, or his positive self-image, in the face of discrimination?

6. Guillaume also discusses the values that he learned from his parents. What are those values, and why are they important in this essay?

7. In paragraph 11, Guillaume discusses his sons' growing sense of their own identity and he explains that there is a difference between the two boys. What does this explanation tell us about how children form their identity?

8. Do you, like Guillaume, see yourself as belonging to several groups, or do you see yourself as belonging to just one? Explain.

Vocabulary Expansion

Vocabulary for analyzing cultures. To explain your culture to someone, you could, like Guillaume, begin by identifying its parts.

Exercise 1
Complete the following activities.

1. The circular diagram represents a culture. In each of the six wedge-shaped sections of the circle, write an aspect of culture, such as *architecture*.

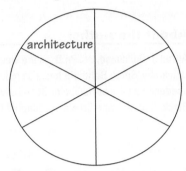

2. In the word-family chart below, write the six nouns you used in the culture circle. Check the dictionary to see if there is an adjective in the word family of each noun. If you find one, add it to the chart. (You may not find adjectives for all your nouns.)

Nouns	Adjectives
architecture	architectural

WRITING

Assignment

You will analyze one of the following topics by logical division. That means you will divide the topic into parts and discuss each part. First you will write a paragraph, and later you will expand it to an essay. Select a topic from the list on page 81 that you will be able to divide into parts and whose parts you will be able to develop well.

1. Tell what your culture or ethnic identity is. Identify and describe three or four aspects of your culture or ethnic identity.

2. Write about your home country in terms of its geographic parts or your native city in terms of its neighborhoods.

3. Analyze a holiday or celebration that is observed in your culture. Divide that celebration into parts according to time, place, or people's roles.

4. Write about the life of a person in your country in terms of its parts. For example, Mahatma Gandhi's life can be analyzed by *time* (periods of his life: youth, mid-life, old age), *places* he lived (England, South Africa, India), or *roles* he played in his life (student, lawyer, social reformer, religious and political leader). The person you choose does not need to be famous. If you write about an ordinary person, you can analyze either the person's entire life or a day in his or her life.

What Logical Division Is and Why It Is Important

Logical division helps us understand things that are big, complicated, unfamiliar, or abstract by dividing them into parts. For example, to understand a country such as China, we can divide it into geographic regions (northern, eastern, southern, western) and study each region. Or we can divide it according to the languages people speak in different parts or the way people make their living in different areas. We can also use logical division to study China over time, looking at the many stages in its history.

Finding a basis of division. A **basis of division** is a way to divide a topic. The two most common bases of division are *time* and *place*. These two concepts will help you analyze, or divide into logical parts, many different topics.

Exercise 2

Read each topic idea and decide whether you would analyze it according to time or place. Write *T* (time) or *P* (place). Some topic ideas may be analyzed both ways.

__P__	1. the marketplace in San Salvador
_____	2. New Year's celebration in Japan
_____	3. a traditional meal in Morocco
_____	4. economic zones in Portugal
_____	5. ethnic groups in the former Yugoslavia
_____	6. language groups in India
_____	7. the Great Wall of China
_____	8. the life of Albert Einstein

Compare your answers with your classmates'. Discuss any differences in your responses.

Place and *time* are not the only bases of division you can use in a logical division paper. When you analyze the life of a person like Albert Einstein, you can use *roles* (scientist, teacher, father) as well as *time* and *place*. When you write about a culture, you can select *aspects* such as music or architecture to discuss.

Your **purpose** (why you have chosen to write about a topic and the message you want to express about the topic) will determine the parts or aspects of your topic that you discuss. For example, if you wanted to show that Einstein was a better scientist and teacher than father, you would use *role* as an organizing principle. If you wanted to show that Einstein's life in Switzerland was more productive than his life in Germany or the United States, you would use *place* or *time*.

Prewriting

Select a topic. Analyze the topics on page 81, or consider how you could divide each one into parts. Ask yourself what purpose you would have in writing about each topic. Notice how Dion, a student from Fiji, analyzed each topic before he selected one to write about. Dion chose topic 3, the celebration of Fiji Day, because it has three parts that he thought he could develop well.

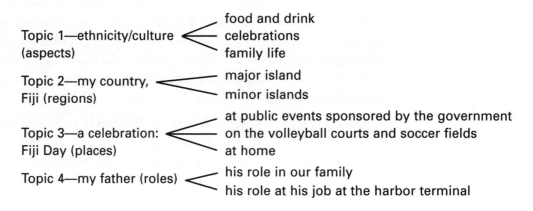

Topic 1—ethnicity/culture (aspects)
- food and drink
- celebrations
- family life

Topic 2—my country, Fiji (regions)
- major island
- minor islands

Topic 3—a celebration: Fiji Day (places)
- at public events sponsored by the government
- on the volleyball courts and soccer fields
- at home

Topic 4—my father (roles)
- his role in our family
- his role at his job at the harbor terminal

Choose a topic that has two or more parts you can develop well. (The ideal number of parts is three, but two or four will work as well.) Then follow the series of prewriting steps listed below. As you read through the steps, you will see how Dion prepared to write a paragraph about Fiji Day.

STEP 1 Draft a **topic sentence**.

Dion drafted this topic sentence.

On Fiji Day we have a wonderful time in Sula at public events, in casual matches on the volleyball courts and soccer fields, and at home.

STEP 2 Develop each part of your topic by making a **brainstorming list** for it. If you have two parts, make two lists; if you have three parts, make three lists, and so on.

Dion decided to divide Fiji Day celebrations according to place. Because he had three locations to discuss, he made three lists.

At Public Events
government officials' speeches
singing competition between church choirs

On the Volleyball Courts and Soccer Fields
young people gather and form casual teams
after they play, they sit on the grass and chat
winners tease the losers, but there is no serious competition

At Home
relatives help prepare the meal which includes <u>palusami</u>, a mixture of
    chicken or beef, onion, and tomato wrapped in a taro leaf and cooked
    in coconut milk
the head of the household makes <u>yaqona</u>, our traditional drink, and offers it
    to the guests in coconut shell cups

STEP 3 Make an **outline**. Your outline must have three levels: **topic sentence, supporting points**, and **development**.

Dion marked his topic sentence (*TS*), his supporting points (*SP*), and finally his development (*DEV*).

On Fiji Day we have a wonderful time in Sula at the public events, on the volleyball courts and soccer fields, and at home. (TS)

I. The public events give a feeling of national pride and provide some fine traditional Fijian entertainment. (SP)
  A. Public speeches are delivered by elected officials. (DEV)
  B. Awards are presented for the young people's essay contest. (DEV)
  C. There is a singing competition between church choirs. (DEV)

II. Soccer and volleyball games give us a chance to meet and play together with friends. (SP)
  A. Winners tease the losers, but there is no serious competition. (DEV)
  B. Players stay to chat after the game. (DEV)

III. At home, a big celebration is underway. (SP)
   A. Friends and relatives arrive early to help make <u>palusami</u>, a mixture of chicken or beef, onion, and tomato wrapped in a taro leaf and cooked in coconut milk. (DEV)
   B. The head of the household makes <u>yaqona</u>, our traditional drink, in a large bowl and offers it to the guests in a coconut shell cups. (DEV)
   C. After the drinking, everyone eats <u>palusami</u>, rice, and salad. (DEV)

When your outline is complete, you will be ready to write your first draft. Dion wrote the following paragraph.

Fiji Day

On Fiji Day we have a wonderful time in Sula at the public events, on the volleyball courts and on the soccer fields, and at home. At the public celebrations, government officials' speeches and fine traditional Fijian entertainment stir feelings of national pride. Awards are presented to young people for the annual essay competition, and there is a singing contest between church choirs. All Fijians love sports, and on the beaches and in the parks, informal games of volleyball and soccer give young people a chance to play together and socialize. Sometimes winners playfully tease the losers, but there is no serious competition. After the games, players stay to chat with their friends. Finally, at home a big celebration is underway. Friends and relatives arrive early to help make *palusami*—a mixture of chicken, onion, and tomato, wrapped in a taro leaf and cooked in coconut milk. The head of the household makes the traditional drink, *yaqona*, in a large bowl and offers it to the guests in coconut shells. After the *yaqona* drinking, everyone eats *palusami*, rice, and salad. Fiji Day is our most popular celebration because it incorporates all the things Fijians love most: our national heritage, sports, food and drink, and socializing with family and friends.

Exercise 3

With a partner or a small group, review Dion's paragraph.

1. Find the three levels of development in Dion's paragraph. Put <u>one line</u> under the first level (topic sentence), <u>two lines</u> under the second level (supporting points), and brackets ([ ]) around the third level (development).

2. How would you divide this paragraph if you were to expand it into a five-paragraph essay? Put slash lines (/ /) to show where the introduction and each of the three body paragraphs would end. Discuss what kind of information you might add to the text in order to expand it into an essay.

After selecting a topic from the list on page 81 that you think you can explain well in terms of its parts, follow the sequence of prewriting steps Dion used.

First Draft

Now you are ready to write the first draft of your paragraph. Following your outline, begin with your topic sentence, add supporting points and development, and finish with a concluding sentence. After writing, put your draft away for a while before you return to it. In the Revising section of this chapter, you will expand your paragraph into a simple essay.

REVISING

Composition Focus

Before you expand your paragraph to an essay, check it to make sure that it communicates effectively. Follow the directions in the following Review and Revise box.

Review and Revise 1: First-Draft Paragraph
Review your paragraph. Ask yourself if it has the three levels a paragraph should have: a clear topic sentence that presents the main idea, supporting points, and development. Review your topic sentence to see whether it informs the reader that you are going to divide your topic into parts. If your topic sentence or your paragraph needs improvement, revise it now.

Expanding a paragraph to an essay. We read paragraphs as units of information. We can read a paragraph of ten or twelve sentences and keep all the ideas in mind. However, when paragraphs become longer than that, we find it difficult to focus on the whole paragraph at once.

Therefore, when you have too much supporting information in a paragraph, you need to break it down into smaller paragraphs. In order to expand your one-paragraph composition to an essay, you will change your composition in the following ways:

1. Topic Sentence ⟶ Thesis Statement

   The topic sentence of your paragraph will become the thesis statement of your essay.

2. Supporting Points ⟶ Body Paragraphs

   The supporting points will become the topic sentences of your body paragraphs.

3. **Development** ⟶ **More Development**

You will add more development to complete the body paragraphs of the essay. This is the most important part of changing a paragraph to an essay.

4. **Concluding Sentence** ⟶ **Conclusion**

The concluding sentence of your paragraph will become the conclusion of your essay.

In this chapter, you will learn how to develop the supporting points into body paragraphs and write a **simple essay**. In Chapter 5, you will learn how to write an introduction and conclusion for a **complete essay**.

Outlining and expansion. When you expand a paragraph into an essay, you keep the same main idea statement and supporting points. Therefore, it is usually not necessary to make a new outline. The only thing you might add to your original outline is some additional development.

Exercise 4

A. Read the paragraph and the simple essay about the culture of Kenya. You will see that the essay is an expansion of the paragraph. Then do the activities that follow.

PARAGRAPH

The Cultures of Kenya: Enduring Aspects of a Diverse People

Although Kenya has many different ethnic groups and these groups have been affected to various degrees by European colonization, the cultures of people across the nation share some common characteristics. One enduring aspect of the cultures of Kenya is the family. Traditionally, Kenyan people received all their education from their parents and grandparents. Today there are schools to educate children, but the family is still very important as a social unit. Another enduring aspect of Kenyan cultures is respect for the old. Traditional society was organized around not only family life but also relationships with a group of people of the same age. These same-age groups went through all the stages of life together until they became the much-respected elders who made decisions for the community. Today old people are still respected, but they don't have the responsibility of leadership that they once had. Another enduring aspect of Kenyan cultures is dance. Traditionally, dances marked all the important events in life. Kenyans in both the countryside and the cities still dance, but most dancing is done simply for pleasure these days. The traditional music of Kenya has been influenced by music from the United States and Europe, and new styles of music and dance have evolved. To sum up, the cultures of Kenya's ethnic groups have undergone many changes, but family, respect for elders, and dance still have an important place in the lives of the people of Kenya.

SIMPLE ESSAY   **The Cultures of Kenya: Enduring Aspects of a Diverse People**

INTRODUCTION

Although Kenya contains many different ethnic groups and these groups have been affected to various degrees by European colonization, the cultures of people across the nation still share common characteristics: Families are important to them, they respect their elders, and they enjoy dance.

BODY PARAGRAPH

One enduring aspect of the cultures of Kenya is the family. Traditionally, people received all their education from their parents and grandparents in the form of stories, songs, and proverbs. Although this is no longer the case today because schools educate the children, the family is still a vital social unit. Most people in Kenya live on scattered farms with their families or extended families and their nearest neighbors are relatives. Usually everyone in their region is related to them in some way. Clans or large extended families cooperate in community projects such as the building of schools. To some extent, the growth in recent decades of large-scale farms and cities has put a strain on rural family life. Fathers often go away to work for extended periods of time, leaving mothers and aging parents to manage the family farms. This is a hardship for families, but the money that fathers send home helps with expenses such as school tuition.

BODY PARAGRAPH

Another enduring aspect of Kenyan cultures is respect for the old. Traditional society was organized around not only family life but also relationships with a group of people of the same age. These same-age groups went through all the stages of life together until they became the much-respected elders who made decisions for the community. Formerly, councils of elders were the only government the people had. They made decisions, judged wrong-doing, and initiated social activities. Today Kenya's central government and its regional branches have taken over these functions. Although Kenyans still show respect for elders with gestures and greetings, old people do not have the leadership role they once had.

BODY PARAGRAPH

Another enduring aspect of Kenyan cultures is dance. Traditionally, dances marked all important events in life—coming-of-age ceremonies and weddings, wars or hunts, planting and harvesting. Traditional dances did not allow much self-expression; they were learned and performed in the same way that generations before had learned them. The dances told stories and thus formed part of the education of the young people in the community. For the most part, these traditional dances are only performed by professional dancers now, but all Kenyans still enjoy dancing. The traditional music of Kenya has been influenced by jazz, rock, and hip-hop music from the United States and Europe, and, as a result, new styles of music have evolved, such as *benga,* which combines traditional rhythms and modern instrumentation. Kenyans enjoy dancing to *benga* and many other styles of music that are a fusion of old and new.

CONCLUSION   Traditional cultures in Kenya have undergone many changes, but family, respect for elders, and dance still have an important place in the lives of the people of Kenya.

B. Compare the paragraph and the simple essay.

1. *Main Idea Statement.* Find the main idea statement in the paragraph (topic sentence) and in the essay (thesis statement). Draw <u>one line</u> under them. What is the difference between the two main idea statements?

2. *Supporting Points.* Find the supporting points in the paragraph and in the essay, and draw <u>two lines</u> under them. Where are the supporting points in the essay? What transition words are used to mark the supporting points?

3. *Development.* Find the development for the supporting points in the paragraph and the essay and put brackets [ ] around it. How many sentences did the writer add to each supporting point in order to expand his ideas into an essay?

C. With a partner, compare how you each marked the text. Discuss your observations with your teacher and classmates.

D. With your teacher and classmates, make *one* outline showing the structure of the paragraph and the essay.

Review and Revise 2: Preparing to Expand Your Paragraph
Review your first-draft paragraph and the outline you prepared before writing. Put slash marks (/) in your paragraph to show where you will divide it when you expand it to an essay. You may find it helpful to cut the paragraph up with scissors and then tape each piece to a separate piece of paper for expanding and revising. Or, if you are working on a computer, you can simply insert spaces between the various parts of your paragraph.

From topic sentence to thesis statement: Adding supporting points. In Chapter 3, you learned that a topic sentence has two parts, the topic and the controlling idea. The same is true of thesis statements. Because an essay contains a lot of information, it is helpful to the reader if its controlling idea names the supporting points. In a logical division essay, naming the supporting points means naming the parts. Compare the topic sentence and thesis statement below.

Topic sentence
Chinese New Year celebrations have three **parts.**

Thesis statement
Chinese New Year celebrations have three **parts**: the preparations, New Year's Eve and New Year's Day, and the two weeks following New Year's Day.

The controlling idea of the thesis statement names the parts of the celebration (*the preparations, New Year's Eve and New Year's Day*, and *the two weeks following New Year's Day*). This helps the reader anticipate what will appear in the body paragraphs of the essay.

Vocabulary for logical division. In addition to the word *part*, other nouns can be used in the controlling idea of a logical division essay.

Time	Space	Parts or Qualities
period	district	aspect
stage	region	characteristic
	zone	element
		feature
		quality

Exercise 5

Complete each thesis statement with an appropriate word from the chart above. Mark each thesis statement below *C* (complete) if the thesis names the parts of the controlling idea or *I* (incomplete) if it does not name the parts.

___I___ 1. The Island of Cyprus has two distinct ethnic ____regions____.

_____ 2. The culture of Haiti has three _____: the people's African heritage, the French language, and cultural influence from Latin America.

_____ 3. Each of Uruguay's four agricultural _____ has a certain type of product: fresh fruit and vegetables, milk and dairy products, grain, and meat.

_____ 4. Over time, the celebration of Christmas that we see in the United States today has developed in a series of _____.

_____ 5. The Brazilian dance called the *samba* has three important _____: rhythm, lyrics, and dance steps.

_____ 6. Dag Hammarskjöld, who was secretary-general of the United Nations from 1953 to 1961, is remembered for these _____: tactfulness, self-discipline, and a strong sense of duty.

_____ 7. The three dominant buildings of Thailand's Royal Palace symbolize three significant _____ in the country's history

_____ 8. The cellist Yo-Yo Ma is greatly admired for two _____: his personal warmth and the sensitivity of his playing.

_____ 9. The celebration of Holy Week in Guatemala has two important _____: the religious objects that are carried in processions through the streets and the colors worn by the people in the processions.

_____ 10. The city of Salzburg, Austria, has three unique _____: The oldest is the medieval part with narrow, winding streets; the second oldest is the baroque part with wide boulevards and large public buildings; and the newest is the modern, industrial part with factories and high-rise apartment buildings.

> **Review and Revise 3: Supporting Points in Thesis Statements**
> Look at your composition. The topic sentence of your first-draft paragraph will become the thesis statement of your simple essay. Check the controlling idea of your thesis statement to see whether it lists the supporting points of your essay. If not, expand it so that it includes your supporting points.

Parallel structure in thesis statements. When your thesis statement lists your supporting points, the supporting points must be **parallel**. That is, they must be the same part of speech.

Underline parallel elements in the following examples.

1. In our region, most men work in offices, stores, and factories.

2. Our culture is unique because of its architectural, musical, and artistic traditions.

What elements are parallel in sentence 1? What part of speech are they? What elements are parallel in sentence 2? What part of speech are they?

In sentence 1, the words *offices, stores,* and *factories* are parallel. They are all nouns. It would be wrong to write the sentence this way:

INCORRECT: In our region, most men work in offices, stores, and industrial.

For more on parallel structure, see Appendix IA, page 283.

Offices and *stores* are nouns. *Industrial* is an adjective. That is why the sentence above is not parallel and is therefore incorrect.

Exercise 6

Each statement contains a list that is not parallel. Find the word in each list that is not parallel and change its form so that the words are parallel. Then underline the parallel items.

1. The economy is based on ~~agricultural~~, mining, and industry.

   agriculture

2. The inhabitants of the two regions share a common history, language, and architectural.

3. The names of cities and towns come from religion, history, or natural.

4. The language, art, and educational of this community have barely changed over the last 100 years.

5. The land can be divided in three parts: forest, grasslands, and dry.

6. The community has well-organized educational, political, and law organizations.

7. The city has three kinds of buildings: public, commercial, and houses.

Review and Revise 4: Parallel Structure in Thesis Statements
Look at your thesis statement again. If you have used a list in the controlling idea of your thesis, make sure that it has correct parallel structure.

Linking the thesis statement to the body paragraphs: Cohesion. When we read, we look for connections. If the parts of a paragraph or essay have clear connections, we say that the paragraph or essay has **cohesion**.

In essays, the most important connections are between the thesis statement and the topic sentences of the body paragraphs. These connections will be very clear in your essay if you:

1. name the supporting points in your thesis statement.

2. put the supporting points in the body paragraphs in the same order as they appear in your thesis statement.

3. repeat the words you have used in the controlling idea of your thesis statement in the topic sentences of your body paragraphs or use *synonyms* (words that have the same or similar meaning).

4. use transitions such as *another, second,* and *finally* in the topic sentences of your body paragraphs.

Exercise 7

Work with a partner. One of you should read the essay "Fiji Day" below, and the other should reread "The Cultures of Kenya: Enduring Aspects of a Diverse People" on pages 87–88. Find signals of cohesion in your assigned essay, and complete the chart that follows.

Fiji Day

On Fiji Day we have a wonderful time in Sula at the public events, on the volleyball courts and on the soccer fields, and at home.

At the public celebrations, government officials' speeches and fine traditional Fijian entertainment stir feelings of national pride. Politicians remind us of the value of our independence and the importance of harmony in our multiethnic society. Men wearing grass skirts and women wearing tapa cloth perform *meke*, a performance of dance and singing which tells a story. Awards are presented to young people for the annual essay competition, and there is a singing contest between church choirs.

All Fijians love sports, and on the beaches and in the parks, informal games of volleyball and soccer give young people a chance to get together and socialize. Fiji Day comes in early October, when the weather is not too hot or humid, so the games can last for hours. Sometimes the winners playfully tease the losers, but there is no serious competition. After the games, players sit on the grass and chat, catching up with old friends and making new acquaintances.

Finally, at home, friends and relatives arrive carrying baskets of breadfruit as the women prepare a feast. They gossip in the kitchen as they make *palusami*—a mixture of chicken, onion, and tomato, wrapped in a taro leaf and cooked in coconut milk. Someone plays the guitar while the head of the household makes the traditional drink, *yaqona*, in a large bowl and offers it to the guests in coconut shells. People sit on the hand-woven mats in a circle, celebrating as their ancestors have done: Upon receiving the cup they clap once, drink, say "Bula," and clap three times in appreciation. After the *yaqona* drinking, everyone eats *palusami*, rice, yams, salad, and fish roasted in banana leaves. The celebration can last long into the night.

Fiji Day is our most popular celebration because it incorporates all the things Fijians love most: our national heritage, sports, food and drink, and socializing with family and friends.

Culture, Identity, and Homeland | 93

Signals of Cohesion in _____

(Name of Essay)

1. **Words** or **phrases** from the controlling idea of the thesis statement that are **repeated** in the topic sentences of the body paragraph:

_____

_____

2. **Synonyms** used in the topic sentences of the body paragraphs that refer to words or phrases in the controlling idea of the thesis statement:

_____

_____

3. **Transitions** that link the topic sentences to the thesis statement and the body paragraphs to one another:

_____

_____

Discuss the signals of cohesion that you found with your partner. Why are signals of cohesion important? Do these two essays illustrate good cohesion?

Review and Revise 5: Cohesion
Check your thesis statement and the topic sentences of your body paragraphs for cohesion. If you have not used repeated words, synonyms, and transitions to link the thesis and the body paragraphs, add them now.

Development of body paragraphs. The most important part of expanding a composition from a paragraph to an essay is developing its body paragraphs. The two main types of development are **examples** and **explanation**.

1. **Examples** are references to specific things or events that help readers understand general or abstract ideas. In Chapter 3 you learned to introduce examples with _for example_ and _such as_.

   > In the celebration of Nawruz, or Persian New Year, symbolic things are displayed on a table. _For example_, there are silver coins, which represent prosperity, and eggs, which represent fertility. There are also herbs _such as_ sumac and rue.

2. **Explanation** means providing information of various types to readers. Explanation can include:

   a. giving the meaning of words or symbols

   > In the Nawruz celebration, the table is covered with a _sofreh_. This is a special tablecloth for the occasion.

b. presenting a reason that something occurs

> Nawruz has its roots in the Zoroastrian religion. It is celebrated on March 21 because that is the birthday of the Zoroastrian prophet Zarathustra.

c. telling the process by which something occurs

> Preparation for Nawruz begins weeks in advance. First, the whole house must be cleaned from top to bottom. Then new clothes are purchased, or old clothes are washed so that they can be worn on the holiday. Finally, special foods must be purchased and prepared according to tradition.

d. describing how something looks or sounds

> Nawruz is a time of light-hearted fun. In the evening, people gather around bonfires, talking and laughing as they try to jump over the flames, following an ancient custom.

Exercise 8

Read the following essay. Two of the body paragraphs are well developed, but one needs additional examples and explanations. Write a message to the writer, telling him or her which paragraph needs development and suggesting ways to develop that paragraph.

The Original Shanghainese

The population of Shanghai has grown very fast in recent years with a great influx of migrants from all over China, so there are now two groups of people in Shanghai: long-time Shanghai residents and newcomers. The members of each group identify themselves by their language, clothing, and food.

Language separates long-time Shanghai residents from newcomers. Although Mandarin has replaced Shanghainese as the official language of the city, long-term residents prefer to speak the local dialect, Shanghainese, in social situations. New residents in Shanghai come from all parts of China, so they speak many different dialects.

Clothing also distinguishes long-time Shanghai residents from newcomers. Long-term residents are very fashion conscious. Young people wear blue jeans, while older adults prefer suits. Men and women alike respect brand names, which they sometimes display on handbags, footwear, or even business suits. Women wear muted color combinations. Newcomers often dress in traditional Chinese jackets and work clothes. The newcomer women tend to wear brighter colors than the long-term residents.

Not only language and clothing, but also food serves to identify long-time Shanghai residents and newcomers. The long-time residents eat rice porridge, flat bread, and fried dough sticks for breakfast, while the newcomers from the provinces prefer steamed bread or soup. Also, because Shanghai is an international city, the original Shanghainese are more likely to sample Western foods. For example, for lunch a long-time Shanghai resident might order a sandwich and a soda, while a newcomer would select a traditional meal of rice, vegetables, and bean curd.

As Shanghai's population has grown, it has become apparent that there are two social groups in the city. The residents of Shanghai identify themselves as either long-term residents or as newcomers by the way they speak, dress, and eat.

To the writer: _____

_____

_____

_____

Review and Revise 6: Development of Body Paragraphs
If your body paragraphs lack examples or explanation, add some now. Try to use various types of development (examples as well as explanations, which include the meaning of words, reasons, processes, or description) in your essay.

Language Focus

Adjective clauses. An adjective clause is a dependent clause that modifies a noun. Adjective clauses begin with the relative pronouns *who, whom, which, that, whose, where,* and *when.* Adjective clauses provide a way to combine short sentences and show relationships between ideas. Look at the following examples.

1a. King Sejong ruled Korea during a time of peace and prosperity. He was responsible for the invention of the Korean alphabet.

RELATIVE
PRONOUN

1b. King Sejong, ***who*** *ruled Korea during a time of peace and prosperity,* was responsible for the invention of the Korean alphabet.

2a. The Korean alphabet has fourteen consonants and ten vowels. It is relatively easy to learn.

RELATIVE
PRONOUN

2b. The Korean alphabet ***which*** *has fourteen consonants and ten vowels,* is relatively easy to learn.

For more on adjective clauses, see Appendix IA, page 261.

In the examples above, notice that the relative pronouns ***who*** and ***which*** follow the nouns that they modify. In example 1b, ***who*** refers to *King Sejong,* and in example 2b, ***which*** refers to *Korean alphabet.*

Exercise 9

A. This essay contains seven adjective clauses. Underline the adjective clauses and circle the nouns they modify.

[1]The (Nile), <u>which is the longest river in the world</u>, flows through northeastern Africa from Lake Victoria to the Mediterranean Sea. [2]The history of the relationship between the Nile and the people of Egypt has two parts: the period before the Aswan Dam was built and the period since.

[3]Over 4,000 years ago, the Nile made ancient Egypt a birthplace of civilization. [4]The river brought water to this extremely dry land, where agriculture would not have been possible without its annual flooding. [5]The floodwaters also distributed a fine dark soil called silt, which is rich in nutrients. [6]The ancient Egyptians learned to trap the waters of the Nile for irrigation and raise enough food to support their thriving civilization. [7]The Nile also provided food in the form of fish and waterfowl, and the plant called *papyrus* grew along its banks, from which the ancient Egyptians made paper. [8]While Egyptians still depend on the Nile today, their relationship to the river and the river itself have changed.

[9]The Nile was altered in 1971, when the Aswan High Dam was completed. [10]The river does not flood its banks anymore, so the Egyptian people, most of whom live along its banks, no longer have to worry about annual floodwaters destroying their homes. [11]Egyptian farmers today are able to raise food year round because there is a constant supply of water, whereas in centuries past, they could produce only one crop a year. [12]When the dam went into operation, new lands were opened to farming in the Upper Nile, but at the same time, agricultural lands were lost in the delta region, where saltwater from the Mediterranean flooded the fields and made them unusable.

[13]The two-part history of the Nile has an important lesson: [14]People have benefited from this great river, which has allowed civilization to flourish for over 4,000 years, and so people must take responsibility for the Nile's future.

B. Now read the essay without the adjective clauses. Notice how much information the clauses contribute.

Exercise 10

Read each paragraph and the list of sentences following it. Find a place in the paragraph for each sentence, change the sentence to an adjective clause, and insert it in the paragraph. To help you, the part of the sentence which must be changed to a relative pronoun (*who, which, where,* or *when*) is underlined. Rewrite the three paragraphs with the added adjective clauses on a piece of paper. Punctuate all the adjective clauses in this exercise with commas.

> **Example**
> Another region in Brazil is known as the Pantanal, which means *swampland* in Portuguese. . . .

1. This paragraph is from an essay that describes geographic regions in Brazil.

   [1]Another region in Brazil is known as the Pantanal. [2]This vast lowland area in western Brazil is completely flooded in the rainy season from November to April. [3]The Pantanal is not suitable for farmland because of its poor soils, but it has been used for cattle grazing since the eighteenth century. [4]The Pantanal has remarkably varied wildlife including jaguars, wild pigs, giant river otters, large crocodilians called caimans, and capybaras. [5]There are at least 700 species of birds, including twenty-six kinds of parrots. [6]There are 260 species of fish. [7]In the dry season, when the lakes and ponds shrink to small pools, flocks of birds and caimans gather to feast upon the numerous fish trapped in them. [8]Brazilians say, "O Pantanal é vida," and the Pantanal is truly a very important part of the web of life on the South American continent.

   a. Pantanal means *swampland* in Portuguese.

   b. In the eighteenth century cowboys first staked out tracts of land as large as 12,000 square kilometers.

   c. Capybaras are the biggest rodents in the world.

   d. Many of the species of fish survive on fruits and nuts during the annual floods.

   e. "O Pantanal é vida," means "The Pantanal is life."

2. This paragraph is from an essay about aspects of Arab culture.

[1]Another important aspect of Arab culture is hospitality. [2]In Arab countries from Morocco to Iraq, visitors are very warmly welcomed. [3]Relatives, friends, and even strangers are always offered coffee or tea and perhaps some bread or sweets, and if they happen to arrive at mealtime, they are urged to stay and eat. [4]Guests cannot refuse these offers without offending their host. [5]This tradition of hospitality dates back thousands of years. [6]To survive in the desert, nomadic tribesmen had to depend on one another, so it became a matter of honor to give and receive hospitality. [7]The Quran and the books known as the *hadith* have helped preserve this tradition of hospitality by urging people to practice kindness. [8]But the holy books do not say that kindness and hospitality must be given without limit. Guests must know when to leave, and hospitality must be returned. [9]Hospitality can strengthen the bonds between the members of society only when its rules are followed well.

    a. <u>Their host</u> feels that how well he treats his guests is a measure of the kind of person he is.

    b. Water and food are scarce <u>in the desert</u>.

    c. <u>The Quran</u> is the chief holy book of Islam.

    d. <u>The *hadith*</u> relate the life story and teachings of the prophet Mohammed.

    e. <u>Hospitality</u> is actually part of a system of mutual obligations.

3. This paragraph is from an essay about economic zones in Mexico.

[1]The *maquiladora* zone is in the north, especially in the cities of Tijuana, Ciudad Juarez, and Matamoros. [2]*Maquiladoras* produce plastics, clothing, furniture, appliances, and electronic and automobile components. [3]*Maquiladora* owners take advantage of the relatively low cost of labor in Mexico. [4]The *maquiladora* workers have migrated to this border region from central and southern Mexico. [5]Most *maquiladoras* are owned by U.S., Japanese, and European companies such as IBM, Sony, and BMW. [6]As long as trading conditions remain favorable, international companies are likely to continue opening new *maquiladoras*.

a. <u>Tijuana, Ciudad Juarez, and Matamoros</u> are located near the U.S. border.

b. <u>Plastics, clothing, furniture, appliances, and electronic and automobile components</u> are shipped to the United States and other countries around the world.

c. Workers <u>in Mexico</u> earn a fraction of what U.S. industrial workers earn.

d. <u>The *maquiladora* workers</u> cannot find employment in their villages and towns.

e. <u>Large U.S., Japanese, and European companies such as IBM, Sony, and BMW</u> can import machinery and materials to Mexico duty free.

For the use of commas with adjective clauses, see Appendix IA, page 263.

> **Review and Revise 7: Adjective Clauses**
> Make sure your body paragraphs are well developed. Check to see if your composition has some adjective clauses. If you think your body paragraphs need more development, look for ways to use adjective clauses to include more information in your body paragraphs.

PEER REVIEW AND FINAL DRAFT

Now that you have revised your composition, it is time to share your writing with others. Exchange papers with one or two classmates. Turn to page 335 in Appendix II, and fill out the Peer Review form.

After considering your classmates' suggestions, prepare a final draft of your composition to hand in to your teacher. Before handing in your paper, check for correct use of parallel structure. Proofread for spelling and punctuation mistakes as well.

CHAPTER REVIEW

Look back at what you have accomplished in Chapter 4. Check (✓) what you have learned and what you have used as you have written and revised your composition.

Chapter 4 Topics	I understand this	I have used this
using logical division by time, place, or another organizing principle to analyze a topic (pages 81–82)		
expanding a paragraph to an essay by developing the supporting points in body paragraphs (pages 85–88)		
expanding main idea statements and using parallel structure to list supporting points in thesis statements (pages 88–90)		
using repeated words, synonyms, and transitions to link your thesis statement to the topic sentences of your body paragraphs to increase cohesion in your essay (pages 91–93)		
using adjective clauses to include more information in sentences and develop body paragraphs (pages 95–99)		

Full Pockets, Empty Pockets

◆ Writing a Cause-and-Effect Essay

Around the world people find themselves in very different living conditions—some rich and comfortable, some harsh and miserable—and they often live their whole lives without realizing that their situation is not typical of the other 6 billion Earth-dwellers. A look at the contrast that exists today invites serious questions.

This chapter will help you

- write a complete essay with an introduction and a conclusion.
- practice two methods of organization: time order and order of importance.
- use transitions to make the essay's organization clear.
- use the language of cause and effect.

READING FOR WRITING

Before You Read

1. Discuss these questions with a partner or a small group.

   a. What is globalization? Do you think globalization has affected your life? If so, explain.

   b. Every country has an economy, but economies are not all alike. Some economies are large and powerful; others are small and weak. In your opinion, what explains the differences?

2. Use the Internet or your local library to become familiar with some terms used in this reading. You may want to divide the items under question a and b so that a small group or pair of students can research one item and report back to the class. (The paragraph in the reading where the term appears is shown in parentheses.)

   a. The following economic concepts are mentioned in this reading. What do they mean?

      per capita income (paragraph 2)

      GDP (paragraph 3)

   b. Several multinational organizations are mentioned in this reading. When was each one formed and what is its purpose?

      OECD (paragraph 4)

      G8 (*formerly G7*) (paragraph 13)

      United Nations (U.N.) (paragraph 14)

      World Bank (paragraph 14)

      International Monetary Fund (IMF) (paragraph 14)

3. In the field of economics, explanations about the high growth rates of some economies and the slow growth rates of other economies are very controversial. That means everyone has an opinion, and there is little agreement. As you begin to read the following excerpt from the textbook *Global Connections: Canadian and World Issues*, look at the vocabulary for clues that reveal the authors' opinion. For example, words such as *strong*, *benefit*, and *growth* can suggest a positive attitude, and words such as *weak*, *harm*, and *decrease* suggest a negative attitude.

disparity: inequality

Global Economic Disparity°

by Bruce Clark and John Wallace

1 Most observers agree that economic globalization has created more wealth in the world. Unfortunately, the economic wealth has not been shared equitably among all nations and all peoples. While the wealthier nations have seen their economies grow, poorer countries have not.

2   For the world's poor, the situation has been described as "a race to the bottom." The United Nations has reported that per capita incomes in 100 countries, with a combined population of 1.6 billion, have dropped from the maximum levels ever reached. This decline has not been just a recent phenomenon°. Remarkably, almost 20 countries, from Armenia and Tajikistan to Nicaragua and Sudan, reached their maximum per capita income in 1960 or before, with 50 more reaching theirs in the 1960s and 1970s.

phenomenon: a thing or event that can be observed or studied

3   By the end of the 1990s, the world found itself in the sad situation in which its 13 richest countries had per capita incomes of more than US$20,000, while the 26 poorest countries had per capita GDPs of less than $350 per year. While 200 million people saw their incomes fall between 1965 and 1983, the situation was even worse between 1980 and 1993, when more than five times that many experienced a decline in income.

4   At the same time, there has been a much smaller number of economic winners, some of whom have enjoyed remarkable success. The traditional winners, like most of the members of the Organization for Economic Co-operation and Development (OECD), have maintained their growth. A few countries, such as the so-called "Asian tigers" (Taiwan, South Korea, Singapore, and Hong Kong), have produced a model for growth and prosperity° that the developing world has tried in vain° to copy.

prosperity: wealth
in vain: without success

The Nature of the Problem of Disparity

5   Less than 20 percent of the Earth's GDP is produced in the developing world, and yet this is where 80 percent of its people live. In the next 25 years, the Earth's population is likely to increase by about two billion. Of these people, 97 percent will be in the developing world, and the vast majority of them will be poor. Such poverty produces a great reduction in opportunities for human development.

6   Supporters of economic globalization contend that an important reason that some countries are poor is that they are isolated from the world's economic system. They say globalization will bring much greater prosperity to these countries. Opponents respond by saying that globalization will only make a bad situation worse.

Causes of Disparity

7   As you look at the reasons that follow, remember that disparity is often a product of poor or unfair decisions in the past, rather than a result of fundamental differences in the resource base° of different countries. The obvious solution for the future would be to make better decisions.

Impact of Colonialism°

8   Most developing countries were, at one time or another, colonies. Colonization produced distortions° in the economic structures of these countries that still have a huge impact, even though they may have been independent for a half century or more.

Population Growth

9   In general, developing countries have experienced (and are still experiencing) substantially° higher rates of population growth than the developed world. This means that economic growth in developing countries has provided at best a miserable level of existence for more and more people, rather than a higher standard of living for a more stable° population.

Foreign Debt

10   In 2000, developing countries owed US$2.5 trillion to creditors° in developed countries. (One trillion is one thousand billion!) These debts were so great that many debtor° nations, after paying the interest on their loans, had little left to invest in vital economic development, education, and health care.

War

11   The poorest countries, especially those in Africa, have often had to deal with the devastation of wars and civil unrest° arising from tribal conflicts and the ambitions of warlords. Some civil conflicts, like those in Colombia, Mozambique, and the Democratic Republic of the Congo, have been going on for decades.

Leadership Issues

12   Many of the poorest countries in the world have had to deal with leaders who had little interest or skill in improving the economic lot° of the citizens of their countries. Far too often they have used their positions to steal millions—and in some cases, billions—of dollars for their own use.

Trade Inequities°

13   The Group of Eight (G8) nations (with the exception of Russia) have traditionally used tariff° and non-tariff barriers° to restrict imports from developing countries. For example, the tariffs placed by these countries on cloth and clothing produced in Africa and the Middle East are four times as high as the tariffs on similar products from other G8 countries. At the same

resource base: the resources a country owns, including water, minerals, forests

colonialism: the practice by which a powerful country rules a weaker one

distortions: changes that are not beneficial

substantially: a lot

stable: unchanging

creditor: someone who loans money

debtor: someone who borrows money

civil unrest: conflict between groups in a nation's population

lot: condition

inequity: unfairness

tariff: a tax on imported goods

non-tariff barrier: subsidy or government action to stop the movement of goods into a country

commodity: a product that is bought and sold

potential: ability to grow in the future

critical: important

First World Nation: a wealthy nation (Developing nations are sometimes called Second or Third World Nations.)

time, the G8 nations subsidize their agricultural products so that they are often as cheap or cheaper than commodities° from developing countries. Trade policies in the developed world that are fair to all would help poorer countries to reach their economic potential° without relying on direct aid from richer countries.

Local Control

14   Citizens of developing countries complain about the lack of local control that they feel over their own affairs. They point out that far too many critical° decisions are made outside their countries by the United Nations, the World Bank, and the International Monetary Fund, by the governments of the First World Nations°, and by the management of transnational corporations.

15   The solution to the problem of global inequity is complex. It requires an understanding of each of the factors listed above and of how they interact in each country. Those who work to solve the problems of poor countries must also remember that the problems and solutions for each country are different.

About the Authors

Bruce Clark and John Wallace are high school instructors in Canada who have written several textbooks together. They both hold multiple degrees in geography and education, and together they have over sixty years teaching experience.

Understanding the Reading

With a partner or a small group, discuss the questions.

1. The poorest people in the world lack a great many things that you may have. For example, they may not have three meals a day. Make a list of the things you believe the poorest people lack. After making your list, rank the items in order of importance from the least important (number 1) to the most important.

2. Do the authors have an optimistic or a pessimistic view of the global economy today? What words or phrases in the title and first four paragraphs provide clues to their point of view? What do you think was their purpose in writing this passage?

3. This reading can be seen as having three main parts (paragraphs 1–4, 5–6, and 7–14). What role does each of the three parts play in the reading?

4. In paragraph 6, Clark and Wallace present two opposing opinions of the impact of economic globalization on the disparity among nations. What are these two views? In your opinion, which view is correct? Why?

5. What view do you think Clark and Wallace have regarding the effect of economic globalization on poor countries?

6. a. In paragraphs 7–14, Clark and Wallace list seven reasons that developing countries are not catching up with the developed countries. Looking back at the text, check (✓) three problems that you think can be addressed, or fixed, in some way. (It is helpful to have an example in mind, so try to focus on the economic problems of *one* country when you do this.)

   b. Look at the three causes of global inequality that you have identified in 6a and describe a way to reduce or eliminate the problem. For each cause, tell *who* should do *what* to reduce inequality. For example, referring to paragraph 14, you could say, "To reduce the problem of lack of local control in poor countries, the wealthy countries and international organizations such as the World Bank and the IMF should agree not to interfere with local leaders' right to set their own economic policies."

Vocabulary Expansion

Adjectives used as nouns. In English, some adjectives are used with *the* to refer to classes of people. Some examples are *the poor*, *the wealthy*, *the old*, and *the young*. The following three sentences all have the same meaning. Which sentence is the most concise?

This magazine is read by **people who are young**.

This magazine is read by **young people**.

This magazine is read by **the young**.

Exercise 1

A. Change the sentences, replacing the adjective clause *people who are . . .* with an adjective used as a noun.

1. In societies and between countries, there is often envy of people who are rich.

   In societies and between countries, there is often envy of the rich.

2. People who are uneducated have a hard time catching up.

   _____

3. It is usually hard for people who are undernourished to be productive.

   _____

4. Governments should not overlook people who are unfortunate.

   _____

5. People who are powerful decide which projects to invest in and which
   to ignore.

   _____

6. Many people feel that people who are prosperous should share their wealth.

   _____

B. Each of the adjectives used as a noun in Part A has an antonym (a word with
   the opposite meaning). For example, the opposite of *the rich* is *the poor.* List the
   antonyms of the adjectives used as nouns in the exercise above.

   1. *the poor*   4. _____

   2. _____   5. _____

   3. _____   6. _____

Verbs used as adjectives. In English it is common to find adjectives that are made
from **participles,** the *-ed* and *-ing* parts of verbs. Verbs have two participles, a
present participle and a **past participle**.

   VERB: develop

   PRESENT PARTICIPLE: developing

   PAST PARTICIPLE: developed

Both present participles and past participles can be used as **participial adjectives**.

   Developing countries want to have more technology.

   Developed countries have a lot of technology.

What is the difference between these two participial adjectives? Which participial
adjective indicates that a process is ongoing? Which indicates that a process is
complete?

   The *-ing* participial adjective indicates that a process is going on. The *-ed*
participial adjective indicates that a process is complete.

   Participial adjectives provide a way to make sentences more concise. It is
sometimes possible to change an adjective clause to a participial adjective.
Compare these two sentences:

   The *inequality which is rising* is a concern to everyone.

   The *rising inequality* is a concern to everyone.

Exercise 2

Replace the adjective clause with a participial adjective in each sentence. First, underline the noun and adjective clause. Then, to select the appropriate participial adjective, decide whether the verb in the adjective clause indicates a process that is ongoing or a process that is complete.

1. Countries that have industrialized usually have a large middle class.
   Industrialized countries usually have a large middle class.

2. Countries that are industrializing need tariffs to protect their new industries.

   _____

3. Economies that are growing need infrastructure such as roads and telephone lines.

   _____

4. Rivers and beaches that have been polluted can be restored.

   _____

5. Factories that are polluting should be required to clean up their operations.

   _____

For more on participial adjectives, see Appendix IA, page 268.

6. There will be demand that is increasing for technology to reduce pollution.

   _____

Exercise 3

In order to learn the words that are new to you in Exercises 1 and 2, write statements about your country and its economy on a piece of paper. Underline these new words in your example sentences.

WRITING

Assignment

Choose one of the following topics and write an essay.

1. Write about the effects of globalization on your country, region, or city.

2. Write about the reasons that your country has a strong or weak economy.

3. Write about the economic effects of an event in your country, region, or city. Some examples of events that can bring about positive or negative economic effects are the following: a new government policy (formal plan of action), a treaty (an agreement between nations), introduction of new technology, a war, or an environmental disaster.

4. Write about a job that you would like to have in the future. Tell why that job would be beneficial to you. (If you currently have a job that you feel is right for you, you can write about your current job.)

What Cause and Effect Is and Why It Is Important

When we experience change, we want to know *why* things happen and what their *effects* will be. Whether it is a war, an accident, or just the experience of catching a cold, we ask the same questions: What are the reasons that this happened? What will the results be? Understanding cause and effect helps us analyze events, and knowing how to write about cause and effect is essential to being a competent writer.

In this chapter, you will learn to write a cause-and-effect essay. Brainstorming your topic before you write will help you discover several causes (reasons) or effects and organize them.

Organizing a cause-and-effect essay: Time order and order of importance. Generally, cause-and-effect essays are organized by either **time order** or **order of importance**. When organizing a list of causes or effects, look for time order first. If you don't see any time relationships, use order of importance.

Look at the sample question and the two different sets of answers. What is the difference between the first and second set of answers?

Why did the family become wealthy?

1. • They saved money from growing wheat.

   • They bought more land and grew more wheat.

   • They bought equipment to save labor.

   • They bought a mill to process the wheat so that they could sell directly to retailers.

2. • They had five healthy sons.

   • They were quite well educated.

   • They worked very hard together.

The first set of answers gives the process, step-by-step, that the family used to gain wealth. This is time order. The second set of answers lists the reasons they became wealthy in order of importance from less to more important, with the most important last. (People do not always agree on what is most important, so individuals might organize a list by order of importance differently.)

Exercise 4

A. Look at the following thesis statements and lists of supporting points. Number the supporting points to show how you would organize them. You may organize the points by time order or by order of importance. You may want to work with a partner or a small group.

1. **THESIS:** Government investment in higher education has several effects.

   __2__ Over time, the skills of the workforce increase.

   __1__ College enrollment increases.

   __3__ The country's economy shows greater productivity.

2. **THESIS:** Inflation, or an increase in consumer prices, has several effects.

   _____ When prices rise, people buy less.

   _____ When factories slow down, workers are laid off.

   _____ When people buy less, factories must slow their rate of production.

3. **THESIS:** There are several reasons that a product costs more when it is imported.

   _____ Sellers can ask the highest price that they think customers will pay.

   _____ There are transportation costs involved in moving the product from the country where it was made to the country of sale.

   _____ Exchange rates and tariffs affect the price of imported products.

4. **THESIS:** When a country opens its markets to imports, there are several effects.

   _____ The new items compete with domestic goods.

   _____ Domestic industries have to adjust by lowering production costs and reducing prices.

   _____ People rush to buy the new items.

5. **THESIS:** There are several reasons that development doesn't always reduce inequality in a country.

_____ Economic growth may benefit only part of the population, only those in a certain region or only those who are well educated.

_____ Most new jobs may be for unskilled, low-wage workers.

_____ Development increases the price of land. When the price of land is high, workers have to pay a large part of their salary for housing.

6. **THESIS:** Poor people need bank credit for several reasons.

_____ When people suffer hardships such as natural disasters or illness, small loans can make the difference between life and death.

_____ People can sometimes escape poverty if they can borrow small amounts to start small businesses.

_____ There is a lot of unemployment in poor communities. If there are loans, there will be more business, so unemployment will decrease.

Note that when one point is clearly much more important than the others, the normal order of importance (least to most important) is sometimes reversed. Writers often put a point that is obviously important first because readers anticipate it. For example, item 6 above says, "small loans can make the difference between life and death." A matter of life and death is of obvious importance, so many writers would put this idea first.

B. Discuss your answers with your class.

Prewriting

Before you write, do the following prewriting activities. As you read through the steps, you will see how Chong Ho, a student from South Korea, prepared to write about the effects of economic growth on his city, Seoul, the capital of South Korea.

STEP 1 Make a **list**, and, if possible, discuss it with friends or classmates. Then use your list to draft a **thesis statement**.

Chong Ho made a list of all the effects of economic growth he had seen in Seoul.

many more cars, some fancy cars
air pollution

more roads, bridges, and buildings

more factories; people now manufacture electronics and automobiles whereas they used to make shoes and clothing

the city's boundary is constantly expanding

loss of farmland

new suburbs are continually being built; entire satellite cities arise from farmland over the course of two or three years

although people have little leisure time, golf is popular, and some people belong to private clubs to play

people who were farmers now dwell in high-rise apartments

people used to cook at home only; now they can afford to eat out

After discussing his list, Chong Ho was able to focus on the two most important effects, which he used to draft his thesis.

DRAFT THESIS
STATEMENT

Over the past forty or fifty years, my city, Seoul, has experienced great economic growth. This growth has had two major effects: The city has grown, and the people have a better standard of living.

STEP **2** | **Number** the items on your list according to how they relate to the controlling idea of your draft thesis statement. **Cross out** the items that do not relate to the supporting points that you plan to address in your body paragraphs.

Chong Ho went back to his list and numbered items relating to urban growth (1) and items relating to the standard of living (2). He crossed out the items that did not relate to either point.

(2) many more cars, some fancy cars
~~air pollution~~
(1) more roads, bridges, and buildings
(2) more factories; people now manufacture electronics and automobiles whereas they used to make shoes and clothing
(1) the city's boundary is constantly expanding
~~loss of farmland~~
(1) new suburbs are continually being built; entire satellite cities arise from farmland over the course of two or three years
(2) although people have little leisure time, golf is popular, and some people belong to private clubs to play
(2) people who were farmers now dwell in high-rise apartments
(2) people used to cook at home only; now they can afford to eat out

STEP 3 Make a **cluster** for each supporting point to make sure that you have enough information for each body paragraph. (A cluster is a diagram of connected circles that shows cause-and-effect development.) Clustering will help you see the relationships between your supporting ideas.

Chong Ho made one cluster about each of these two major effects: urban growth and the standard of living.

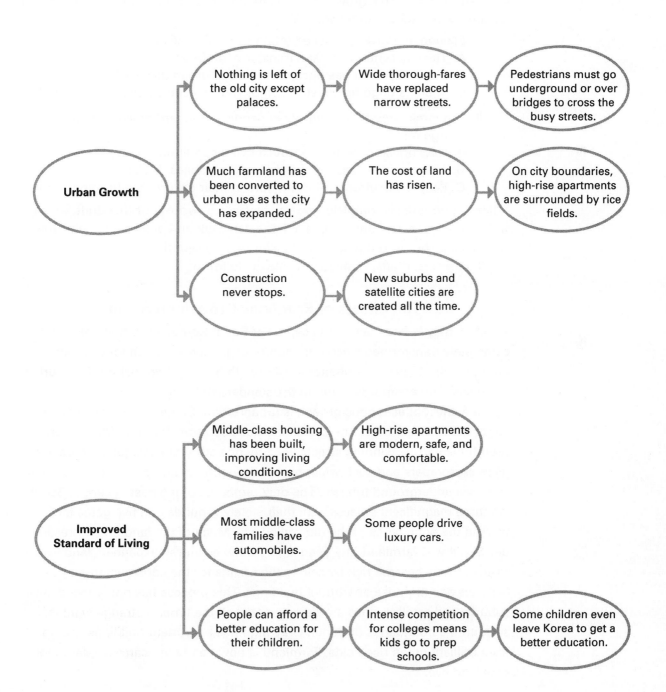

STEP **4** | Make an **outline** that shows three levels of development. You may organize the supporting ideas on your outline according to **time** or **importance**.

Chong Ho labeled the three levels of development: thesis statement (*TS*), supporting points/topic sentences for body paragraphs (*SP*), and development of the supporting points (*DEV*).

Over the past forty or fifty years, my city, Seoul, has experienced great economic growth. This growth has had two major effects: urban expansion and an improved standard of living. (TS)

    I. Economic growth produced urban expansion. (SP)
       A. The city center has been transformed. (DEV)
       B. Much farmland has been converted to urban use. (DEV)
       C. There is ongoing construction of suburbs and satellite cities. (DEV)

    II. Economic growth has improved people's standard of living; there is now a large middle class. (SP)
       A. New housing means improved living conditions. (DEV)
       B. Most middle-class families have automobiles. (DEV)
       C. People can afford to invest more in their children's education. (DEV)

When your outline is complete, you will be ready to write your first draft, which will be a simple essay consisting of a thesis statement and body paragraphs. You will develop your introduction and conclusion later—in the process of revising.

After several drafts, Chong Ho wrote the following draft.

The Effects of Economic Growth on Seoul

1   My family is from Seoul, the capital of South Korea, a city that has been completely transformed since our country began a great push for economic growth in the 1960s. This phenomenal growth has had two major effects: urban expansion and an improvement in the standard of living.

2   One effect of economic growth is urbanization. Seoul is now many times larger than it used to be. The city center has been transformed. Where there used to be narrow winding streets lined by one-story houses, today there are glass skyscrapers and such wide, busy thoroughfares that pedestrians can only cross via underground tunnels. The only remnants of the past in central Seoul are three magnificent palaces with their stately grounds and five gates that marked the boundaries of the old walled city. Much of the land under present-day Seoul was farmland fifty years ago. As the economy expanded, land values rose. Farmers became rich by selling their fields for the construction of factories and high-rise apartment buildings. This process has not stopped; new suburbs and satellite cities are being created all the time. A strange sight is seen on the boundaries of Seoul: Gray high-rise apartment buildings rise up from brilliant green rice fields. Farmland is now nearly as scarce as places for people to live.

3   Another effect of economic growth is the rise of the middle class. Before the industrial age in Korea, there was almost no middle class. Now there is a large middle class that can afford to dine out in traditional Korean restaurants or enjoy American-style fast-food snacks. They can afford automobiles, cell phones, and computers, and they may even find a little time for golf. The government has used the profits from a growing economy to invest in education. This means that all Koreans attend good public schools, so even children from lower-class families have a chance to go to universities. Competition for the best universities is intense, however, so parents who can afford it send their children to prep schools that coach the youngsters to pass the entrance exams. Those who are able may even send their children overseas to improve their chances of getting ahead.

4   Forty or fifty years of dramatic economic growth have transformed Seoul. As a result, its residents, who now number around eleven million, have had to adapt to a very urban environment that is continually changing. Fortunately, this rapid growth has resulted in more equality in Korean society, which has made it easier to accept the changes.

Exercise 5

With a partner or a small group, review Chong Ho's essay and discuss the following questions.

1. Can you find three levels of development in Chong Ho's essay? Tell a partner what they are.

2. Does Chong Ho's essay have good cohesion? Check the order of the supporting points in the thesis statement and in the topic sentences of the body paragraphs. Look for repeated words or phrases and synonyms, and underline them. Circle the transitions.

After selecting a topic from the list on pages 108–109, follow the sequence of prewriting steps Chong Ho used.

First Draft

If you have followed the steps listed above, you are well prepared to work from your outline and write the first draft of your essay. Remember that each supporting point (SP) on your outline becomes the topic sentence of a body paragraph. You will find instruction in writing an introduction and a conclusion in the Composition Focus section that follows.

REVISING

This part of the chapter will show you how to expand and improve the first draft of your cause-and-effect essay. As you work through the lessons presented here, pay close attention to the Review and Revise boxes, which will give you suggestions for revising your essay.

Composition Focus

Essay introductions. Just as a one-paragraph composition begins with a topic sentence that introduces the topic and focuses the reader's attention on the controlling idea, an essay begins with a one-paragraph **introduction** that serves the following purposes:

- The introductory paragraph identifies the topic.
- It gets the reader's attention.
- It leads the reader to the thesis.
- It states the thesis.

Reread the introduction to Chong Ho's essay.

My family is from Seoul, the capital of South Korea, a city that has been completely transformed since our country began a great push for economic growth in the 1960s. This phenomenal growth has had two major effects: urban expansion and an improvement in the standard of living.

Now discuss the following questions with a partner.

1. Where does Chong Ho first introduce the topic? Draw a circle around the words that first introduce the topic.

2. Does Chong Ho engage your interest? If so, put brackets around the phrases that you find engaging.

3. Where does Chong Ho present the main point of the essay? Underline the thesis statement.

You should have noted that Chong Ho introduces the topic with the words *Seoul, South Korea* and *economic growth* in the first sentence. In the same sentence he offers background information about himself, *My family is from Seoul,* and background information about Korea, *our country began a great push . . . in the 1960s.* At the end of the paragraph, he presents the thesis statement containing the controlling idea, *This phenomenal growth has had two major effects: urban expansion and an improvement in the standard of living.*

Strategies for writing an introduction to a formal essay. Essay introductions not only identify the topic, lead the reader to the thesis, and state the thesis. They also must engage readers' interest. Here are some popular strategies that writers use to catch readers' attention.

1. *General Statement.* A common technique is to begin with a general statement and follow with statements that become increasingly specific as they move toward the thesis statement of the essay. For example, Chong Ho might have begun his essay this way:

   > The last fifty years have seen a great deal of economic development around the world. Growth has been especially rapid in the countries known as the "Asian tigers." Among them, South Korea is known as a growth leader.

2. *Background.* A paper about a historical event or a current problem or situation can begin with background information.

   > After the Korean War, South Korea needed to rebuild, and its leaders chose a path of economic development. In the 1960s, the South Korean government instituted land reform, which improved agricultural production, and it also invested heavily in education. In the 1970s, it invested in industries such as shipbuilding, chemicals, and electronics.

3. *Anecdote.* Another way to begin an essay is with a brief anecdote or story.

   > My uncle left Seoul twenty years ago and moved to the United States. When he came back to visit last autumn, he could not believe the transformation in his hometown. The neighborhood where he had grown up had disappeared, and now there were tall skyscrapers and busy thoroughfares where he used to play tag with his friends in the alleyway. The fields on the edge of town where he had picked strawberries after school had long ago disappeared, replaced with factories, warehouses, and high-rise apartments.

Exercise 6

With a partner or a small group, discuss the following questions.

1. Of the three introduction strategies you have seen above, which do you think is most appropriate for Chong Ho's essay about urban growth and an improvement in the standard of living in Seoul?

2. Chong Ho chose to include some personal information in his introduction. When is personal information appropriate in an introduction?

Exercise 7

Read the following introductions, and identify their types (as described on page 117) on the lines below them. Underline the thesis statement in each introduction.

1.   **The Industrial Revolution in Europe**

By around 1750, Europeans had discovered that coal and iron could be made into steel, and inventors were using this new material to create steam engines and machinery for manufacturing. At the same time, changes in the laws concerning agricultural land had displaced agricultural workers and made agriculture more productive. With new technology and surplus labor and food, conditions were right for what is called the Industrial Revolution. It is called a <u>revolution</u> because <u>it had enormous effects on life in Europe: People moved to the cities and a new social class of urban workers formed, trade increased, and with the new wealth, the standard of living improved.</u>

_____background_____

2.   **Foreign Aid**

Humans are social creatures and often turn to others for help in time of need. Just as individuals ask their relatives and neighbors for assistance when they cannot pay their bills, countries ask their allies for help when they face an economic downturn. In the global community, foreign aid, meaning gifts or special low-interest loans given by rich countries to poor countries, is essential for two reasons: Foreign aid reduces the suffering of people who have been displaced by war and natural disasters, and it helps struggling economies catch up over time.

_____

3.   **Globalization**

The other day I was riding a bus and I witnessed the effects of globalization with my own eyes and ears. Two women—one wearing a T-shirt bearing the name of an Italian company and the other with a French name on her jeans— were speaking about what Indian movies they had seen, what African music they enjoyed, and what South American newspapers they had been reading on the Internet. One of the women got a call on her cell phone and started to speak in Farsi. I was intrigued. I couldn't have imagined this transfer and mixing of information, goods, and cultures ten or fifteen years ago. This phenomenon would not have been possible without investments in communication, improvements in the technology of transport, and the creation of multinational corporations.

_____

4. **The Solution to Global Poverty**

Over the past twenty-five years the disparity between rich and poor countries has been growing at an alarming rate. A comparison of the legal systems in wealthy and poor countries reveals the major cause of the disparity: Poor countries do not have effective legal systems. If poor countries had laws regulating private ownership and business transactions, the poor would be much better off. In developing countries, three conditions are necessary to achieve prosperity: a system of documenting what people own so that they can borrow money to start or expand businesses, laws that standardize business transactions and make corruption illegal, and police and courts that enforce the laws.

Exercise 8

These two cause-and-effect essays have thesis statements, body paragraphs, and concluding paragraphs, but they do not have introductory paragraphs. On another piece of paper, write an introductory paragraph for each, using one or more of the suggestions for writing introductions listed on page 117. (You can combine methods if you like.) Include the thesis statement that is given, placing it at the end of your introduction.

1. **Why I Left the Farm**

THESIS: The reasons I did not want to stay on my family farm were the difficulty of farm work and my desire to learn to program computers.

First of all, I left the farm because life there was extremely hard and frustrating due to lack of water and poor soil. There was no irrigation to water the crops that we planted, so we prayed for rain every year. Periodically, there was a drought. As a result of the drought, there was not even enough water for the cattle to drink, and we had to let the crops die. In addition, the soil was poor in nutrients, and we did not have the money to buy fertilizers to improve it. There were, however, some years when we had a good crop of fruit and corn, but then we had another obstacle to face. Since we didn't have a truck to transport our produce, we had to sell it to people in our village who could transport it to the market town. They would pay us very little because they knew we had no choice but to sell our goods to them.

Second, I left the farm because I knew that I would not have any possibility of getting an advanced education if I remained there. The farm was far from any major city. I attended high school in the nearest town, but there was no college in the area. When I was in my freshman year in high school, a counselor came to our class and asked what we wanted to do after we graduated. Even though I had never seen a computer, I raised my hand and said that I wanted to learn how to be a programmer. I had little idea about what programmers actually do, but I thought programming would be a very exciting and important job. But at the time, studying computer science seemed to be little more than a dream because I knew my father could not provide me with more education. But three years later I graduated from high school at the top of my class. This led to my receiving a scholarship that paid my way through two years of technical training, and eventually I got a good job.

From the time I was about ten, I realized that I did not want to spend my life toiling on a hot, dusty farm. I felt sad to leave my parents to do the work on the farm alone, but now I am able to send them some money to help them out.

2. Urbanization

THESIS: In general, cities develop as a result of two factors: a "push" that makes people leave their farms and a "pull" that draws them to the cities.

One reason cities develop is that economic hardship on the farm pushes people to search for other kinds of work. Farming does not bring in regular income; there are good years and bad ones. If a farmer operates on a small profit margin, a drought or plague of insects or other pests can force him to abandon his land. Also, a small farm can support only a limited number of people. Therefore, when a farmer has a large family, some of the sons and daughters have to leave when they reach adulthood and are ready to marry and settle down.

The other reason cities develop is that urban centers pull or attract people from the farms with a promise of good salaries and exciting new experiences. Generally, work in cities pays more than farming. However, farmers who leave to go to the cities take a risk: They do not know how long it will take to find a job, how much they will make, or how they will house and feed themselves in the meantime. But most people who migrate from farms are young single men, and they are able to assume some risk. They may even enjoy the adventure. Cities offer young men from the countryside new kinds of entertainment and new people to meet. In fact, a final reason for the growth of population in cities is that young migrants frequently marry and have families within a short period of time after their arrival in cities.

Urbanization is a growing trend around the world as people leave the agricultural way of life behind. It is easy to understand why individuals migrate to cities to escape economic hardship and to have new experiences.

After writing the two introductions, take turns reading them aloud in small groups. Guess which strategies your classmates used.

Review and Revise 1: Essay Introductions

Look at the introduction to your essay. Make sure that it contains a thesis statement that names the topic and the controlling idea of your paper. Ask yourself if the introduction catches the reader's attention. If you can improve your introduction now, revise.

Organization of body paragraphs and transition signals. If you make your essay cohesive, readers will be able to follow your ideas easily. (To review cohesion, see page 91.) If you arrange the supporting points in your essay according to time order or order of importance, readers will be able to understand your thinking. Use the transition signals in this chart to tell readers which plan of organization you have used:

Transitions to Indicate		
Time Order	**A Sequence**	**Order of Importance**
First/First of all . . . Then . . . After that . . . Finally . . .	One reason/result . . . Another reason/ result . . .	The most important reason/effect . . .

Exercise 9

The topic sentences of the body paragraphs in the following essay lack transitions. Read the essay, decide which pattern of organization it has (*time order* or *order of importance*), and add appropriate transitions from the chart.

Singapore's Economic Success

1   When Britain withdrew from Singapore in 1971, the tiny island nation at the tip of the Malay Peninsula had no way to support itself. Its only resource was people. From the start, the Singapore government determined that the country's survival would depend on foreign investment and expertise. Furthermore, the government itself would need to play an active role in guiding economic development. As a result of these strategies, Singapore developed one of the most productive economies in the world.

2   The Singapore government found Asian investors who were willing to open light industries such as textile and toy manufacturing. It converted the land that had been occupied by the British to industrial parks, and it developed its infrastructure—highways, port, and airport. To make it easy for foreign companies to set up business, the government established the Economic Development Board, which helped investors secure land, power, and water. Singapore also gave early investors tax-free status for five years.

3   Singapore successfully attracted high-tech investors from the United States who were willing to open semiconductor factories and, later on, computer-assembly plants. To help Singaporean workers develop the skills they needed to work with this advanced technology, the government provided free training institutes. To make sure that the labor force was disciplined, the government enacted extensive labor laws, and to make sure that it was cooperative, the government formed the National Wages Council. In the council, representatives from labor unions, management, and the government set guidelines for annual wage increases which both allowed for growth and prevented strikes.

4   Singapore has been readying itself for the future by promoting its biotechnology, chemical, information, and service industries. The government sees investing in people as a top priority. It has sent its brightest students to the best universities overseas and has expanded its college and university campuses at home. To encourage innovation and provide high-level jobs, it has built a science park where corporations and institutes conduct research in biotechnology and information science. Singapore also encourages talented students from other Asian countries to immigrate with offers of scholarships and jobs.

5   As a result of its economic strategies, Singapore has attracted investments from more than 3,000 multinational corporations and achieved almost 100 percent employment over the past few decades, and it can claim one of the highest per capita gross domestic products in the world today.

Pattern of organization: _____

Compare your choice of transitions with a partner's, and discuss how you made that choice.

Review and Revise 2: Organization of Body Paragraphs and Transition Signals
Make sure that you have arranged your supporting points according to a logical plan of organization and that your thesis statement and the topic sentences of your body paragraphs are cohesive. Check your draft to see whether it has enough transition signals. If you need transition signals, add them.

Essay conclusions. Just as the last sentence in a one-paragraph composition signals to the reader that the writer is finished, a concluding paragraph signals the end of an essay. The most important reason for the **conclusion** is to make the reader *feel* that the essay is finished.

A conclusion can answer any questions that have not been addressed in the body of the essay, but it must not raise new questions. Any new information that is added must be sufficient without explanation. For examples, see page 120. In the conclusion to "Why I Left the Farm," the writer informs us that he is able to send his parents some money to help them out. In the conclusion to "Urbanization," we learn that urbanization is a growing trend around the world and that the writer understands why young people are moving to cities. Neither of these pieces of added information raises questions that require further explanation.

Strategies for writing a conclusion to a formal essay. Here are several strategies you can use in conclusions. Most conclusions are a combination of these strategies.

1. *Summary.* In a conclusion, you should help readers remember the key points of the essay by summarizing them. Summarizing means repeating the same key words and phrases used in the thesis statement and topic sentences of the body paragraphs or using synonyms. For example, in the conclusion of the model essay "The Effects of Economic Growth on Seoul," Chong Ho referred to his thesis when he wrote in the final paragraph, *Forty or fifty years of dramatic economic growth have transformed Seoul. . . . Fortunately, this rapid growth has produced more equality in Korean society.*

2. *Suggestion.* Many essays are about problems, and the most common way to conclude them is by suggesting solutions. For example, an essay that tells how rapid urbanization can produce unhealthy living conditions may conclude by saying, *People should get as much information as they can before moving to a city where they may not find clean drinking water, decent shelter, or adequate health care.*

3. *Prediction.* An essay about a problem may conclude with a prediction or warning about the future. For example, an essay about overpopulated cities and unhealthy living conditions may conclude by warning, *We will see increased cancer in children and people of all ages if we allow cities to grow without adequate regulation of polluting industries.*

4. *Opinion.* You may conclude by offering your own perspective. For example, in an essay that presents the effects of urbanization, you may finish by saying that you think the positive outcomes from urbanization are greater than the negative.

Note that many essays present an opinion in the thesis and support the opinion with arguments in the body paragraphs. But if the main purpose of the paper is to explain, you can withhold your opinion for the conclusion and present it in a brief statement there.

Exercise 10

The following two essays have good introductory and body paragraphs, but there are problems with their conclusions. On the lines below each essay, tell what is wrong with the conclusion. Then, on another piece of paper, write better conclusions for them, using some of the strategies listed on page 123.

1. ### Globalization in Naucalapan

Globalization refers to the exchange of not only goods and services but also cultural information. Globalization has been good for the economy of Mexico, but the impact that it has had on the community that I used to live in, Naucalapan de Juarez, has not been good. The environment, the people's entertainment, and their cultural traditions have been negatively affected by globalization.

One problem caused by globalization is the destruction of the environment. Naucalapan is one of Mexico City's fastest-growing suburbs. It is the home of some of the biggest factories in the city, manufacturers of clothing, athletic shoes, drugs, plastics, machinery, and more. The pollution these factories produce is affecting the environment. The birds are dying, and the residents can't drink the tap water due to the industrial waste discharged in the canals or nearby lakes. There is less and less open space, and today there are rows of city blocks where not a single tree can be seen. New factories move in constantly and new workers, most of whom are from the countryside, arrive to find jobs. These newcomers have no money, so they have to sleep in the parks and streets. The new factories also provide employment for new management-level workers who need housing, too, and this creates a demand for new homes. Developers are constructing houses over what is left of our open space, and the government doesn't seem to care at all because it can collect taxes on the buildings that are built.

Another problem caused by globalization is the corruption of televised entertainment. Because it is no longer pleasant to be outside in Naucalapan, people stay inside and watch television more and more. But television isn't the way it used to be. Mexican television used to censor explicit language, controversial topics, and graphic violence, but since it started buying programs from the United States, television has changed dramatically. It now shows brutal murders and airs frank talk about sex that the community doesn't want its children exposed to.

The most important result of globalization is that the traditional holidays have been changed. The religious meaning and family celebration of Mexican holidays have been replaced with customs from the United States which always seem to involve spending money. People used to go to church on Easter, but now they hunt for eggs. On October 31, people used to remember and pray for their dead ancestors, but now it's Halloween, a day for dressing up as witches and going to parties. Last but not least is Christmas. This used to be the most sacred holiday, but now it is just an excuse to get as much as possible from Santa Claus.

We have to respect the environment. People should recycle their cans and bottles and not throw them on the street. Not recycling is wasting valuable resources.

Problems with the conclusion: _____

_____

_____

2.   Globalization in Peru

Globalization refers to a shift from distinct national economies to a global economy and involves an exchange of cultural information. Lima, Peru, where I come from, is not immune to this phenomenon. I see both positive and negative changes every time I go back for a visit.

The benefits of globalization are in the area of communication. Peruvians are now able to keep in touch with the outside world affordably. My parents are happy that they can call my sister and me in the United States and my brother in Uruguay cheaply, and the transmission is so clear that it seems we are in nearby towns. Many young people access the Internet regularly. They know what books are being published in New York and London, what styles are worn in Paris and Tokyo, and what technological changes are taking place in Silicon Valley and Bangalore. Through the information superhighway, Peruvians are keeping up with the world.

While globalization has been beneficial to Peru in a number of ways, it has increased inequality. Rapid economic growth means modern airports, computers, express highways, and air-conditioned malls with the latest international fashion for a few, but it has not improved conditions for the many. Big corporations have been investing in Peru, and the government has been forced to keep wages down to attract these investments. As a result of globalization, the gap between rich and poor Peruvians has been increasing at an alarming rate.

Peru has a long history that goes back to the Incas. For thousands of years, change was very slow, but change is now much faster. I think it is time for the Peruvian government to address the problems created by globalization.

Problems with the conclusion: _____

_____

_____

> **Review and Revise 3: Essay Conclusions**
> Check the conclusion of your essay. Make sure that it does not introduce new ideas that will need development. If your conclusion does not give the reader the feeling that the essay is complete, revise it.

Language Focus

The vocabulary of cause and effect: Nouns and verbs. English has several nouns and verbs that are used to discuss cause and effect. Look at the chart.

Nouns	Verbs
cause	cause
reason	result in
factor	lead to
result	affect
effect	

1. *Nouns that refer to a cause*

   - We use the noun ***reason*** to explain the thinking behind our actions.

     The *reason* I took English composition was so that I could write more confidently.

   - We use ***cause*** for events that are beyond our control.

     The *cause of* the landslide was the heavy rain.

   - We use the noun ***factor*** when there are two or more reasons or causes.

     There are two *factors* in the company's success. One *factor* is that it faced little competition in the market. The second *factor* is that it had a very popular product.

2. *Nouns that refer to an effect*

   The two nouns we use to talk about what happens as an outcome of an event are ***effect*** and ***result***. These words are generally the same and can often be used interchangeably.

   The *result/effect* of the company's expansion was an increase in profit.

However, there is a slight difference: We use *result* when the cause-and-effect relationship is direct and obvious. We use *effect* when the cause-and-effect relationship is more indirect or complicated.

The *result* of the plane crash was the death of the travelers.

The *effect* of the plane crash was the passing of new airline safety laws.

3. *Cause-and-effect verbs*

Cause, **result in**, and **lead to** all describe change and are followed by a result. However, there is a slight difference in meaning: We use *cause* when the effect is direct and immediate. We use *lead to* or *result in* when the result is less direct or is delayed.

The election of the new president *caused* excitement.

The election of the new president *led to/resulted in* economic growth.

Cause, lead to, and *result in* can be followed by noun objects, as in the examples above. But they also can be used with other patterns, as in the following examples.

The election *caused* people to celebrate. (*cause* + someone or something + infinitive)

The election *led to/resulted* in Parliament writing new laws. (*lead to/result in* + someone or something + gerund)

To find out what can follow a verb, check your dictionary.

Exercise 11

With a partner, fill in the blanks in the following passage with the cause-and-effect nouns and verbs listed below. Use each word only once, and write the part of speech of the word, *(n.)* or *(v.)*, in parentheses under it.

Nouns	Verbs
cause	cause
effect	lead to
factors	result in
reason	
results	

Addressing Inequality

There are two (1) _____reasons_____ that rich nations should help poor nations:
(n.)
Assistance would reduce suffering now, and it would create a better future.
First, economic assistance would improve the health of people in poor nations
immediately. Disease is a major (2) _____ of human suffering.
( )
Two (3) _____ are responsible for disease in poor nations: lack of
( )
sanitation (sewage systems) and lack of medical treatment. With clean water
and medicine, the suffering caused by disease could be greatly reduced.
Treatment of disease would also (4) _____ economic growth in poor
( )
countries, because when people are healthy, they can work and feed
themselves.

Second, in order to have a brighter future, people in poor countries need
education. Providing education would (5) _____ increased
( )
productivity, too. Furthermore, statistics show that educating people has a
positive (6) _____ on the next generation in that educated parents
( )
have smaller families and raise healthier children. If people have smaller,
healthier families, they will have a higher standard of living.

One economist suggested a way to raise money to help the poorest
nations: Impose a tax on international financial transactions and use those
funds to improve conditions in poor countries. Rich countries trade the most.
Taxing the rich to help the poor would (7) _____ no hardship for the
( )
rich. The poor would see immediate (8) _____: better health and
( )
education.

Cause-and-effect vocabulary: Conjunctions and transition words. We can show
cause-and-effect relationships between clauses with subordinating conjunctions,
coordinating conjunctions, and transition words. Notice the punctuation in these
examples.

1. *Subordinating conjunction*

For more on commas,
see Appendix IB,
page 315.

┌─────── EFFECT ───────┐┌─────── CAUSE ───────┐
The people's lifestyle improved **because** the country's economy grew.

┌─────── CAUSE ───────┐┌─────── EFFECT ───────┐
Because the country's economy grew, the people's lifestyle improved.

2. *Coordinating conjunction*

┌──────── CAUSE ────────┐ ┌──────── EFFECT ────────┐
The country's economy grew, **so** the people's lifestyle improved.

3. *Transition word*

┌──────── CAUSE ────────┐ ┌──────── EFFECT ────────┐
The country's economy grew. **Therefore**, the people's lifestyle improved.

For more on
semicolons, see
Appendix IB, page 319.

┌──────── CAUSE ────────┐ ┌──────── EFFECT ────────┐
The country's economy grew; **therefore**, the people's lifestyle improved.

Exercise 12

On another piece of paper, combine the pairs of sentences using the words in parentheses. You may need to change the order of the clauses. Make sure you use correct punctuation.

1. The countries with the most technology are richest. Technology is vital to development. (so)

   Technology is vital to development, so the countries with the most technology are richest.

2. Technology can help fight disease and improve the use of agricultural land. Poor countries need technology. (because)

3. Technology is often shared when countries trade with each other. Countries that are isolated from international trade are unlikely to acquire technology. (therefore)

4. Landlocked regions such as central Brazil or inland China are isolated from international trade. They cannot easily acquire technology. (so)

5. Today people can work on the Internet from remote areas. The Internet can help isolated regions overcome the disadvantages of distance. (therefore)

6. Innovation, or the development of new technology, requires both universities and the investment of private companies. The poorest countries cannot acquire technology without help. (because)

Compare your sentences with a partner's. Did you use commas, periods, and semicolons in the same way?

Overview of cause-and-effect vocabulary and structures. Some structures are followed by a cause, and some are followed by an effect.

Vocabulary and Structures Followed by a *Cause*		
Coordinating Conjunctions	**Subordinating Conjunctions**	**Prepositions**
for[1]	because[2] since[2] as[2]	due to[3] because of[3] as a result of[3]

1. When *for* is used as a coordinating conjunction, it has the same meaning as *because. For* is more formal than *because* and is used less often.

   The amount of money transferred between countries has increased, *for* most countries have removed their restrictions on the flow of money.

   The amount of money transferred between countries has increased *because* most countries have removed their restrictions on the flow of money.

2. *Because, since,* and *as* are subordinating conjunctions that introduce reason clauses.

   Multinational corporations have prospered *because* they have found new markets for their goods.

   Multinational corporations have prospered *since* they have found new markets for their goods.

   Multinational corporations have prospered *as* they have found new markets for their goods.

For more on adverb clauses, see Appendix IA, page 270.

   Note that *because* only introduces reason clauses, but *since* and *as* introduce other kinds of clauses as well.

3. *Due to, because of,* and *as a result of* are multi-word prepositions, and, like all prepositions, they are followed by nouns. (Do not confuse *because of* with *because. Because* is followed by a clause.)

   Communication improved *due to* the Internet.

   Transportation of goods became faster *as a result of* shipping containers.

   The trucking industry has grown *because of* international trade.

   The trucking industry has grown *because* international trade has created a demand for truck transportation.

Vocabulary and Structures Followed by an *Effect*		
Verbs	**Transition Words**	**Coordinating Conjunctions**
cause	therefore	so
result in	consequently	
lead to	as a result	

Note that the verb *affect* is used to discuss cause and effect, but it is not listed here because it is not followed by a result. Instead, it is followed by the person or thing that experiences the result. Compare these examples:

The crop failure *caused/resulted in/led to* hunger. (Hunger is the result.)

The crop failure *affected* the farmers' children. (The children experienced the result.)

The crop failure *affected* the economy. (The economy experienced the result.)

Exercise 13

Practice using the cause-and-effect vocabulary and structures from this chapter. On a piece of paper, rewrite the sentences below, making one sentence by using the words in parentheses.

Note that some words may need to be left out and verbs may need to be changed or removed when you combine the sentences.

1. The cost of computers is lower today. Small businesses can afford them. (due to)

   Due to the lower cost of computers today, small businesses can afford them.

2. The Internet benefits consumers. It allows them to compare prices. (as)

3. The Internet allows people to share new discoveries quickly. Innovations in technology are adopted more quickly. (because)

4. The Internet reduces the cost of buying and selling goods. It helps small companies. (for)

5. The Internet has affected workers who program computers or process data. They now compete with workers in other countries. (as a result of)

6. The use of electronic transfers has grown. There is an increased international flow of money. (so)

7. A government has less control over multinational corporations than over national corporations. Multinational corporations can move to another country. (therefore)

Check the punctuation of your sentences.

> **Review and Revise 4: Cause-and-Effect Vocabulary and Structures**
> Review your draft. Underline the cause-and-effect vocabulary and structures you have used. Make sure your composition has a variety of vocabulary and structures. If it does not have enough variety, revise it.

Exercise 14

This is a plan for an essay that discusses the causes and effects of migration. The introduction and conclusion have been written, but the body paragraphs are in outline form. Because this essay discusses both causes and effects, the thesis statement has two parts. The first part introduces the causes of migration and is at the end of the introduction. The second part introduces the effects of migration and is in paragraph 3, a one-sentence transition paragraph. Both parts of the thesis statement are underlined.

Divide into small groups. Each group should develop one of the four body paragraphs for this essay with explanations or examples. In each body paragraph, use transitions (from page 121) or the cause-and-effect signals from pages 130–131 to show logical relationships and make the essay cohesive.

The Causes and Effects of Migration

I.   *Migration* is the relocation of groups of people. *Emigration* refers to movement *out of* the home country; *immigration* refers to movement *into* a host country. <u>From the time people first appeared on the Earth, some of them have chosen to migrate because they have believed that migration would improve their lives.</u>

II. Migration involves risk and expense, so in order to move, people must have good reasons.

    A. environmental change
    B. discrimination or persecution
    C. wars
    D. unemployment or lack of opportunity

III.   Migration has a number of effects. It affects the homeland that migrants leave, the host country that they settle in, and the migrants themselves.

IV. The homeland may be affected either positively or negatively.

    A. benefits to the homeland
        1. If the homeland is overcrowded, emigration can bring some relief.
        2. If the migrants work abroad and send money home, the home economy will benefit.
    B. disadvantages to the home economy
        1. If professionals leave, the home economy may slow down.

V. The host country can be affected either positively or negatively by immigration.

    A. benefits to the host country
        1. Migrants can contribute to the local economy as both workers and consumers.
    B. disadvantages to the host country
        1. crowding
        2. Conflict can build up between the newcomers and the settled population.

VI. The immigrants themselves may experience both positive and negative effects.

    A. benefits to immigrants
        1. a better standard of living
        2. increased knowledge as a result of having lived in two cultures
    B. disadvantages to immigrants
        1. economic hardship
        2. language barrier
        3. discrimination

VII. Migration has been a part of human existence throughout history. English has an expression that describes the urge to migrate, "The grass is greener on the other side of the fence." As long as people see better opportunities, they will continue to move, with various results for themselves and the countries they emigrate from and immigrate into.

Read the entire essay aloud to the class, having each group present its completed paragraph. Discuss transition words that you have chosen to give the essay coherence.

PEER REVIEW AND FINAL DRAFT

Now that you have revised your composition, it is time to share your writing with others. Exchange papers with one or two classmates. Turn to page 336 in Appendix II, and fill out the Peer Review form.

After considering your classmates' suggestions, prepare a final draft of your composition to hand in to your teacher. Before handing it in, check the punctuation of your sentences. Proofread for spelling and grammar errors as well.

CHAPTER REVIEW

Look back at what you have accomplished in Chapter 5. Check (✓) what you have learned and what you have used as you have written and revised your composition.

Chapter 5 Topics	I understand this	I have used this
writing an introduction that gets the reader's attention and identifies the topic and controlling idea of the essay (pages 116–117)		
organizing causes or effects by time order or order of importance (pages 109–110)		
using transition signals to help the reader follow the organization of the paper (page 121)		
writing a conclusion that gives the reader the sense that the essay is finished (page 123)		
using the language of cause and effect (pages 126–131)		

CHAPTER 6

Marriage and Family

◆ Writing a Comparison/Contrast Essay

In every part of the world, families are important. Therefore, how people meet one another, marry, and arrange family life are serious matters—not only for individuals, but also for whole societies. Historically, cultures around the world have developed very different values and customs regarding courtship, marriage, and family life. In recent times, however, with the growth of industrialization and cities, families everywhere are experiencing similar changes and adapting in similar ways.

This chapter will help you

- use an appropriate pattern of organization for a comparison/contrast essay.
- learn more about introduction strategies.
- balance development in comparison/contrast essays.
- improve cohesion in your essays.
- use the language of comparison/contrast.

READING FOR WRITING

Before You Read

Complete the following questionnaire by yourself. Then freewrite on the topic of marriage for ten minutes.

QUESTIONNAIRE. Our attitudes about marriage are shaped by our cultures. To reflect on your thoughts about this important social institution, select the answers that best express your opinions.

1. Marriage _____ necessary to a meaningful adult life.

   a. is

   b. is not

2. Choosing a marriage partner is _____ matter.

   a. an individual

   b. a family

3. The purpose of marriage is _____.

   a. finding one's true love

   b. bringing children into the world and providing a safe, secure environment for them

   c. fulfilling one's parents' expectations

   d. strengthening the social position of one's family

   e. *other*: _____

Lifestyle Changes in Japan

by Sumiko Iwao

1 Like many other countries, Japan is in the midst of major social change. The area of Japanese life that has changed the most since World War II is the family. The greatest shifts have been seen in women's lives, but men's lives have been altered as well.

Changes in Women's Lives

2   Two of the most significant changes in the lives of Japanese women are the extension of their average lifespan and the decrease in the average number of children they have. In 1935 the average lifespan for women in Japan was just

skyrocket: to increase suddenly and dramatically

career track: a pathway in which a person moves upward from one job to another

short of 50 years; in 1994 it had skyrocketed° to 82 years. In the early postwar years, the average Japanese woman gave birth to four children, but by 1995, the number of births per woman had dropped to 1.43. The drop in the birthrate is, in part, a result of women's growing participation in the workforce.

3   Women have been steadily increasing their rate of employment outside the home, and Japanese companies are coming to rely more on women in all parts of their operations—on the factory floor as well as in the office. It had been the tradition to assign women to a special secretarial career track° and to deny them access to both shop floor and managerial positions. Recently, however, more and more manufacturers are taking steps to make it possible for women to do blue-collar jobs which were once reserved for men. Women have been given access to the management track as well, and as a result, the number of women pursuing managerial jobs has grown substantially.

4   It used to be that women would quit working as soon as they married, but that is no longer the case. However, many women interrupt their careers for several years to raise a family. When broken down by age, the female workplace participation rate represents an "M" shaped curve. A low percentage of women between the ages of 30 and 34 are working because they leave the labor market temporarily to take care of young families. This represents the dip in the "M." These same women return to work when they have completed childrearing.

Labor Force Participation Rates for Women in Japan

Source: Bureau of Statistics. Management and Coordination Agency, *Labor Force Survey*.

5   The significance of marriage has also changed for women. New employment opportunities for female workers have made it much easier for women to make a life for themselves outside the framework of marriage.

overwhelming: very large and impressive

opinion survey: questions asked of a large number of people to find out what they think

autonomy: independence

wedlock: marriage

toil: to work hard

colleague: a fellow worker, especially a fellow professional

Marriage used to be a necessity for women to survive, but today it has clearly become an option, and a woman has the freedom to choose whether to marry or remain single.

6   The overwhelming° majority of women in Japan do want to marry, however. Recent opinion surveys° indicate that only a very small number, 6 percent, are determined to remain single all their lives. But since single women can get just about everything they desire without marrying—a challenging job with a good salary, a nice apartment, and even male companionship—they are delaying marriage. In the last 40 years, the average age at which people married for the first time rose steadily, from 26 to 28 years for men and from 23 to 26 for women. The trend among women to wed later is closely related to education. The more education a woman has received, the more likely she is to delay marriage.

7   Young married women, more highly educated and more financially independent than ever before, are also seeking new demands from the relationship with their husbands. They desire to maintain their freedom and autonomy° even after wedlock°. This has seen the divorce rate begin to rise in Japan, although it remains considerably lower than in other advanced industrial countries. Japan's numbers are rising, however, and the younger generation has an increasingly tolerant view of divorce.

8   Divorce among older couples is a new phenomenon in Japan. It is in part a product of the tradition in older couples for the husband and wife to form two separate social worlds. For this generation, the man usually leaves management of the home and education of the children in the wife's hands while he toils° long and hard at the office. His detachment from household affairs has the effect of making his wife psychologically independent. However, divorce is still seen as a last resort, as it brings sacrifice for both women and men.

Changes in Men's Lives

9   In contrast to the dramatic changes that have taken place in women's lives, men's lives have changed to a lesser degree. Furthermore, there is a difference between men of the older generation and younger men. Men in older age groups have wives who are full-time housewives. They did not have women as their classmates in their college days. For them, women and children still form a single group in need of a man's protection.

10   By comparison, younger men are accustomed to women classmates and coworkers. They are quite open to accept a person by his or her ability. They find nothing unusual or unsettling about having a female boss or female colleagues°. When married, these men hope their wives will continue working even after the children are born. They share as much as possible in the domestic responsibilities (though the value of their contribution is still up for debate).

individualistic:
independent, not
influenced by other
people

11   In the workplace, the younger generation is much more individualistic° than their parents were. Their fathers thought it natural to place work before family and personal wishes, but young Japanese are much more interested in placing their individual needs and concerns before their company's. Japan's rapid economic development since World War II, often described as an "economic miracle," was partly due to the Japanese custom of putting the well-being of the group as a whole before individual needs and desires. Such behavior enhanced group harmony, which in turn reinforced° the importance of a group-centered society.

reinforce: to support

pseudo: false

12   For many Japanese men, the workplace became a pseudo° family. These businessmen worked until late at night and then, before returning home, went out drinking with work colleagues. On the weekends, they met again for golf. Their life was focused on their work, and work prevented them from spending time on personal hobbies or meeting new friends.

13   I expect these men sacrificed their private life to their company because they were working toward building up their country and also they thought they would be rewarded sufficiently and fairly by the company for their service. However, the so-called restructuring° now underway in the Japanese economy has left many of them disillusioned°. Their years of hard work have been rewarded by "a seat by the window," a Japanese expression meaning that a worker is pushed aside in the office, although not formally laid off.

restructuring:
reorganizing a
company, usually to
reduce the number of
management levels
disillusioned:
disappointed because
of a mistaken belief

14   The children of these men have watched what happened to their fathers. They have learned quickly that instead of being dependent on the company, they should do what they themselves wish to do as individuals. This generation does not hesitate to take paid holidays if they are entitled to do so. Or if they have a previous engagement, they will refuse to stay late in the office to do overtime work. Some see this change among the younger generation as negative, while others see it as positive.

optimist: a person with
a positive point of view
pessimist: a person
with a negative point
of view
crossroads: a point in
life when one is forced
to make a decision

15   Whether optimist° or pessimist°, all would agree that Japan is at a crossroads° in her history. In the last 60 years, the Japanese family has experienced major changes. While women's lives have changed the most, men's lives have been altered as well. On every level of society, the Japanese are adapting to these changes.

About the Author

Sumiko Iwao is a professor at Musashi Institute of Technology in Japan. She is also a member of the Gender Equality Congress in the Office of the Japanese Prime Minister, where she advises the government with respect to gender equality. Dr. Iwao received her Ph.D. in psychology from Yale University and has taught at Harvard University. "Lifestyle Changes in Japan" was adapted from a speech Dr. Iwao gave in Lima, Peru, in 1996.

Understanding the Reading

With a partner or small group, discuss the following questions.

1. Sumiko Iwao makes several comparisons in this speech. What are they? Which comparison did you find most interesting, and why?

2. a. In this chapter, you will write an essay that compares two things. To do this, you will select two or three **points of comparison**. To help you prepare for the chapter assignment, compare the lives of women in two countries. First, find the aspects of Japanese women's lives that Iwao discusses, and write them in the column in the chart under *Points of Comparison*. Then, write the names of two countries at the top of the other two columns. (One may be Japan, if you wish.) Complete the chart with information about each point of comparison. (It is not necessary to do research to complete this exercise. Just use your general knowledge.)

Points of Comparison	Women in _____	Women in _____
lifespan (paragraph 2)		

   b. Make three or four comparative statements about women in the two countries you chose. For example, *Women in Country X are living longer than they used to, while women in Country Y are not living as long as they used to.*

3. Do you see a cause-and-effect relationship among the changes in Japanese women's lives? What do you think is the root cause (the first change which led to the other changes)? Fill in the bubbles in the cause-and-effect cluster (see also Chapter 5, page 113), starting with the root cause in the bubble on the left and showing the effects in the bubbles to the right. You may add bubbles if you wish.

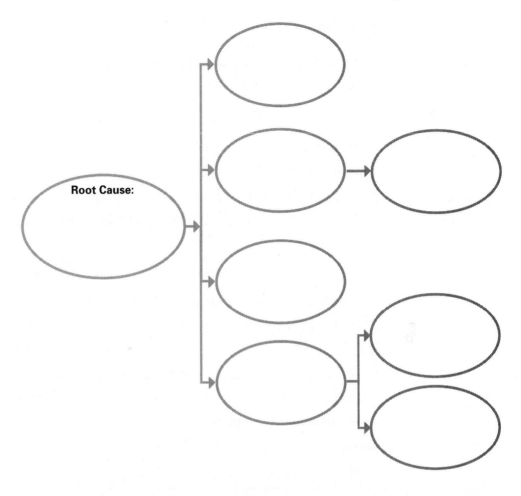

Compare your cluster with your classmates'. Do you agree about the causal relationships? If not, explain your reasons.

4. When a society experiences dramatic change, both positive and negative effects can be seen. In your opinion, what is one positive and one negative effect of the social change in Japan?

5. *Status* refers to a person's position in society relative to other people. How have the changes in Japanese society affected the status of women? Explain.

6. What vocabulary and grammatical structures does Iwao use to present comparisons? Give examples of three different words, phrases, or sentence patterns from the reading that show a comparison.

Vocabulary Expansion

Word families. You have learned that in English there are word families—groups of words with the same root and different suffixes. The suffixes show what parts of speech the members of word families are.

Exercise 1

Look at the word-family lists above each paragraph. Each box contains the nouns, verbs, and adjectives in a word family. Complete the paragraphs with words from the lists. Some words will need to be made plural; others will be singular.

> 1. marriage (*n.*)   married (*adj.*)   marital (*adj.*)   marry (*v.*)

Most young people expect to (a) _____ marry _____, so magazines often print articles about love and (b) _____. These articles tell single people how to find partners, how to plan a wedding, and, once they are (c) _____, how to solve their (d) _____ problems.

> 2. symbol (*n.*)   symbolic (*adj.*)   symbolism (*n.*)   symbolize (*v.*)

Wedding ceremonies contain a great deal of (e) _____. For example, in traditional Western-style weddings, the white bridal gown is a (f) _____ of the bride's purity, and the rings (g) _____ the bride and groom's commitment to each other. Diamond wedding rings are popular because the diamond is the hardest, most enduring mineral, and therefore it is (h) _____ of the couple's lasting love.

> 3. partner (*n.*)   partnership (*n.*)

Marriage is a lifelong (i) _____, so the choice of a marriage (j) _____ is a critical decision. When looking for a spouse, one should avoid people who do not like to share responsibility, people who do not always tell the truth, and people who cannot make a decision and live with the consequences.

> 4. relate (*v.*)   relative (*n.*)   relation (*n.*)   relationship (*n.*)

Sociologists and anthropologists refer to family members as "kin," but most English speakers call their aunts, uncles, cousins, and grandparents (k) "_____" or (l) "_____."

Some families are close-knit. Aunts, uncles, and cousins talk to each other often, and they can (m) _____ to each other easily. Other families do not have such strong (n) _____. They do not see each other often, and when they do get together, they may have trouble communicating.

> 5. cooperate (*v.*)   cooperation (*n.*)   cooperative (*adj.*)

Marriage is an economic and social union. People need to (o) _____ in order to live well. If there is (p) _____ between not only the husband and wife but the couple and other members of their families, life is better for everyone. That is why, in traditional extended families, it is most important that the person who joins the family through marriage be (q) _____.

> 6. commit (*v.*)   committed (*adj.*)   commitment (*n.*)

Marriage is a serious (r) _____. When two people marry, they (s) _____ themselves to remain together whether they are healthy or sick, rich or poor, happy or unhappy. However, over the years, marital relations can change. Loving, (t) _____ spouses can become discontent or even unfaithful partners. That is why a significant number of marriages end in divorce.

> 7. individual (*n.*)   individualism (*n.*)   individualistic (*adj.*)
> individuality (*n.*)

In pre-industrial times, marriage was an agreement between families. To arrange a marriage meant to bring a new person into a family. People identified themselves first as members of families and second as (u) _____.

Economic development has changed this. It has promoted (v) _____, the belief that the rights of the individual are the most important rights in society. The reason that economic development has had this effect is that when a person is employed away from his or her family, he or she acquires a new sense of (w) _____. But opinions about this trend vary, and some people say that a person who insists too much on his or her own way of doing things is too (x) _____.

WRITING

Assignment

Choose one of the following topics and write an essay using one of the comparison/contrast patterns of organization shown below and on page 145.

1. Compare single life and married life.

2. Compare the lives of men and women in your country or culture.

3. Compare young people's expectations for marriage and the reality of married life.

4. Compare courtship and/or marriage in your parents' or grandparents' times and courtship and/or marriage in your time.

5. Compare women's roles in two generations.

What Comparison/Contrast Is and Why It Is Important

Comparing is something you do automatically. You routinely compare things like neighborhoods, schools, and vacation destinations. When you compare two things, you use **points of comparison**. (For example, when you answered item 2 in Understanding the Reading on page 140, you compared the lives of women in two countries in terms of their lifespan, number of children, employment, and so on.) As you consider the composition topics, you will also look for points of comparison. For example, if you are going to write about topic 1, single life and married life, you will search for points of comparison such as free time, money, and companionship.

When you compare two things, you will find both differences and similarities. (The word *compare* means *find differences and similarities*, while *contrast* means *find differences only*.) Many comparison/contrast essays present only differences, but you may prefer to focus on similarities.

Organizing a comparison/contrast essay. Whether you decide to write about differences or similarities, you will have to choose between two patterns of organization, **point-by-point** or **side-by-side**. The two sample outlines that follow compare single life and married life.

Point-by-Point Organization
Introduction and thesis statement

I. Point of Comparison 1
Single life
Married life

II. Point of Comparison 2
Single life
Married life

III. Point of Comparison 3
   Single life
   Married life

Conclusion

Side-by-Side Organization
Introduction and thesis statement

I. Single Life
   Point of comparison 1
   Point of comparison 2
   Point of comparison 3

II. Married Life
   Point of comparison 1
   Point of comparison 2
   Point of comparison 3

Conclusion

Exercise 2

Look at the following outline, and decide what pattern of organization (side-by-side or point-by-point) it has. On another piece of paper, rewrite the outline, using the other pattern of organization.

THESIS: Marriage in traditional societies differs from marriage in industrialized societies.

I. The purpose of marriage
   A. In traditional societies
      1. A marriage creates an alliance between two families.
      2. Through marriage, children are born who will continue the family line.
   B. In industrialized societies
      1. Marriage serves the needs of individuals.
         a. status and security
         b. an opportunity to have legitimate children

II. The selection of a marriage partner
   A. In traditional societies
      1. A marriage partner is usually selected by the parents of the bride and groom.
   B. In industrialized societies
      1. Individuals choose their own partners.

III. Marriage customs
    A. In traditional societies
        1. Customs symbolize the exchange between two families.
           a. the dowry
    B. In industrialized societies
        1. Customs symbolize the exchange between two individuals.
           a. wedding rings

Pattern of organization: _____

Point-by-point organization is used more often than side-by-side because it helps readers focus on the points of comparison. Point-by-point is particularly useful for papers that contain a lot of information. However, side-by-side is more dramatic and therefore is effective for discussing a change over time or for contrasting an impression of reality with the way things really are. For example, to compare young people's idealistic ideas about marriage with the reality of married life, you might write the first body paragraph about a fantasy of marriage as an extended courtship during which the wife receives frequent gifts of flowers and jewelry. The second body paragraph might be about the unromantic reality of the first few months of marriage when the couple has to decide who will pay the bills, clean the floor, and take out the trash.

When you select a topic, consider both point-by-point and side-by-side (make brief outlines with each to compare them), and then choose the pattern of organization that will be most effective for your essay.

Combining similarities and differences in the comparison/contrast essay. While many comparison/contrast essays discuss only differences or only similarities, some discuss both. If you decide to discuss both, put the aspect you wish to emphasize (either similarities or differences) last. For example, if you decide to emphasize differences, you can (1) mention similarities in the introduction before concentrating on differences in the body, or (2) include a body paragraph about similarities before discussing differences in one or more additional body paragraphs.

Prewriting

Once you have selected a topic, following the prewriting steps will help you gather information and organize it effectively.

Marie, a student from France, decided to write about the differences in the lives of men and women in her culture because she knew several married women who had jobs and children, and she had concluded that their lives were more difficult than their husbands'. She did her prewriting in the following way.

STEP 1 | Write down the two things that you plan to compare, and make a **list** for the first one. Then create a **parallel list** for the second one.

First, Marie wrote a list about men, which you see on the left. Then she created a parallel list about women.

<u>Men</u>

- tend to work away from home more hours than they work at home
- tend to have more leisure time than their wives; tend to spend their leisure time doing outdoor activities or watching sports on television either alone or with friends
- tend to be employed at higher positions and paid more
- tend to have higher status in society

<u>Women</u>

- tend to work at home nearly as many or even more hours than they work away from home
- tend to have less leisure time than their husbands; tend to spend their leisure time with their children
- even when as well educated as men, tend to be hired at lower positions and paid less
- tend to have lower status in society

STEP 2 | At this point, you may need to **narrow your topic** and cross out the items on your list that do not fit in your topic focus. Then write a **thesis statement**.

Marie decided to focus on men and women's work, so she crossed out the point about leisure time. Then she drafted a thesis statement.

Today in France, when married couples both work outside the home, the lives of the husband and wife differ.

STEP 3 | Look for **points of comparison** on your lists and check (✓) them. If you can, discuss them with your classmates and teacher. Then write **focused questions** and answers to develop each one.

Marie decided on three points of comparison, which she wrote as focused questions. She then answered each one.

1. How much time do men and women spend working outside and inside the home?
   —Men tend to work away from home more hours than they work at home.
   —Women tend to work at home as many or more hours than they work away from home.

2. What type of work do men and women do outside and inside the home?
   —Men tend to hold managerial positions.
   —Women tend to hold lower-level positions such as clerks and food processors.
   —Men tend to choose which household tasks they will perform.
   —Women do not choose which household tasks they will perform.

3. How are men and women rewarded for the work they do outside and inside the home?
   —Men tend to be given more promotions and to be paid more.
   —Women, even when as well educated as men, tend to be given fewer promotions and paid less.
   —Men are rewarded for their work at home because it is not expected.
   —Women are not rewarded for their work at home because it is expected.

STEP 4 Consider the two **patterns of organization** (point-by-point and side-by-side), and select one. Make an **outline**, using each **focused question** as a **point of comparison**.

Marie decided to use point-by-point organization. She made the following outline.

Today in France, when married partners both work outside the home, their lives differ <u>in terms of the amount of time they spend on work, the type of work they do, and the rewards they receive both outside and inside the home.</u>

I. Time they spend on work
   A. Men
      1. spend more hours working away from home
      2. spend less time working at home
   B. Women
      1. some hold part-time jobs near their homes
      2. some hold full-time jobs and struggle to do work at home in less time

II. Type of work they do
   A. Men
      1. managerial positions outside
      2. select the household tasks they do
   B. Women
      1. lower-level positions outside
      2. cannot choose the household tasks they do

III. Rewards they receive
   A. Men
      1. higher salaries and more promotions
      2. efforts in the home are acknowledged more
   B. Women
      1. lower salaries and fewer promotions
      2. efforts in the home are not acknowledged

With her outline complete, Marie was ready to write a first draft. She wrote several drafts before completing the following draft.

The Lives of Working Husbands and Wives in France Today

Today a significant number of French women work outside the home, some full time and others part time. However, when housewives and mothers enter the labor market, their lives do not become exactly like their husbands'. In fact, the lives of working husbands and wives differ in terms of the time they spend on work, the type of work they do, and the rewards they receive both outside and inside the home.

First, men and women spend different amounts of time working both away from and in the home. Men spend, on average, more time working away from home than women do because most men hold full-time jobs. At home, men average only twenty minutes of work per day while women average about four hours. Many women with young children opt to take part-time jobs so that they can spend more time caring for their children. Women who hold full-time jobs struggle to complete their household tasks and care for their children in less time; for example, they may attempt to do laundry, cook dinner, and help their children with homework all at the same time.

Second, the type of work that men and women do differs. In the workforce, more men than women rise to the managerial level, whereas more women occupy low-level jobs such as secretaries, food processors, and domestic workers. At home, men often see housework as voluntary for them and therefore tend to select the tasks they perform. Thus, the husband may vacuum for twenty minutes and then leave the rest of the housework for his wife. Unless they can afford to hire other women to clean for them, women have no choice but to do all the housework their husbands cannot or will not do.

Third, the rewards men and women receive from work are different. In the workforce, men are paid higher salaries and are promoted more quickly. At home, men receive more praise from their partners for their efforts than women because men are not expected to do housework. Women in the workforce are paid lower salaries and awarded fewer promotions, and at home, because they are expected to do housework, their efforts are not acknowledged as often as their husbands'.

The differences we see in the lives of working men and women lead to lower status for women: Women work fewer hours and so cannot advance in their jobs; women hold lower-level positions in the workforce, in part because employers do not view them as able to commit themselves fully to their jobs; and due to their shorter hours and lower-level positions, women earn less. Because they are not bringing home as much money as their husbands, women continue to do more housework, and housework does not bring women status or rewards. To break this cycle, men must share equally with women in household responsibilities, and employers must give women opportunities equal to those they offer to men.

Exercise 3

With your classmates, discuss the following questions.

1. Does Marie's essay discuss similarities, differences, or similarities and differences?

2. Which strategy (general statement, background, anecdote) did Marie use in her introduction?

3. Does Marie's thesis statement mention the supporting points of the essay? If so, what are they?

4. Which pattern of organization (point-by-point or side-by-side) did Marie use?

5. Which strategies (summary, suggestion, prediction, opinion) did Marie use in her conclusion?

After selecting a topic from the list on page 144, follow the sequence of steps Marie used.

First Draft

Once you have completed an outline, you are ready to write your first draft. You may, if you wish, write the thesis statement and the body of the essay before you write the introduction and conclusion.

REVISING

If you can, put your first draft aside for a day or two before you begin revising. You should be able to see your work with fresh eyes when you come back to it. Revising carefully can make the difference between a paper that is good and one that is excellent. As you proceed through the lessons and exercises in this chapter, review your draft, and follow the instructions in the Review and Revise boxes.

Composition Focus

The introduction of the comparison/contrast essay. In Chapter 5, you learned about three kinds of introductions: general statement, background, or anecdote (see page 117). In a comparison/contrast essay, you can use another kind of introduction: the **turnabout**. For example, you could write about similarities in the introduction, and then turn about and focus on differences in the body.

Furthermore, introductions may contain more than one strategy. For example, you could begin an introductory paragraph with a general statement about marriage, then give some background information about marriage in a particular culture, and finally present a thesis statement about the differences in marriage customs between two generations in that culture.

Exercise 4

Read the following introductions, and identify the strategy or strategies used as *general statement, background, anecdote,* or *turnabout.* Underline the thesis statement <u>once</u> and the controlling idea <u>twice</u>.

1.   **Indian Women's Rights Before Marriage Laws and Today**

India is a land of many cultures and a long history. Traditionally, India had a great variety of marriage customs, some of them very unfair to women. Since India's independence from Britain in 1947, the Indian Parliament has enacted a number of laws which have given more rights to women and greatly improved their lives. <u>As a result of these laws, women's lives have changed <u>in terms of the age at which they get married and the conditions under which they may divorce</u>.</u>

Strategy: _____ *background* _____

2.   **Civil and Church Weddings in Colombia**

Last year I was fortunate to attend two wonderful weddings in my country, Colombia. In May, my cousin Linda married Geraldo in a civil ceremony, and in September, my long-time friend Maria married Ignacio in a Catholic wedding ceremony. Both weddings were joyous occasions, but they were different in a number of ways. In Colombia, civil weddings and church weddings differ in terms of their elaborateness and their social significance.

Strategy: _____

3.   **Men and Women's Reasons for Marrying**

Men and women marry for many of the same reasons. Both men and women marry because marriage is valued by society, and therefore, marriage gives both higher social status. Marriage offers both men and women psychological benefits as well in that married people have more support and companionship than single people. However, some of the motivations of men and women differ: Men tend to be more interested in the attractiveness of their spouses, and women tend to be more interested in the wage-earning capacity of their partners.

Strategy: _____

4.   **Marriage in Greece and Turkey**

Religious organizations are deeply concerned with preserving family life, so in a country with one dominant faith, marriage customs tend to be shaped by religion. Greece and Turkey are both countries with a single dominant religion: The Greek Orthodox faith is the principal religion of Greece, and Islam is the principal faith of Turkey. Because of this difference in religion, Greek marriages and Turkish marriages differ in that Turkish parents play a larger role in selecting the marriage partner than Greek parents do, and Greek and Turkish ceremonies contain different symbolism.

Strategy: _____

Review and Revise 1: Strategies for Writing Introductions
Look at your essay. If you have already written an introduction, determine what strategy you have used. Ask yourself if another strategy might work better. If you have not written an introduction, choose one of the strategies discussed on pages 117 and 150, and write your introduction now.

For more about noun clauses, see Appendix IA, page 287.

The controlling idea in thesis statements. In Exercise 4, you identified thesis statements and their controlling ideas. You may have noticed that controlling ideas for comparison/contrast essays can be introduced by *in* or *in terms of*. *In* is followed by a *that*-clause, and *in terms of* is followed by a noun, a noun phrase, or a *wh*-noun clause. Look at the examples below.

In + That- *Clauses*

CLAUSE

Muslim and Christian weddings differ in <u>that Muslim ceremonies are held in</u>

CLAUSE

<u>a mosque or a home</u> <u>while Christian weddings are usually held in a church</u>.

In Terms Of + *Noun(s), Noun-Phrase(s), or* Wh-*Noun Clause(s)*

NOUN

Muslim and Christian weddings differ in terms of <u>location</u>.
Muslim and Christian weddings differ in terms of

NOUN PHRASE   NOUN PHRASE

<u>the selection of the marriage partner</u> and <u>the location of the ceremony</u>.

Muslim and Christian marriages differ in terms of <u>how they are arranged</u> [WH-NOUN CLAUSE]

and <u>where the ceremony is held</u> [WH-NOUN CLAUSE].

When you introduce two or three points of comparison after *in* or *in terms of*, you must use correct parallel structure (see page 90). Look at the example.

NOT PARALLEL: In Japan, Christian weddings differ from traditional Shinto weddings in terms of the location of the ceremony, the presiding official, and the bride and groom wear Western clothing instead of kimonos.

The location of the ceremony and *the presiding official* are noun phrases, but *the bride and groom wear Western clothing instead of kimonos* is a clause. To correct the parallel structure, the clause must be changed to a noun phrase.

PARALLEL: In Japan, Christian weddings differ from traditional Shinto weddings in terms of <u>the location of the ceremony</u>, <u>the presiding official</u>, and <u>the clothing worn by the bride and groom</u>.

> For more on parallel structure, see Appendix IA, page 283.

Exercise 5

Work with a partner. Read the following passage about the changes in marriage in Japan. Using the information in the passage, complete the following statements using *in* or *in terms of*.

In Japan in the 1950s, marriage was a family matter. The father had the authority in the family, so he would arrange the marriages of his children. An eldest son lived all his life in the family home with his parents and carried on the family line, so his marriage was particularly important. For this reason, when an eldest son reached the age of twenty-five, his father would seek the assistance of a go-between, or matchmaker, who would show him photographs and give him family histories of six or seven young women. The father would then choose one young woman whose family was similar to his own and set a date for a meeting between the two families called an *omiai*. During the *omiai*, the parents would do almost all the talking while the young people would sit with eyes cast down. Afterward, if all had gone well, the young man and woman would be asked to give their consent. In those days, there were more available women than men, so young women and their families had to agree to any reasonable match. Once the marriage was agreed upon, the bride and groom would not see each other again until the wedding day.

Since the 1950s, Japan has changed a great deal. Today marriage is largely an individual matter. Fathers do not have as much authority in the family as they once had, and eldest sons do not always remain at home, though, if they move out, they usually settle near their parents. Young people choose their own marriage partners, often after meeting one another at college or work. Today very few seek the help of go-betweens, but those who cannot find a spouse on their own use the services of computer matchmaking companies, which provide applicants with photographs and information about dozens of potential mates. Because many women are delaying marriage and a few are deciding to remain single, the number of available men is now greater than the number of available women, so young men have to agree to any reasonable match. Typically, a young man selecting a potential spouse through computer dating will first send e-mails to a few candidates, then select one to date, and finally, if the dating goes well, ask her to marry him. Young people still want to have their parents' approval in the selection of a partner, but a lack of parental approval will not necessarily stop them from marrying.

1. In Japan, the role of fathers has changed _in that they no longer arrange the marriages of their children._

2. The role of eldest sons has changed as well _____

   _____

   _____

3. A go-between and a computer dating service are similar _____

   _____

   _____

4. An *omiai* and a date differ _____

   _____

5. Courtship in Japan today differs from courtship fifty years ago _____

   _____

Now share your responses with your classmates.

> **Review and Revise 2: The Controlling Idea in Thesis Statements**
> Review your thesis statement. If you have not included points of comparison in your thesis statement, try using *in* or *in terms of* to add them. If you use parallel structure in your thesis statement, check it to make sure that it is correct.

Balanced development in the comparison/contrast essay. Whether your essay compares two events, two situations, two customs, or two ideas, it must present these two things in a balanced way. Therefore, when revising a comparison/contrast essay, you must make sure all parts of your paper are equally well developed.

Exercise 6

This essay does not have balanced development. That means that the two things it is comparing, the raising of boys and the raising of girls, are not equally developed. Read the essay and locate the places where more development is needed. Finally, add information to the text to improve the balance.

Raising Boys and Girls

1   [1]Even though women's and men's roles have changed in the last fifty or sixty years as women have started working outside the home, the raising of boys and girls has not substantially changed. [2]Boys and girls are still raised differently in terms of how they are dressed, what toys they are given, and where and how they are allowed to play.

2   [3]From the first day of their lives, boys' and girls' clothing differs in terms of color and style. [4]Boys' colors are bold blues, reds, or greens, while girls are usually dressed in pink or other pastel colors. [5]Boys' clothing tends to be functional, while girls' has decorative details such as ribbons, bows, and ruffles. [6]Many outfits for babies and young children have pictures on them, and those images clearly mark them as for boys or girls. [7]Boys' clothing has images of trains, trucks, or sailboats.

3   [8]When parents and relatives select toys for young children, they choose playthings that reflect traditional male and female roles. [9]Boys are given toys that move such as trucks and cars, or cannons or guns that shoot objects into the air, as well as toys that allow them to build structures or carry out science experiments. [10]Girls are given toys that replicate the home environment.

4   [11]When boys and girls are old enough to play independently, they are treated differently in terms of how and where they are allowed to play. [12]Boys are allowed to go outside where they can run, climb trees, and wander through the neighborhood. [13]They can get wet or muddy, and no one gets upset with them. [14]Girls, on the other hand, are told to remain inside and stay clean.

5   [15]The way parents raise their children has an effect on their future lives. [16]Boys and girls learn about their gender, or social roles as males and females, from their earliest experiences—from how they are dressed, what they are given to play with, and how and where they are allowed to play. [17]Parents should realize that the roles their boys and girls will play in the future will not be as distinct as the male and female roles of the past. [18]Their girls will grow up to be women who will work outside the home, and their boys will grow up to be men who will share in household responsibilities. [19]Therefore, parents should raise boys and girls more uniformly to prepare them for the future.

> **Review and Revise 3: Balance in the Comparison/Contrast Essay**
> Review your own essay for balance. Make sure that the two things you are comparing are equally well developed. If development in your essay is not balanced, revise it.

Cohesion in the comparison/contrast essay. As you learned on page 91, you can make your essay cohesive if you link your thesis statement to the topic sentences of your body paragraphs and link the topic sentences of the body paragraphs to one another in the following ways:

1. Name the supporting points in your thesis statement.

2. Put the supporting points in the same order in your body paragraphs as they appear in your thesis statement.

3. Repeat key words used in the controlling idea of your thesis statement in the topic sentences of your body paragraphs, or use synonyms.

4. Use transitions such as *one*, *another*, *first*, and *finally* in the topic sentences of your body paragraphs.

Notice which strategies are used in these examples.

Thesis
In <u>my grandmother's time</u> a woman's life was very different from what it is today: <u>Taiwanese women's lives have changed</u> in terms of <u>their responsibilities, their rights, and their social status</u>.

Topic sentences
First, <u>Taiwanese women's lives have changed</u> since <u>my grandmother's generation</u> in terms of <u>what their duties are</u>.

Second, <u>Taiwanese women's lives have changed</u> since <u>my grandmother's generation</u> in terms of <u>what they are permitted to do</u>.

Finally, <u>Taiwanese women's lives have changed</u> since <u>my grandmother's generation</u> in terms of <u>how much they are respected by others</u>.

Here are three more ways to link your thesis statement and the topic sentences of your body paragraphs.

1. **Word forms.** Use the members of a word family to link your thesis and topic sentences.

   Thesis
   Extended families and nuclear families differ in three ways: the *education* of children, the *division* of work, and the *distribution* of property.

   Topic sentences
   First, the way that babies and young children are *educated* in extended families and nuclear families is different.

   Second, the way that work is *divided* among family members in extended families and nuclear families is different.

   Finally, the way that property is *distributed* in extended families and nuclear families is different.

2. **Similar sentence beginnings.** Use similar prepositional phrases or subjects and verbs at the beginning of the topic sentences to link the topic sentences to one another.

   Thesis
   Family life in two-career television families differs from actual family life in two-career families in terms of the way family members communicate with one another, care for children, and manage household duties.

Topic sentences

In situation comedies and similar programs, family members in two-career families have a lot of time to talk to each other, but in real life, working parents and their children are too busy to interact.

On TV, men are shown caring for children as often as women, but in real life, mothers care for children more often than fathers.

On the air, dual-career couples seldom argue about or even appear to do housework, but in real life, getting housework done is a big problem for dual-career couples, and they often disagree about who should do the chores.

3. **Correlative conjunctions.** Use the correlative conjunctions *not only . . . but also* to link the topic sentences of the body paragraphs to one another.

Thesis

Married and single people lead very different lives in terms of their ability to live economically, to find companionship, and to plan for the future.

Topic sentences

Married people can share basic expenses and save money, while single people have to manage household expenses on their own.

Married people have companionship almost any time they want it, whereas single people have to make an effort to find company.

Not only are married people better off economically and socially than single people, *but* married people can *also* face the future with greater certainty.

For more on correlative conjunctions, see Appendix IA, page 285.

> **Review and Revise 4: Cohesion**
> Check the thesis statement and the topic sentences of the body paragraphs in your essay for cohesion, noticing which strategies you have used. If you have not used at least one or two of the strategies listed above in your essay, revise now.

The conclusion of the comparison/contrast essay. As you learned on page 123, in conclusions you try to give readers a sense of completion. Use summary, suggestion, prediction, opinion, and other strategies to accomplish this.

Exercise 7

A. Examine the conclusions of the two model essays in this chapter, and check (✓) the methods that were used in each.

"The Lives of Working Husbands and Wives in France Today" (pages 149–150)	"Raising Boys and Girls" (pages 155–156)
_____ summarizing	_____ summarizing
_____ predicting	_____ predicting
_____ recommending	_____ recommending
_____ offering an opinion	_____ offering an opinion
_____ drawing conclusions about why or how things occur	_____ drawing conclusions about why or how things occur

B. Write a conclusion for the following essay using the methods that you think were successful in the essays you have just reviewed.

Later Is Better

Because I am now approaching thirty years of age, I have had the opportunity to see most of my friends get married. Some married in their late teens, and, unfortunately, some of those early marriages haven't lasted. Others married in their mid- or late twenties, and these later marriages appear more stable. I have concluded that there is a significant difference between early and late marriage in that mature couples know better what they want in life, are more able to make joint decisions based on their shared goals, and are more willing to make sacrifices.

To succeed in marriage, people must know what they value in life. Young people in their late teens or early twenties are still in the process of getting to know themselves. Trying to discover what they want in life, they may move from one place to another, start school and later drop out, and even alter their idea of an ideal partner. Because people change so much at this age, a person who marries at eighteen may look at her spouse five years later and ask herself, "Is this the same person I married?" On the other hand, those who marry after the age of twenty-five have had time to experience life. They have studied a range of subjects in school or held various jobs; they have dated a number of people and have developed a good sense of what they want in a mate. After the age of twenty-five, people are less likely to undergo major shifts in their interests or values. Therefore, more mature marriage partners are less likely to grow apart.

To succeed in marriage, people must not only know what their own values and goals are, but they must also know how to establish common goals with their spouses and decide together how to reach those goals. Some eighteen-year-olds expect everything to go their way. Others are very impatient and expect problems to be solved quickly. Even the most mature eighteen-year-olds are not practiced in the give-and-take of negotiations with a peer. People of twenty-five or older, in contrast, have learned that they cannot always get what they want. They know that it takes time to work problems out. Through their experience in other relationships, they have learned to cooperate and compromise, so they are more successful at agreeing upon common goals with their spouses.

Finally, to succeed in marriage, people must be ready to sacrifice. Teenage newlyweds are sometimes shocked to discover that they can't watch their favorite TV program when their spouse wants to watch another, that they can't buy a new CD player because they need the money to pay the rent, or that they can't hang out with their old buddies every Friday and Saturday night. They become angry and refuse to give up what they want. More mature newlyweds will also discover that adjusting to married life can be difficult, but they are better able to meet the challenge. Because they have learned that to get along with others requires compromise, they can give up their favorite TV show, wait to buy the CD player, and forgo seeing their old buddies. Such sacrifices create a bond of trust between the couple.

_____

_____

_____

_____

_____

_____

_____

Review and Revise 5: Strategies for Writing Conclusions
Check the conclusion of your essay. Determine which strategies you have used, and ask yourself whether you want to include other strategies. Make sure that your conclusion does not introduce new ideas that require development. If your conclusion can be improved, revise it.

Language Focus

The vocabulary of comparison and contrast. English has many ways to signal similarity and contrast. Look at the chart.

Vocabulary and Structures That Signal Similarity				
Coordinating Conjunctions	**Subordinating Conjunctions**	**Correlative Conjunctions**	**Transitions**	**Other Parts of Speech**

and (can be used with adverbs such as *also*)	as
	just as
		both . . . and
		neither . . . nor
			likewise
			similarly
			in the same way
				alike, similar (adj.)
				also, as well,
				  so, the same,
				  too (adv.)
				similarity (n.)
				like (prep.)

Exercise 8

Choose a signal of similarity from the chart above to complete each sentence. Write *c.c.* (coordinating conjunction), *s.c.* (subordinating conjunction), *cor.c.* (correlative conjunction), *tr.* (transition), *adj.* (adjective), *adv.* (adverb), *n.* (noun), or *prep.* (preposition) in the parentheses.

1. _____ Like _____ Moroccan brides, Sudanese brides have their hands and feet decorated with designs made of a vegetable dye prior to the wedding. (prep.)

2. One _____ between Hindu and Christian weddings is the use of marriage vows. (   )

3. At Catholic weddings in _____ Spain _____ Mexico, the groom gives the bride coins which represent his willingness to support her. (   )

4. Greek and Kazakh weddings are _____ in that the bride and groom drink from a common cup that symbolizes their union. (   )

5. _____ young Italians usually live with their parents until they marry, young Greeks remain at home until married as well. (   )

6. In Chile, a couple transfers the rings from their right to left hands during the marriage ceremony, _____ an Egyptian couple does the same. (   )

7. In Ecuador, the godparents of the bride and groom participate in the wedding ceremony. _____, in Bolivia, the bride and groom's godparents take part in the wedding ceremony. (   )

For more on commas, see Appendix IB, page 315.

To avoid repetition in comparative statements, use synonyms and auxiliary verbs.

1. Instead of repeating the same words, phrases, and clauses, use **synonyms** and **synonymous phrases**.

   In Ecuador, the godparents of the bride and groom *participate* in the wedding ceremony. Similarly, in Bolivia, the godparents of the bride and groom *take part* in the wedding ceremony.

2. Instead of repeating long verb phrases, use **auxiliary verbs**.

   In Ecuador, the godparents of the bride and groom participate in the wedding ceremony, just as godparents *do* in Bolivia.

3. With *and*, use auxiliary verbs along with adverbs.

   In Ecuador, the godparents of the bride and groom participate in the wedding ceremony, and godparents *do the same* in Bolivia.

   In Ecuador, the godparents of the bride and groom participate in the wedding ceremony, and godparents *do* in Bolivia *also/as well/too.*

   In Ecuador, the godparents of the bride and groom participate in the wedding ceremony, and *so do* godparents in Bolivia.

Vocabulary and Structures That Signal Contrast			
Coordinating Conjunctions	**Subordinating Conjunctions**	**Transitions**	**Other Parts of Speech**
but	while whereas	however in contrast by comparison on the other hand	differ (v.) difference (n.) different (adj.) unlike (prep.)

Exercise 9
Choose a signal of contrast from the chart on page 162 to complete each sentence. Write *c.c.* (coordinating conjunction), *s.c.* (subordinating conjunction), *tr.* (transition), *v.* (verb), *n.* (noun), *adj.* (adjective), or *prep.* (preposition) in the parentheses.

1. In South Africa, weddings are held on Sundays, _____ but _____ in the United States, weddings are held on Saturdays. (*c.c.*)

2. _____ a bride in Yemen, who wears a dress of gold fabric, a bride in Pakistan wears a dress of red fabric. (   )

3. Christian weddings and Muslim weddings are _____ in that, in a Christian wedding, the bride and room make vows, while in a Muslim wedding, they sign a contract. (   )

4. Christian weddings include an exchange of rings to symbolize the bride and groom's union. _____, Hindu weddings include an exchange of necklaces or flower garlands. (   )

5. One _____ between weddings in India and weddings in the United States is the fact that in India the bride's family often pays a dowry to the groom's family. (   )

6. In Singapore, intermarriage, that is, marriage between people of different religions, is common. In India, intermarriage is unusual, _____. (   )

7. Weddings in the Netherlands _____ from weddings in Switzerland in that in the Netherlands, guests throw flowers on the couple after the wedding ceremony, and in Switzerland, they throw rice. (   )

8. Dancing and feasting go on from three to eight days after a Russian Orthodox wedding ceremony, _____ wedding receptions usually last only four or five hours in the United States. (   )

Exercise 10

Practice using the comparison/contrast signals. On another piece of paper, rewrite each sentence using the suggested structure. Remember to use synonyms and auxiliary verbs to avoid repetition, and check your punctuation.

1. Twenty-five years ago, Russians lived under a socialist system, but today they live under a capitalist system. (whereas)

   Twenty-five years ago, Russians lived under a socialist system, whereas today they live under a capitalist system.

2. In Russia today, women are as well educated as men, and they were under the socialist system, too. (just as)

3. Unlike twenty-five years ago, when, under the Soviet system, most Russian women between the ages of twenty and sixty were employed, today many Russian women are unemployed. (however)

4. Under the socialist system, women did the same heavy work in agriculture and manufacturing that men did. In contrast, today most of the job opportunities for women are in office work or sales. (while)

5. Today in Russia, some female employees work part time or have flexible schedules, but a generation ago, all female employees worked full time. (by comparison)

6. Twenty-five years ago, Russian women did all the housework, and they continue to do all the work at home today. (just as)

7. For Russian women, one important difference between the socialist and capitalist systems has been that working women had affordable child care under socialism, whereas they have to pay a substantial amount for child care under capitalism. (differ)

8. In contrast to the Soviet period, when by law women made up 34 percent of the lawmakers in the government, today women make up less than 10 percent of the lawmakers. (but)

9. During the Soviet period, women were seen in only two roles, as mothers and as workers. Today in Russia women are seen in a variety of roles, including those of fashion models, television personalities, and journalists. (difference)

Compare your answers with your classmates'. Discuss any questions you have with your teacher.

Review and Revise 6: Signals of Similarity and Contrast
Underline the comparison/contrast signals in your essay. Review your essay to see whether it is easy for a reader to follow. If you think adding more signals would make your paper easier to read, add them now. Make sure you have used commas, periods, and semicolons correctly.

PEER REVIEW AND FINAL DRAFT

Now that you have revised your composition, it is time to share your writing with others. Exchange papers with one or two classmates. Turn to page 337 in Appendix II, and fill out the Peer Review form.

After considering your classmates' suggestions, prepare a final draft of your composition to hand in to your teacher. Before turning it in, check your spelling, grammar, and punctuation, especially in sentences with comparison/contrast signals.

CHAPTER REVIEW

Look back at what you have accomplished in Chapter 6. Check (✓) what you have learned and what you have used as you have written and revised your composition.

Chapter 6 Topics	I understand this	I have used this
using point-by-point or side-by-side comparison/contrast organization (pages 144–145)		
applying strategies for writing introductions to comparison/contrast essays (pages 150–151)		
using *in* or *in terms of* to state the controlling idea in the thesis statement of a comparison/contrast essay (page 152)		
using balanced development in the body of a comparison/contrast essay (page 155)		
using the strategies of cohesion to link the thesis statement and the topic sentences of the body paragraphs (pages 156–158)		
applying strategies for writing conclusions to comparison/contrast essays (pages 158–159)		
using the vocabulary of comparison and contrast (pages 161–162)		

◆ Writing a Classification Essay

Whenever people interact with each other, you usually find the three Cs—cooperation, competition, and conflict. Whether people cooperate, compete, or get into conflict in a particular situation depends, at least in part, on their culture and its rules. This chapter will focus on people at work and, in particular, on how workplaces are organized and how people relate to each other on the job.

This chapter will help you

- plan and write a classification essay.
- develop body paragraphs using various rhetorical strategies.
- write cohesive body paragraphs.
- maintain consistent point of view.
- use direct quotations and paraphrase to report information from outside sources in your writing.

READING FOR WRITING

Before You Read

Freewrite on the following topic for ten minutes, and then discuss it in a small group.

Think of a time when you were a member of a group or team that was working toward a shared goal—perhaps working on a school project, preparing for a family celebration, playing a sport, or collaborating on the job. Reflect on your experience and ask yourself these questions.

1. How did the group members cooperate?

2. Was there competition between the group members? What form did it take?

3. Was there conflict between the group members? If not, how was conflict avoided?

NUMMI: A Case Study in Employee Involvement

by David I. Levine with Paul S. Adler and Barbara Goldoftas

joint venture: a business project run by two companies

plant: a factory

1 Employee involvement means giving employees the opportunity to improve how they do their jobs. Giving workers a chance to make meaningful suggestions about work procedures and working conditions is generally considered to be a good idea, but few businesses in the United States have committed to it as thoroughly as the New United Motor Manufacturing Inc. (NUMMI) located in Fremont, California. General Motors (GM) and Toyota opened NUMMI in 1984 as a joint venture°, utilizing the old GM plant° and equipment and employing almost the same workforce as GM had employed. The agreement stated that GM would supply the facilities and Toyota would supply the car designs and manage the new factory. Because the Toyota management at NUMMI has given workers far more opportunities to participate than the old GM management did, NUMMI is a suitable case study° for examining the effects of employee involvement.

case study: an analysis of a particular business that contains lessons for other businesses

2 Management of the old GM plant in Fremont had been based on the principle of scientific management which was developed by F. W. Taylor at the turn of the twentieth century. Scientific management emphasizes the division between planning and doing—managers and engineers make all the plans, while frontline° workers perform all the work. In the scientific management system, work is divided into small, easily learned tasks. Each worker performs a task repeatedly and competes with other workers for

frontline: refers to the people who actually do the labor

Toyota factory workers in the United States.

bonus: extra money paid as a reward for good work

collaborative: refers to work done by two or more people together

bonuses°, promotions, and continued employment. Work is not seen as collaborative°, and workers have little opportunity for making suggestions to improve their jobs.

3   The NUMMI plant opened with a number of important changes. Former GM employees arriving to work for NUMMI found that senior executives parked in the same lots and ate in the same cafeterias as they did, and managers worked in accessible open offices and even wore the company uniform. Employees were given a significant increase in training, more job security, expanded opportunities for promotion within the organization, and a bonus system based on factory-wide productivity° and customer satisfaction. Most significantly, a new production system and the use of teams transformed the nature of work at the plant.

productivity: the rate at which goods are produced, and the amount produced

4   The Toyota production system is based on three principles: just-in-time production, quality, and continuous improvement. The just-in-time production principle requires Toyota plants to operate on a very lean° system: They do not keep large supplies of parts on hand; instead, they work closely with suppliers to assure that small shipments of high-quality parts are delivered just in time for use on the assembly line°. This saves the cost of maintaining a large inventory° and makes it easier to address problems with parts. Just-in-time production also demands that workers respond quickly to problems.

lean: not wasteful

assembly line: a series of workstations where workers each do one part in putting together a product as it passes in front of them

inventory: a collection of parts or supplies that are ready for use

defective: not made correctly

5   The quality principle dictates that, as much as possible, the production process should be error-proof. Under the GM system, defective° parts proceeded from one manufacturing process to the next; management did not trust workers to examine the parts and instead relied on teams of inspectors to catch defects at the end of the assembly line. By contrast, NUMMI aims to find defective parts immediately. One way that problems with defective parts

are addressed is through the use of the andon cord. Located above each workstation, the andon cord permits each worker to stop the assembly line when a problem arises. When the cord is pulled, a musical tune plays, and a flashing light on an overhead board alerts everyone of the problem. At the old GM plant, workers were unable to stop the assembly line, and so could not correct problems, but the NUMMI-United Auto Workers contract stipulates° that when workers fall behind or see a defect they cannot repair, they are "expected, without being subject to discipline, to pull the cord." NUMMI executives have said that the ability of ordinary workers to stop the line symbolizes the relationship of trust between management and labor. "We had heavy arguments about installing the andon cord here," said NUMMI president Kan Higashi. "We wondered if workers would pull it just to get a rest. That has not happened."

6   The third principle of the Toyota Production System is continuous improvement. As at the old GM plant, each task at NUMMI is designed to be performed in a standardized fashion, with motion-by-motion instructions that describe exactly how it should be done. However, NUMMI's approach differs from GM's in two crucial ways. First, teams of workers, not industrial engineers, define the procedures. Second, at NUMMI, the best procedure remains an ever-shifting target, which means that workers must make an on-going effort to improve their jobs. Work teams make suggestions, and through the *ringi* system, their suggestions are communicated up the chain-of-command to high-ranking officials. At each stage in the communication process, the suggestions are discussed until consensus° is reached.

7   Teamwork is a key part of the Toyota system. NUMMI uses several types of teams, including work teams, problem-solving teams, and pilot° teams. Employees who work together on a single section of the assembly line form work teams. Work teams must not only make recommendations about quality, safety, and procedures but also rotate jobs. NUMMI encourages job rotation because it reduces ergonomic° problems that result from performing the same task repeatedly, and it also gives workers a broader understanding of their jobs. Teams must plan their job rotation and balance their assignments to equalize workloads. This builds up group cohesiveness° and mollifies° team members' concerns over which jobs are overloaded (more work than the pace of the line allows for completion) or underloaded (more time is available than is necessary to perform a task).

8   Problem-solving circles at NUMMI usually meet for weeks or months, typically over company-provided lunches, primarily to discuss issues concerning quality and productivity, although safety is also a valid° topic. These circles are quite successful in solving the problems they identify.

9   Pilot teams have the important responsibility of helping the organization prepare for annual changes in car models. For example, in 1993, NUMMI

---

stipulate: to state that something must be done

consensus: an agreement reached by a group of people through discussion

pilot: refers to testing out a new project or model

ergonomic: refers to design of work tools and equipment

cohesiveness: close ties among a group of people

mollify: to make someone feel less angry and upset

valid: reasonable

was to begin producing an entirely new model which would require a significant redesign of the production process. To prepare for this changeover, a team of designers, manufacturing engineers, suppliers, and production workers began visiting Japan in 1991. Some pilot team members even worked on the assembly line in Japan, where the new model was already in production. This early preparation had a number of benefits. For instance, a NUMMI engineer and a Toyota colleague found that the bumper did not fit into the designated channel° on the body of the car. By finding the problem early, the engineers were able to solve it at minimal cost.

channel: a long, narrow opening

10   In spite of the careful preparation and coordinated teamwork, NUMMI faced serious problems during the changeover in 1993. Parts manufactured by suppliers did not fit well, so workers had to force them into place, which led to ergonomic problems. These health and safety problems were worsened because workers had not been sufficiently trained to allow job rotation. Some of the training sessions had been scheduled outside normal work hours, and a number of workers had failed to attend. After the problems emerged, NUMMI increased the rate of production and did not provide enough training to allow full job rotation for one year, which led to a very large number of worker complaints. These problems illustrate that, even in a highly cooperative setting, workers and management have different interests. No amount of involvement can fully resolve all workplace conflicts.

notwithstanding: in spite of

plague: to repeatedly affect negatively

11   The problems of 1993 notwithstanding°, NUMMI has had a very positive record overall. The old GM plant had been plagued° with serious problems of low quality, high absenteeism, and a large number of worker complaints. Although most of the technology and most of the workers were the same as in the old factory, NUMMI in its first few years reduced worker-hours per car by approximately 40 percent, led U. S. auto plants in quality, and reported a very high level of worker satisfaction. NUMMI's significant improvements in productivity, quality, and worker morale° are due, at least in part, to its efforts to achieve significant employee involvement.

morale: the confidence that a group has in themselves and their organization

About the Author

David I. Levine, Ph.D., is a professor at the Haas School of Business at the University of California, Berkeley, where his research focuses on labor markets and workplaces. He is interested in workplaces with high levels of employee decision making. This reading is adapted from Dr. Levine's book, *Reinventing the Workplace: How Businesses and Employees Can Both Win.*

Understanding the Reading

With a partner or a small group, discuss the following questions.

1. What is *employee involvement*? Why does Levine say that NUMMI is a good case study for examining the effects of employee involvement?

2. According to Levine, how is the scientific management system different from the Toyota management system?

3. What are the three principles of the Toyota production system?

4. How are teams at NUMMI classified (grouped) in the reading?

5. The Toyota management team at NUMMI came from Japan, and the workforce consists of U.S. workers. While the reading does not discuss cultural differences at the plant, we can assume that the managers and the workers had to adapt to each other's cultures. In a situation like this, what would you recommend to managers and workers from different cultures who must learn to work together?

6. Paragraph 10 says that "even in a highly cooperative setting, workers and management have different interests." In your opinion, what are the goals of corporate management in most businesses, and what are the goals of factory workers? Which of those interests can conflict?

7. The reading does not discuss any negative aspects of the worker involvement approach. From the perspectives of corporate owners, managers, and workers, what might be some objections to using this approach?

8. Quotations are used in paragraph 5. Who or what is quoted? Are the quotes effective in terms of the selection of sources? Do you think a worker at the plant should have been quoted as well? Identify another place in the reading where a quote could have been included.

Vocabulary Expansion

Compound nouns. A compound noun consists of a noun modifier and a noun that have been used together so frequently that they are considered a single noun. Some are written as one word, some as two words, and others as two words with a hyphen. To know whether a compound noun is one word, two words, or hyphenated, you have to check your dictionary. There is no rule that governs the form of compounds.

One-Word Compound Nouns	Two-Word Compound Nouns	Hyphenated Compound Nouns
teamwork	assembly line	job-sharing
businesswoman	voice mail	worker-hour
spokesperson	computer program	go-getter
brainstorming	authority figure	

Exercise 1

Below is a list of compound nouns made with **work** and a list made with **pay**. Choose appropriate compound nouns from the lists to complete the paragraph that follows. You may need to check the meanings of some of the words in the dictionary. When you are done, check your answers with a partner.

~~workday~~	working conditions	workstation	paycheck	pay raise
work ethic	workload	workweek	payday	payroll
work experience	workplace			

A Drill Press Operator

Klaus is a metal worker at S. W. Metal Works, where his job is to make holes in metal hooks and pins. His (1) _____workday_____ starts at 4:00 A.M. and ends at 2:00 P.M. His (2) _____ is noisy with the sound of hammers pounding, metal rods falling, and furnaces roaring. It is also fairly dark, but a bright light shines down on the machine called a drill press at Klaus's (3) _____. Klaus needs the light to do his exacting work. In spite of the long hours and unpleasant (4) _____, Klaus likes his job. He enjoys the precision of his work, and takes pride in the mounds of perfectly drilled hooks and pins in boxes on the floor. Klaus is one of the most valued employees at S. W. Metal Works, and his (5) _____ reflects how favorably the management views him. Klaus has earned a (6) _____ every year he has been at S. W. Metal Works because of his skill and diligence. He has always had a good (7) _____: He believes that whatever one's job is, one should approach it with care.

WRITING

Assignment

Choose one of the following topics and write a classification essay.

1. Write about a group that you have been part of such as a sports team, a work team, a group of musicians, a class, a club, or a religious or political group. Classify either people in the group (group members or leaders) or their behaviors.

2. Pretend that you are writing a letter of application to a school or an employer. Introduce yourself in the letter to the school admissions office or the employer by classifying the skills or talents that you would bring to the new school or job.

3. Classify the responsibilities or duties of a job you have held, or interview someone about the duties of his or her job, and write a classification essay about that person's job duties. Alternatively, classify the types of communication required by a job.

4. Classify people according to how they behave in a certain type of situation, such as when they are given a task to complete, when they join a group as a stranger, when they are placed in a competitive situation, or when they are involved in a conflict.

5. Classify the pathways to a successful life. Use people you have known in your life as examples.

What Classification Is and Why It Is Important

Classifying means dividing a large group of things into smaller groups or categories on the basis of shared characteristics. For example, your school may offer 100 courses. You could classify those courses by subject (math, computer science, English), by time of day (morning, afternoon, evening), by the number of students enrolled, by the amount of homework that is assigned, by how interesting they are—and in many other ways. When you classify, you select one **basis of classification** (e.g., time, place, size, or importance), which determines how you will classify the members of the larger group.

In Chapter 4, you wrote a logical division essay. To do that assignment, you may have divided a culture into its various aspects, a country into its various regions, a person's life into stages, or a celebration into parts. Classification is dividing a plural topic—many things—into groups, which are known as **categories** or **classes**.

Finding a basis of classification. There are many ways to classify a group of people or things. For example, if you are classifying work teams, you could use one of the following bases of classification.

time ——————→ How long do the teams stay together?

size ——————→ How big are the teams?

importance ——→ How important are the teams within their companies?

tasks ——————→ What tasks are the teams assigned to do?

Look at the following classification system and thesis statement for a classification essay.

CLASS: work teams

BASIS OF CLASSIFICATION: tasks

CATEGORIES: quality teams, safety teams, new product teams

THESIS: Work teams can be classified according to the tasks they perform. There are teams that collaborate to improve quality, teams that address safety issues, and teams that develop new products.

Notice that you could not use the categories *very important teams* or *teams with more than ten members* here because the basis of classification is the kind of tasks performed by the teams. Be sure that all your categories share the same basis of classification.

Exercise 2

Work with a partner or a small group. Write three ways to classify each topic below.

1. cars <u>by size, by price, by country</u> _____

2. energy sources _____

3. sports _____

4. companies _____

5. leaders _____

Exercise 3

Each of the following classification systems has one flawed category. Cross out the category that does not share the basis of classification common to the other categories. Then write a thesis statement for each classification.

1. CLASS: employees

   BASIS OF CLASSIFICATION: expertise

   CATEGORIES: technical skills, ~~loyalty~~, interpersonal skills, organizational skills

   THESIS: <u>Employees can be classified according to their expertise: There are employees with valuable technical skills, employees with strong interpersonal skills, and employees that excel in organizational skills.</u>

2. CLASS: computer programs

   BASIS OF CLASSIFICATION: tasks

   CATEGORIES: spreadsheet, word processing, graphics, user-friendly

   THESIS: _____

   _____

   _____

3. CLASS: retail customers

   BASIS OF CLASSIFICATION: buying behavior

   CATEGORIES: one-time buyers, potential customers, repeat customers (those who buy a second time), regular customers

   THESIS: _____

   _____

   _____

4. CLASS: work-team members

   BASIS OF CLASSIFICATION: official roles

   CATEGORIES: leaders, researchers, gossips, recorders

   THESIS: _____

   _____

   _____

Prewriting

Before you write, do the following prewriting activities. As you read through the steps, you will see how Daniel, a student from Bolivia who was majoring in business management, prepared to write a classification essay about managers. The following steps will help you prepare to write your classification essay.

STEP **1** After you **identify the class** of things you want to write about, list as many **bases of classification** as you can think of. For each basis of classification, write a *wh-question*.

Daniel had decided to write about managers, so he made the following list of possible bases of classification.

<u>Class</u>: Managers
<u>Possible Bases of Classification</u>
control —————⟶ How authoritarian are they?
intelligence ————⟶ How smart are they?
commitment ————⟶ How committed are they to their jobs?
understanding ——⟶ How well do they understand and relate to their
                                    subordinates and other coworkers?

STEP **2** | Select a **basis of classification**, and identify your **categories**. Draft a **thesis statement**.

Note that classification essays usually have three categories. Although you can write a classification essay with only two categories, such an essay may resemble a comparison/contrast essay. For this reason, it is a good idea to develop a classification system with three categories.

Daniel selected a basis of classification that he thought he could write a well-developed essay about. He chose to classify managers according to how understanding they are because the relationship between managers and workers was important to him. He named three categories of managers and then drafted a thesis statement.

<u>Categories</u>
very understanding, somewhat understanding, not at all understanding

DRAFT THESIS
STATEMENT

Managers can be classified according to how understanding they are. There are managers who are not at all understanding, managers who are somewhat understanding, and managers who are very understanding.

STEP **3** | Make a **brainstorming chart** to list and organize your ideas. Write *wh*-questions in the column to the left, and then make one column for each category.

Daniel made the following chart. He answered each question for each of his three categories. His answers would become the supporting information in the body paragraphs of his essay. When the chart was finished, Daniel could see that he would be able to develop each category in the essay.

	Category 1 **not understanding at all**	Category 2 **somewhat understanding**	Category 3 **very understanding**
What kind of relationships do they have with the people who work under them?	They rarely, if ever, communicate directly with workers.	They only listen when workers have something to say about how the work is done.	They are good listeners and spend time in one-on-one conversation with all the workers.
What is their attitude toward the employees who work under them?	They view the employees only in terms of their capacity to produce for the company.	Although they know that the employees are individual human beings, they tend to see them as having one basic need—to be treated fairly.	They view the employees as individuals. They know that each employee has slightly different needs.
How do they respond to the workers' culture or values?	They are not concerned with the culture that workers bring into the workplace. They believe that workers must adapt to the culture and values of the company.	They observe the rules of politeness of the larger culture but do not allow the cultural rules to interfere with the efficiency of the workplace.	They are very sensitive to the values of their employees.
What is the result of their attitude and behavior?	They achieve poor results: Workers are dissatisfied and distrustful.	They achieve moderately good results.	They achieve positive results: Worker satisfaction and trust are high.

STEP **4** | Decide how you will organize the categories in your chart. Make a **brief outline**.

After considering two possible ways to organize the information in his brainstorming chart, Daniel made this brief outline.

> Managers can be classified according to how understanding they are. There are managers who are very understanding, managers who are somewhat understanding, and managers who are not at all understanding.
>
> 1. managers who are very understanding
>
> 2. managers who are somewhat understanding
>
> 3. managers who are not at all understanding

Daniel was now ready to write a first draft. He wrote several drafts, in which he added examples and other details to support his points, before completing the following draft.

Managers—How *Simpático* Are They?

MIT professor of management Douglas MacGregor (1960, 1985) wrote, "The skills of social interaction are . . . among the most essential for the manager. . . ." During the ten years I worked in machine shops in my country Bolivia, I found this to be true. I worked under a number of managers, and I observed that the better the manager related to his employees, the more successful his business was in both financial and human terms. In my opinion, the most important aspect of managing people is being understanding, or *simpático*, as we say in Spanish. I have concluded that managers can be classified according to how understanding they are. In my years of work, I found that there are managers who are very understanding, managers who are somewhat understanding, and managers who are not at all understanding.

Managers who are very understanding quickly develop a rapport with those who work under them. They are good listeners and frequently spend time in one-on-one conversation with workers. They chat about the workers' families, the local soccer teams, the neighborhood gossip—anything the workers are interested in. As a result of this ongoing communication, they know the employees as individuals with different needs. For example, they know who wants a challenge, who needs reassurance, who gets along with whom, and who should be kept apart. These understanding managers realize that the workers bring their cultural values with them, and they respect those values. For example, in Bolivia, older workers are usually given more privileges than younger workers. In the machine shop, older workers tend to prefer bench work over floor work, and a manager who is sensitive to the society's traditions will allow the older workers to do the bench work, at least some of the time, even though they may not do it as fast as younger workers. These managers may sacrifice a little productivity, but they attain a higher level of worker satisfaction and trust.

Managers in the second category, who are somewhat understanding, earn the respect but not the affection of their employees because they try to balance the interests of the company with the interests of the workers. They greet everyone politely by name, but maintain their distance. They do not spend time chatting with workers about the weather or soccer teams, but will listen carefully when a worker has something to say about production problems. They know the employees as individuals only in terms of their skills, and they believe that one fair system of assigning work and awarding pay increases can address all employee needs. They follow the customs of the society as long as those customs do not interfere with the efficiency of the workplace. For example, in Bolivia, most workers like to go home to eat the midday meal with their families. The somewhat understanding managers permit all the workers to break for their midday meal at the time they prefer and provide them a place to warm their food, but they do not let them go home because those who live too far away would come back to work late. These somewhat considerate managers are fair, but they lack empathy, and, as a result, they achieve only a moderate level of worker satisfaction and trust.

Finally, there is the third category of managers, those who are not at all understanding. These managers alienate workers and make them defensive. They communicate directly with a worker only when there is a problem with performance, and then they issue a warning of disciplinary action. They view the employees solely in terms of their output, and even measure and record each worker's productivity in comparison with the others'. These managers are not concerned with the culture that workers bring into the workplace, but rather believe that workers must adapt to the culture and values of the company. They do not care that people in our country value their jobs for the social contacts that work provides. They do not want workers to develop and maintain friendships in the workplace, and, as a result, often move people around just to keep them from talking on the shop floor. They overlook the fact that older workers can provide leadership to the group and mentor younger employees. As a result, these managers promote a high level of worker dissatisfaction and distrust.

In the workplace, people need communication and understanding, and a manager who is understanding pays attention to these needs. He finds ways to allow workers to enjoy the social contacts that work can offer. He also respects workers' culture and values and does not try to force a new value system on them. A manager who ignores people's needs does so at his own expense, because in the end, satisfied employees do the best work.

McGregor, Douglas. *The Human Side of Enterprise: 25th Anniversary Printing.* New York: McGraw-Hill, 1960, 1985.

Exercise 4

With your classmates, review Daniel's essay, and discuss the following questions.

1. What kind of introduction does Daniel's essay have? How effective is this type of introduction, in view of the fact that the purpose of the paper is to classify managers?

2. What categories do the body paragraphs represent?

3. What do you think of the sequence of the body paragraphs? Would you have ordered them another way? Why or why not?

4. Are the categories developed in a balanced way? How are they developed?

5. Why did Daniel include a citation at the end of the essay? What kind of information does the citation contain?

After selecting a topic from the list on pages 172–173, follow the sequence of steps Daniel used.

First Draft

Once you have completed an outline, write your first draft.

REVISING

As you proceed through the lessons and exercises in this chapter, review your draft regularly, and follow the advice in the Review and Revise boxes.

Composition Focus

Thesis statements. Thesis statements in classification essays can take several forms. In Exercise 3 you wrote thesis statements that looked like this.

┌─CLASS─┐   ┌BASIS OF CLASSIFICATION┐
<u>Employees</u> can be categorized according to <u>how hard they work</u>: There are

┌────CATEGORY 1────┐ ┌────CATEGORY 2────┐ ┌────CATEGORY 3────┐
<u>those who are hard workers</u>, <u>those whose effort is just adequate</u>, <u>and those who are lazy</u>.

Another way to write a thesis statement for a classification essay is this.

┌─CLASS─┐   NUMBER   ┌BASIS OF CLASSIFICATION┐
<u>Employees</u> fall into <u>three</u> categories according to <u>how hard they work</u>:

┌────CATEGORY 1────┐ ┌────CATEGORY 2────┐ ┌────CATEGORY 3────┐
<u>those who are hard workers</u>, <u>those whose effort is just adequate</u>, <u>and those who are lazy</u>.

For more on the use of colons, see Appendix IB, page 314.

Note that the colon (:) is often used in a thesis statement to introduce a list of supporting points.

> **Review and Revise 1: Thesis Statements**
> Review the thesis statement in your essay. If you have not used one of the patterns shown above, consider revising your thesis. Check your thesis for correct parallel structure (as used in the two examples above) and punctuation.

Modifying thesis statements. Both thesis statements in the previous section are factual statements which express certainty. But sometimes simple factual statements are not appropriate. Sometimes a statement needs to be modified to indicate that it may not always be true or may not apply in every situation. To do this, you can use **qualifiers** (words that change the degree of certainty or truth in a statement). Two qualifiers are the adverb *usually* and the verb *tend*.

Employees *usually* fall into three categories . . .

Employees *tend* to fall into three categories . . .

In addition, you will sometimes need to indicate that a thesis statement reflects your personal views rather than general truths. In this case, you can personalize the statement in one of the following ways.

I have observed that employees fall into three categories . . .

It seems to me that employees fall into three categories . . .

In my view, employees fall into three categories . . .

Based on my experience, I have found that employees fall into three categories . . .

Exercise 5
The following thesis statements are written as general truths. Modify them by adding a qualifier or by personalizing them. (Be sure to modify each one differently.)

1. Classroom team assignments can be classified according to their complexity.

   <u>In my view, classroom team assignments can be classified according to</u>
   <u>their complexity.</u>

2. Classroom team members fall into three groups according to their behavior. There are the leaders, the listeners, and the loafers.

   _____

   _____

3. Disagreements in classroom groups are of three kinds: arguments about what the task is, about how to do it, and about who should do it.

   _____

   _____

4. There are several ways to respond to conflict: One can force one's opinion on others, one can withdraw, and one can negotiate.

   _____

   _____

Review and Revise 2: Modifying Thesis Statements
Review your own essay, focusing on the thesis statement. Decide whether you want your thesis to read as a general truth or whether you want to qualify or personalize it. Make any changes to your thesis statement that you feel are necessary.

Rhetorical strategies. So far you have studied seven types of writing, or **rhetorical strategies**: description, narration, example, logical division, cause and effect, comparison/contrast, and classification.

Another rhetorical strategy is **process**. Process means telling how something happens or how to do something. To describe a process, you present the steps. For example, you could describe the process of establishing a business relationship this way:

> The *first* step is to introduce yourself to a new contact. The *second* step is getting to know him or her. The *third* step is letting your new acquaintance know what your business can offer him or her . . .

In your academic and professional writing, you will probably use process frequently. For example, you may have to write lab reports for science classes, directions for the use of workplace equipment, or office memos telling how to complete a job.

Development with various rhetorical strategies. You will find that these eight rhetorical strategies are not only ways to write a complete paragraph or essay but also ways to provide supporting information *within* a paragraph or essay. For example, in the body paragraphs of your classification essay, you could use description, narration, example, cause and effect, comparison/contrast, logical division or classification, and process alone or in combination to develop each category.

Imagine, for example, that you are the manager of an electronics store and you are going to write an essay classifying the customers who come to your store. This essay is a real-world writing assignment, a report for your supervisor, who wants to open more franchise stores similar to yours. Because your supervisor is interested in the profits generated by your store, you are going to classify the customers who shop in your store according to how much money they spend a year. You could use any of the following strategies, or a combination of them, to develop the body paragraphs in your report.

1. *Description/Narration/Examples.* You could develop each body paragraph by describing the tastes of people in each category, giving examples of the products they buy.

2. *Causes (Reasons) and Effects.* You could include the results of a customer survey documenting the reasons customers give to explain why they choose to shop at your store rather than at competing stores.

3. *Comparison/Contrast.* You could compare one group of customers with another group in terms of how often they visit the store or how much time they spend getting information before buying.

4. *Classification*. You could put the major groups of customers that you have identified in **subcategories** such as those who shop alone and those who shop with family members.

5. *Process*. You could explain how each category of customer decides to buy something. For example, one type of customer may come into the store and ask questions, then compare prices at other stores, and finally return to make a purchase.

Choosing a development strategy. To decide which development strategy or strategies will be most effective in your writing, consider your purpose in writing and what your audience wants to know. For example, if your purpose in writing about the electronics store customers is to show your supervisor that your customers represent all kinds of people in your community, you might use description as your strategy. If your purpose is to demonstrate to your supervisor the fine service your store provides, you might use process to show how your salespeople adapt their service for each type of customer.

Exercise 6

In this exercise, you will see three body paragraphs from three different essays, each of which is preceded by a thesis statement. Read each body paragraph, and decide what development strategy or strategies it contains.

1.   **Organizational Structures**

THESIS: All organizations are hierarchical; that is, they contain people in higher positions of authority and people in lower positions who must respond to those with authority. Organizational structures can be classified as tall (having many layers of authority), intermediate, or flat (having few levels of authority).

BODY PARAGRAPH   [1]The flat organization has relatively few levels of vertical hierarchy. [2]For example, a furniture company may have only four levels: a president; vice-presidents; managers in charge of production, distribution, and sales; and unranked employees in the production, distribution, and sales departments. [3]When comparing flat organizations with tall organizations, one notices that communication is much more likely to flow from the bottom to the top in the flatter organization.

Development strategy/strategies: _____*example and comparison/contrast*_____

2.   **How Company Policies Can Encourage Various Kinds of Cooperative Relationships**

THESIS: Managers can create policies that will foster cooperation within their companies. These policies can be classified according to the kind of relationships that they affect: Some policies influence person-to-person relationships within departments, and others influence group-to-group relationships between departments or work teams.

BODY PARAGRAPH

[1]With effective policies, companies can foster cooperation at the person-to-person level. [2]One such policy encourages job rotation. [3]Management can require that workers who have been employed for a certain length of time learn to do a second or third job. [4]When workers rotate jobs, they communicate more and develop empathy for each other. [5]Another kind of policy involves scheduling and work flow. [6]Management can require departments or teams to determine how they will handle projects and meet deadlines. [7]Requiring employees to divide tasks, determine the flow of work, and set their own hours makes them depend on one another. [8]Finally, policies governing reward systems can play a big role in fostering cooperation. [9]When management awards bonuses to entire departments or teams rather than to individuals, it promotes collaboration and decreases competition between individual group members.

Development strategy/strategies: _____

3. **Competition Among My Coworkers**

THESIS: In my work as an underwriter in a bank, I have found that coworkers can be classified in terms of how competitive they are. Some are too competitive, others are competitive in an appropriate way, and others are not competitive enough.

BODY PARAGRAPH

[1]My employer rewards employees in a way that encourages competition, and this makes some workers become too competitive. [2]One such person is Nelly, one of several mortgage underwriters I work with. [3]Mortgage underwriters decide whether or not to loan money to people who want to buy a house. [4]They base their decision on the people's financial qualifications. [5]In my bank, if an underwriter makes good loans, she will get bonuses and promotions, but if she makes bad loans, she may lose her job. [6]Knowing this, Nelly is very picky about choosing customers. [7]If she has a family in jeans and T-shirts with several little children come to her for a loan, she will tell them she is busy and send them to another underwriter. [8]However, if a couple in expensive clothes comes into the bank asking about loan applications, she will get up from her chair, greet them with a big smile, and usher them over to her desk. [9]But later, if Nelly discovers that this couple has a bad credit history, she will suddenly need to leave for a "doctor's appointment," and send the customers to another underwriter. [10]Nelly's strategies have served her well. [11]She has the best track record of all the underwriters in the bank with the fewest bad loans, and consequently she has earned more bonuses than anyone else. [12]But, needless to say, she has not earned the affection of her fellow workers.

Development strategy/strategies: _____

> **Review and Revise 3: Developing Body Paragraphs in Classification Essays**
> Review your own essay, identifying the development strategies you have used in your body paragraphs. Determine whether the strategies you have used are the most effective to develop your categories. Next, decide whether you can improve your body paragraphs by adding another type of development, but keep in mind that body paragraphs should be balanced. For example, if you add a result statement to one body paragraph, you should add result statements to the other body paragraphs. Make any changes to your body paragraphs that you feel are necessary, and then recheck them for balance.

To review pronouns and possessive adjectives, see Appendix IA, page 292.

Cohesion in body paragraphs. You have learned about cohesion in essays (the links between the thesis statement and the topic sentences of the body paragraphs). Cohesion within body paragraphs is also important. To create links within body paragraphs, use **repeated words and phrases**, **synonyms**, **word forms**, **logical connectors** (transitions and coordinating and subordinating conjunctions), **time phrases**, and **pronouns** and **possessive adjectives**.

Exercise 7

In this exercise, you will see the thesis and body paragraphs of an essay called "Kinds of Conflict in Organizations." In each paragraph, some of the following cohesion signals are marked with <u>single</u> and <u>double</u> lines.

conjunctions	time phrases
pronouns and possessive adjectives	transitions
repeated words and phrases	word forms
synonyms	

At the end of each body paragraph, write (1) the name of the type of signal marked with <u>single lines</u> and (2) the name of the type of signal marked with <u>double lines</u>.

THESIS: Workplace conflicts can be classified according to their causes. Most conflicts result from competition over scarce resources, from workers' interdependence, or from poor management.

BODY PARAGRAPH 1   [1]Sometimes <u>conflicts</u> are over resources—money and <u>space</u>. [2]For example, the <u>marketing department</u> and the <u>fiscal services department</u> at <u>A & G</u> Import Company have always <u>competed</u> for bigger <u>budgets</u> and nicer office <u>space</u>. [3]Last year the <u>competition</u> turned into a <u>conflict</u> because of the <u>marketing</u>

department's success. [4]When A & G's sales almost doubled last year, the marketing department was rewarded with a budgetary increase that was almost twice as large as that of the fiscal services department. [5]The accountants were very angry, but could only express their feelings indirectly by delaying the release of information about subsequent sales.

Type of signal: _repeated words_ _____ **Type of signal:** _____

BODY PARAGRAPH 2

[6]Occasionally conflicts result from interdependence. [7]Interdependence means that one group depends on another or that one person depends on another to get a job done. [8]Team members are highly interdependent and therefore are very likely to get into conflicts. [9]For example, four months ago a three-person team at L & M Hardware was assigned the task of developing a new household tool that both hammers nails and tightens screws. [10]One team member was supposed to research tools that were already on the market, another was supposed to investigate the kinds of home repair projects people most often do, and a third was supposed to study the materials that popular tools are made of. [11]The problem is that the third team member has done little research on materials and so is holding up the progress of the group. [12]The other two team members have begun quietly complaining about him, but so far the boss has not taken notice of the conflict within this team.

Type of signal: _____ **Type of signal:** _____

BODY PARAGRAPH 3

[13]Sometimes a manager who does not make workers' responsibilities clear is the cause of problems. [14]Managers need to distribute work fairly among employees and make sure that they understand their duties. [15]If a manager fails to make work assignments, conflict is likely to result. [16]For example, at the Sunset Restaurant, the manager lets the three chefs and their helpers in the kitchen decide among themselves how the work should be divided. [17]The older chefs are lazy, so the younger chef does all the planning and ordering, and, as a result, she feels resentful. [18]When the kitchen is busy, the chefs cook the main dishes and leave the side dishes for the assistants. [19]However, they don't tell the support people what to prepare, and, consequently, a dinner sometimes goes to the table with the wrong items on it. [20]When complaints come back to the kitchen, tempers often flare. [21]The chefs accuse the helpers, and the helpers blame them, but the manager is the one who is really responsible.

Type of signal: _____ **Type of signal:** _____

Compare your answers with a partner's, and discuss any questions you have with your teacher and classmates.

> **Review and Revise 4: Cohesion in Body Paragraphs**
> Review your essay. Check the sentences within your body paragraphs for repeated words and phrases, synonyms, word forms, transitions and other logical connectors, time phrases, and pronouns and possessive adjectives. If you find that your body paragraphs lack cohesion, add signals of cohesion now.

Consistent point of view. When you write, you must choose a **point of view**. Point of view refers to the kind of subjects you use in *most* of the sentences in your paragraph or essay. You can use **first person**, **second person**, or **third person** point of view.

> First person: (singular) *I* and (plural) *we*
>
> Second person: (singular or plural) *you*
>
> Third person: (singular) *he, she,* and *it,* and (plural) *they*

To write a cohesive essay, you must use point of view consistently throughout your paper. That means that you should change pronouns only when you need to, for instance, when you are giving an example. In the following excerpt from an essay classifying college freshmen, the writer has used the third person plural point of view throughout *most* of the paper and changed point of view only when necessary to develop examples.

> Many first-time college *students* are overwhelmed by the size and complexity of the campus. *They* don't know *their* way around. For example, *I* got lost twice going to *my* biology class during the first week of school.

Note that some people say that the first person singular pronoun *I* should be avoided in essays, but actually *I* is acceptable in most kinds of writing. In fact, the pronoun *I* is frequently used for including personal opinions or experiences. However, the second person pronoun, *you,* can cause problems because writers tend to shift to *you* unintentionally, making their writing less cohesive.

Exercise 8

As you read the following essay, find and correct the three inappropriate changes in point of view.

Workplace Communication Skills

1   [1]Workplaces demand good communication skills of everyone. [2]When people work together to produce goods or services, they must communicate in order to coordinate their efforts. [3]While the demands vary from job to job, in general, today's workplaces require that people have three kinds of communication skills: writing skills, conversational skills, and oral presentation skills.

2   [4]Nowadays most workplaces have computers, and therefore writing skills are becoming increasingly important. [5]First of all, today's employees should be familiar with the various forms of business communication—e-mails, memos, and letters—and should know when it is appropriate to use each. [6]Second, they have to be able to express themselves in a clear, focused way, and that requires planning ahead—brainstorming, defining their main points, and outlining before they begin to write. [7]Furthermore, you must know how to adjust the style of your writing for various purposes and audiences. [8]Lengthy reports, memos sent to a large number of people, or letters mailed outside the organization should be more formal than e-mails exchanged among coworkers. [9]Finally, in all written communication, correctness is very important because letters and memos tend to be kept as permanent records.

3   [10]Many people believe that talking requires no special skill, but, in fact, to become effective at workplace conversation requires conscious effort. [11]Talking involves two separate skills, listening and speaking. [12]To listen well, people have to put their full attention on the speaker and not be thinking about what they will say next. [13]To speak well, people should imagine themselves in the place of the person who is listening, and adjust their message accordingly. [14]They should be organized, especially if what they want to say is complicated, and that means they should plan what they will say ahead of time. [15]They must also be concise. [16]At work, time is precious, and you don't want to listen to speakers who stumble as they search for ideas or rattle off useless bits of information. [17]Finally, speakers must be honest and make sure that the information they give is accurate.

4   [18]Sooner or later, most employees will need to address a group, whether that means spending a few minutes showing coworkers how to use a new piece of equipment or introducing a major proposal to a client. [19]The most important requirement for giving successful talks and presentations is clarity. [20]Speakers should present their information and ideas as simply and directly as possible so

that the audience will understand and remember what they say. [21]They should also adjust their style for their listeners. [22]Jokes and anecdotes that would be appropriate with a group of colleagues are usually not appropriate with a group of strangers. [23]Finally, you must make sure that all the facts or statistics you include are as accurate and up to date as possible and let listeners know when items are in question.

5   [24]Workers with good communication skills will always be in demand, and as technology grows more complex, the need for good communication will increase. [25]Therefore, people who develop good writing, conversational, and public speaking skills will be the most likely to advance in tomorrow's business world.

After you have found the problems with point of view and corrected the essay, compare your answers with a partner's.

Review and Revise 5: Consistent Point of View
Review the subjects of the sentences in your essay. Make sure that you have used one point of view throughout most of your essay, and that you have changed point of view only when necessary. If you find unnecessary shifts in point of view, correct them. If you are not sure whether a change in point of view is necessary, write a note to your teacher in the margin of your paper.

Language Focus

Using direct quotations and paraphrasing to include ideas and information from outside sources. You have learned that you can develop body paragraphs with the strategies of description, narration, example, cause and effect, comparison/contrast, logical division, classification, and process. In addition, you can use direct quotations and paraphrases from outside sources as supporting information in your body paragraphs. There are various outside sources available to you—the Internet, books, magazines, newspapers, and even your friends and relatives. Quoting and paraphrasing from outside sources will not only help you support your points, but bring variety into your writing.

It is essential that you include your sources for citations. There are two main styles for citations, **MLA** (Modern Language Association), which is used for writing about subjects such as business, literature, and history, and **APA** (American Psychological Association), which is used for science writing. The citations you see in the following pages and in other parts of this chapter are in the MLA style.

To learn how to use citations, see Appendix IC, page 320.

Direct quotations are the exact words of the speaker or writer and are placed inside quotation marks. Give the name of the speaker or writer plus a reporting verb such as *say* (*said*) or *write* (*wrote*). Alternatively, you can introduce a direct quotation with the words *according to*.

> In *Trust and Betrayal in the Workplace*, Dennis and Michelle Reina write, "Leaders have the opportunity to develop trust at work, and their people are looking to them to take the first step" (163).
>
> According to Dennis and Michelle Reina, the authors of *Trust and Betrayal in the Workplace*, "Leaders have the opportunity to develop trust at work, and their people are looking to them to take the first step" (163).

Reina, Dennis S. and Michelle L Reina. *Trust and Betrayal in the Workplace*. San Francisco: Berret-Koehler, 1999.

Paraphrasing means using your own words to convey ideas and information from an outside source. Just as with direct quotations, give the name of the speaker or writer plus a reporting verb such as *say* (*said*) or *write* (*wrote*). Alternatively, you can introduce a paraphrase with *according to*.

For more about reported speech, see Appendix IA, page 288.

> In *Trust and Betrayal in the Workplace*, Dennis and Michelle Reina write that managers have the chance to encourage trust in their workplaces, and their employees expect them to initiate relationships of trust (163).
>
> According to Dennis and Michelle Reina in *Trust and Betrayal in the Workplace*, managers have the chance to encourage trust in their workplaces, and their employees expect them to initiate relationships of trust (163).

When you omit words or phrases from a quoted sentence, use **ellipses** (. . .) to indicate the omitted text.

Original text
Betrayal is an intentional or unintentional breach of trust or the perception of a breach of trust (Reina and Reina, 10).

Quotation with ellipses
Dennis and Michelle Reina write, "*Betrayal* is . . . a breach of trust or the perception of a breach of trust" (10).

Reina, Dennis S. and Michelle L. Reina. *Trust and Betrayal in the Workplace*. San Francisco: Berret-Koehler, 1999.

When you quote text that already has quotation marks, use single quotation marks around the quotation within a quotation.

For more on punctuation in direct quotations, see Appendix IB, page 317.

Original text
It has often been said that "perception equals reality." (Reina and Reina, 17).

Quotation
Reina and Reina write, "It has often been said that 'perception equals reality'" (17).

Reina, Dennis S. and Michelle L. Reina. *Trust and Betrayal in the Workplace.* San Francisco: Berret-Koehler, 1999.

Exercise 9
A. Underline the direct quotations and paraphrases in the following essay. Mark the direct quotations *DQ* and the paraphrases *P*.

Kinds of Coaches

1 [1]Former athletes remember a favorite coach throughout their lives. [2]The coaches they recall are those that mastered the art of communicating with athletes one-on-one and as a team. [3]But not all coaches reach this level of performance. [4]Coaches tend to fall into three categories according to how they relate to athletes: Some are too distant, some are too authoritarian, and some, luckily, are expert.

2 [5]Distant coaches do not form solid relationships with their teams, and this can lead to a number of problems. [6]They fail to notice players' effort, so the players feel unappreciated and probably will not give their best performance. [7]Distant coaches don't provide enough guidance, and this may make players frustrated. [8]If frustration makes some players skip practice, others may do the same, and team discipline and performance will decline overall. [9]Coaching consultant Jerry Lynch says that if coaches are having problems, they should ask their teams to tell them anonymously what aspects of their coaching they need to improve (6). [10]If players feel that the coach doesn't seem to care or doesn't give enough direction, the coach must take immediate steps to improve his or her communication with the team.

3 [11]While distant coaches don't assume enough authority, authoritarian coaches assume too much. [12]They use rules and threat of punishment instead of genuine communication to get players to perform. [13]Often obsessed with winning, these coaches tend to put too much pressure on players and may criticize them individually in front of the whole team. [14]Dave Chambers, director

of the coaching program at York University in Toronto, writes that authoritarian coaches are often disliked or feared by players (8). [15]Authoritarian coaches don't realize that they could get more out of their players by sharing power with them. [16]Stanford Graduate School of Business professor Jim Thompson advises sports coaches, "Get into the habit of asking your players for their ideas and thoughts before you give yours, particularly in post-game meetings"(66). [17]Coaches who follow Thompson's advice find that players appreciate having their opinions and ideas recognized and are thus more willing to put all their effort into the game.

4 [18]Expert coaches, in contrast to distant and authoritarian coaches, succeed because they form genuine relationships with each player and with the team as a whole. [19]Expert coaches assess individual players' needs, pull them aside regularly to give them special tips, and never fail to overlook each player's improvement. [20]When players sense that their coach respects and values them, they strive to give him or her their best. [21]Expert coaches also work to achieve unity and harmony on the team, what Chicago Bulls and L.A. Lakers' coach Phil Jackson says is "the group mind" (63). [22]Jackson points out that some young players "will do almost anything to draw attention to themselves, to say 'This is me' . . . rather than share the limelight with others"(89). [23]To help players overcome this tendency, Jackson has used a number of strategies, including having the team meditate on the idea of *unity*. [24]Jackson maintains that when team members understand the concept of team unity, they reach a new, higher level of play (92).

5 [25]Coaching is an art, and although most coaches have good intentions, not all reach the level of expert coaches. [26]To become experts, coaches must believe that winning involves not just the highest scores but helping every athlete do his or her best, sharing power with the team, and teaching athletes to value team unity.

Chambers, Dave. *Coaching: Winning Strategies for Every Level of Play.* Buffalo, New York: Firefly, 1997.

Jackson, Phil. *Sacred Hoops: Spiritual Lessons of a Hardwood Warrior.* New York: Hyperion, 1995.

Lynch, Jerry. *Creative Coaching.* Champaign, Illinois: Human Kinetics, 2001.

Thompson, Jim. *Shooting in the Dark: Tales of Coaching and Leadership.* Portola Valley, California: Warde, 1998.

B. Now, with a partner, discuss the following questions about "Kinds of Coaches."

1. How many direct quotations and how many paraphrases appear in the essay?

2. In addition to *say* and *write*, what other verbs are used to introduce direct quotations and paraphrases?

3. How are the speakers' titles presented? Do the titles come before or after a speaker's name, and are there commas around the titles?

4. Is ellipsis (. . .) used in any of the quotations? If so, which one(s)?

5. Are quotations within quotations used in any of the sentences? If so, which one(s)?

Correct use of sources. When should you use a direct quotation, and when should you paraphrase? In general, you should use a direct quotation in your paper when you have found a clear, effective statement that supports the point you want to make. Be sure that the statement fits into your paper. When you cannot find an appropriate statement to quote directly, you can paraphrase, or put the information in your own words.

Plagiarism. Reporting from sources without properly giving credit to authors for their original ideas and words is **plagiarism**. Plagiarism can take two forms. Presenting the original ideas of published authors in your paper without giving the authors' names is one kind of plagiarism. Copying sentences from a book and using them in your paper without quotation marks is another kind of plagiarism.

When college students plagiarize, instructors view their action as a serious problem. Most instructors automatically fail papers that they believe contain plagiarized material. How can you avoid plagiarism? First of all, you must understand what plagiarism is. Here are some guidelines to follow.

- **Understand the difference between general knowledge and original ideas.** If you read a statement of a fact that most people know, such as *The business world is competitive*, you do not need to attribute the statement to a source. This is general knowledge. On the other hand, if you want to report an idea that seems unique or original to you, you need to include the name of the author. If you are not sure whether an idea is unique or not, be cautious and report the author's name.

- **Know how much you can copy from a source without plagiarizing.** You can use a word or phrase from a source (unless it is used in an original or unique way), but not a whole clause or sentence. If you want to use a whole clause or sentence, you have only two choices: You can use a direct quotation, or you can **paraphrase**. When you paraphrase, you must change the words of the original statement as much as possible.

Exercise 10

A. Read the direct quotations from various people about their jobs. Then, from the two choices that follow each quotation, choose the better paraphrase.

1. "Our company has recently laid off many of its permanent programmers and hired some temporary people. This puts the remaining permanent programmers under strain. We are competing against younger people who are just out of school and know the latest technologies. Furthermore, the temporary employees cost the company less. We permanent employees feel very insecure."   —Lu Dong, Computer Programmer, Telecon, Inc.

   a. Lu Dong, a computer programmer at Telecon, Inc. says his company has recently laid off permanent programmers and hired some temporary people. This puts the remaining permanent programmers under strain. They are competing against younger people who are just out of school and know the latest technologies. Furthermore, the temporary employees cost the company less. As a result, the permanent employees feel very insecure.

   b. Lu Dong, a computer programmer, says that his employer, Telecon, Inc., has recently replaced permanent computer programmers with temporary programmers. Lu Dong and the other remaining permanent programmers are feeling insecure because the temporary workers know the latest technologies and work for less money.

2. "My job has become more difficult in the last two years. Before we got the new computer system, I spent more time helping the customers. Now I have to answer twice as many calls an hour, and I still have to maintain a pleasant tone of voice and be courteous."
        —Celia Hernandez, Telephone Operator, ILD

   a. Celia Hernandez, a telephone operator at ILD, says that before her company purchased a new computer system, her job was easier, and she was able to be more helpful to the public. Since she started to work with the new technology, she has had to cut the time she spends with a customer in half, although she is still expected to use a pleasant voice and be polite.

   b. Celia Hernandez, a telephone operator at ILD, says her job is very hectic, but her supervisor still expects her to use a nice tone of voice and be polite.

3. "As the Internet has come into widespread use, my job has changed substantially. I used to take orders on the telephone all day, but now I use e-mail, and I like it better. In written communication, there is less chance of error."   —Paul LeBlanc, Distribution Coordinator, HB Food Imports

a. According to Paul LeBlanc of HB Food Imports, the international expansion of his company has changed his job. He now communicates by e-mail with HB employees in other countries.

b. According to Paul LeBlanc of HB Food Imports, the Internet has changed his job significantly. He used to spend all his time on the phone taking orders, and now he uses e-mail instead. He prefers e-mail because there is less risk of error with written messages.

4. "Until last year, Nova was run in a very traditional way, with all the authority at the top. Now the culture at Nova is different. Since Nova was bought by a foreign clothing company, it has been operated more democratically. The new managers, who come from a different cultural background, have a more open attitude toward employees. They let people participate in decision making more."

—Silvia Robello, Assistant Production Manager, Nova Designs

a. Assistant production manager Silvia Robello says that the culture of her company, Nova Designs, has changed since it was purchased by an overseas clothing manufacturer last year. Instead of being run as a traditional top-down organization, Nova is now operated in a way that allows more worker involvement.

b. Silvia Robello, assistant production manager at Nova Designs, says that until last year, Nova was run in a very traditional way, with all the authority at the top. Now the culture at Nova is different. Since Nova was bought by a foreign clothing company, it has been operated more democratically. The new managers, who come from a different cultural background, let people participate in decision making more.

5. "My job has changed since Global downsized. I am lucky to still have my job, but it is a lot harder than it used to be. My supervisor was laid off, and I have had to take on his responsibilities. In addition to managing the data entry department, which was my job before, I now have to write reports.

—Peter Delatin, Supervisor, Global Data

a. Peter Delatin, a supervisor at Global Data, reports that he feels lucky to still have a job, but downsizing has increased his responsibilities at work. He had to assume his boss' duties when his boss was laid off. Now he not only manages a data entry department but writes reports as well.

b. Peter Delatin, a supervisor at Global Data, feels lucky to have his job managing a data entry department because his supervisor was laid off.

6. "WBX has expanded globally. We now have offices in seven cities worldwide. Employees are often transferred to foreign countries where they need to learn a new culture. The rules of etiquette are different in each of our seven offices."

—Harvey Wang, Director of Marketing, WBX Industries

      a. Marketing director Harvey Wang at WBX Industries says that he is having a lot of fun traveling all over the world learning new customs and meeting new people.

      b. According to Harvey Wang, a marketing director at WBX Industries, globalization at WBX has meant that employees often go overseas to work in foreign countries and therefore have to learn new cultures. He says that WBX's seven offices, which are located in different countries, all have different customs.

B. After choosing the better paraphrases, discuss the reasons for your choices with a partner. Then answer the following questions.

- What kinds of changes do you make when you paraphrase?
- Is it OK to change words?
- Is it OK to change the grammar?

Exercise 11

A. With a partner, revise one body paragraph in the following essay. (Working in pairs, the rest of your classmates can revise the other two body paragraphs.) You and your partner need to choose one or two suitable quotations or paraphrases from Exercise 10 to use as support in your body paragraph. Rewrite your revised body paragraph on another piece of paper.

Kinds of Organizational Change

1 [1]Competition in the business environment requires organizations to change constantly, adapting to changes in the marketplace. [2]As organizations change, their employees have to make adjustments. [3]Workers today are coping with change in three areas: technology, organizational structure, and culture.

2 [4]The last twenty-five years have seen the most rapid technological change in history. [5]Personal computers, networking systems, fax machines, voice messaging, the Internet, and e-mail have permanently altered the work environment, and more advanced devices and systems are coming out all the time. [6]This means that employees must constantly learn to work with new technology. [7]Some employees find that new technology makes their jobs easier. [8]Other employees find that new technology makes their jobs harder.

3 [9]In recent years, there has also been a great deal of structural change within organizations. [10]Because of global competition, many companies have been downsizing, or reducing the number of employees they hire in order to save money. [11]When companies downsize, employees' job descriptions change. [12]Many companies downsize by reducing the number of management levels they have. [13]When this happens, those who remain after the layoffs have more responsibilities. [14]Other companies have downsized by laying off permanent employees and hiring temporary workers in their place.

4   [15]In this time of global expansion, corporations have opened offices and factories in other nations to secure new markets and find cheaper labor. [16]This has brought about cultural change within organizations. [17]When corporations expand overseas, their workforce becomes multinational. [18]This can lead to shifts in management style and in the social relationships between workers.

5   [19]As a result of technological advances, downsizing, and globalization, workers today are experiencing rapid change. [20]They have to adapt to ever-more sophisticated technologies, structural change that often increases their responsibilities and decreases their job security, and new cultures in their work environment.

B. After you and your classmates have finished expanding the three body paragraphs, assemble them in order. Then read the entire revised essay aloud. Does including direct quotations or paraphrases improve this essay? If so, how?

Review and Revise 6: Using Outside Sources as Support
Review your own essay. If you have included a statement from an outside source, ask yourself if it supports the point you are making in your paper. If you have not used any outside sources, ask yourself whether it would be possible to include a direct quotation or a paraphrase.

PEER REVIEW AND FINAL DRAFT

Now it is time to share your composition with readers. Exchange papers with one or two classmates. Read each other's papers carefully. Turn to page 338 in Appendix II, and fill out the Peer Review form.

After considering your classmates' suggestions, prepare a final draft of your composition to hand in to your teacher. Proofread your work for spelling, grammar, punctuation, and errors.

CHAPTER REVIEW

Look back at what you have accomplished in Chapter 7. Check (✓) what you have learned and what you have used as you have written and revised your essay.

Chapter 7 Topics	I understand this	I have used this
understanding classification: identifying a class, a basis of classification, and categories (pages 173–174)		
writing thesis statements for classification essays (page 180)		
using qualifiers in thesis statements (pages 180–181)		
developing body paragraphs using various rhetorical strategies (pages 182–183)		
using signals of cohesion in body paragraphs (page 185)		
maintaining consistent point of view in a paragraph or essay (page 187)		
using direct quotations and paraphrase to include information and ideas from outside sources (pages 189–191)		

The Science of Everyday Life

◆ Writing a Definition Paragraph and Essay

Science touches our daily lives in many ways. Science can explain how our hearts beat, how our muscles work, and how we see things. It has given us electricity, telephones, computers, and many more conveniences. The road to each discovery begins with the same basic questions we all ask: What is it? How does it happen? And why does it happen that way? In this chapter, we will focus on the first question—What is it?—the question that leads to a definition.

This chapter will help you

- write one-sentence definitions.
- write extended definitions using various rhetorical strategies.
- use pronouns correctly.
- recognize and correct unnecessary repetition.
- learn how to paraphrase in order to avoid plagiarism.

READING FOR WRITING

Before You Read

With a partner or a small group, do the following activities.

1. Science has developed explanations for many things. Do you ever wonder how scientists explain some of the phenomena you experience in your daily life? Write a few questions that you would like to have answered.

   <u>Why is the sky blue in the daytime?</u>

   <u>Why does moisture collect on the outside of a glass of ice water?</u>

   _____

   _____

   _____

   _____

2. The article you are going to read is about the sense of smell. The following sentences contain definitions of some words that will appear in the article or come from the same word family as words in the article. Underline the defining phrase in each sentence.

   a. Physiology, or <u>the study of how the bodies of living things work</u>, is the basis of medical science.

   b. The tissues of the body, that is, groups of similar cells, are classified according to their functions as muscles, connective parts, nerves, and skin or membranes.

   c. The nervous system—the nerves, spinal cord, and brain—makes it possible for a creature to interact with the world.

   d. An axon (a long, thin part of a nerve cell) carries electrochemical messages away from the cell body toward another nerve cell.

   e. Chemistry is the study of the basic properties of solids, liquids, and gases.

   f. A molecule—the basic unit of a substance—cannot be divided without losing its properties.

   g. A compound is a substance that contains different types of molecules.

   h. Evaporation (the process through which a liquid or solid changes to a gas) occurs more quickly when the temperature rises.

   i. Diffusion is the spreading of a gas over an area.

   j. Olfaction—the sense of smell—occurs when the nose detects molecules of odorous substances in the air.

How Do You Smell?

by Susan Gordon Thomas

saturated: filled with

cosmic rays: energy in the form of heat or light that comes from stars

mechanism: a process, the way that something works

1   The space around us is saturated° with information. Light, sound, cosmic rays° and all manner of other waves pass through the lower atmosphere, and the air itself is made up of incomprehensibly large numbers of gaseous molecules. We are aware of the world only through the physiological mechanisms° that let us capture and process certain bits of the available information. With a single sniff of air, for example, a person inhales more than 15 sextillion molecules (15×10^{21} = 15,000,000,000,000,000,000,000 molecules) of oxygen, nitrogen, argon, carbon dioxide, and thousands of minor components. Most of these we cannot detect. But if among these many molecules, there are some of odorous substances, we have sensory equipment to let us become conscious of them.

ambient: refers to the environment or surrounding area

2   To perhaps a more than usual degree, I am acutely aware of smells. I recognize people and places by their distinctive odors, notice subtle changes in friends' scents when their moods change, and appreciate small differences in ambient° smells. For gathering and sorting olfactory information, I have a nose and a brain. With the same physical equipment, a professional "nose"—a master perfumer who uses his or her sense of smell to make a living—can distinguish at least five thousand odorous compounds. The best "nose" can identify close to an amazing ten thousand smells, and further, can analyze complex odor mixtures by smell alone.

receptor: a structure that receives a chemical message

perceive: to notice or recognize

3   Even as a scientist, I know surprisingly little about how I sense a smell. Relatively little research has been done on how human olfaction works. But we do know that there is great variability in people's perception of smells. An individual's ability to detect odors may change from day to day, depending on physiological condition. A cold, we all know, blocks passage of odors to the olfactory receptors°. A certain percentage of the population is anosmic ("smell-blind") to any of dozens of specific odors, and a given odor may be undetected or perceived° differently by different people. For example, men and women differ in their olfactory abilities. Women seem to be more sensitive to smell in general, but men may smell more vividly the odors of coffee, lemon oil, and some petroleum compounds.

4   Most things that we smell are not "pure" substances, but rather are mixtures of many components. A fine perfume might be a blend of three hundred ingredients; cooked cabbage gives off hundreds of different scents, though one or only a few dominate our perception as the characteristic smell. We do not yet fully understand the relationship between the chemical composition of a substance and its odor. However, to be smelled at all, a substance must first be *volatile*: that is, it must vaporize so that the molecules

can travel through the air to reach our olfactory tissue. Boiling or hot foods smell more strongly than cold ones, because the hotter a substance is, the more it evaporates. The smell of hot chicken soup, for example, is much more enticing than that of cold soup. The second requirement is that the molecules be slightly *soluble* (able to dissolve) in both water and lipid (fat), so that they can pass through the watery mucus° covering the olfactory tissue and pass through the fatty layer of the olfactory receptor cells. Beyond these fundamental requirements, the various facts that are known about odorous molecules do not yet form a coherent explanation of what makes some molecules smell a particular way.

5   But let's go back to chicken soup. How do the chicken soup molecules reach the right spot? You might be aware of a slight sensation of odor when you inhale a few of the vaporized molecules in a breath of air. The air is warmed and filtered in your nasal cavity and the molecules reach the olfactory tissue by diffusion. A good voluntary sniff is needed to bring enough odor molecules into contact with the receptors in the olfactory tissue to let you distinguish the smell clearly.

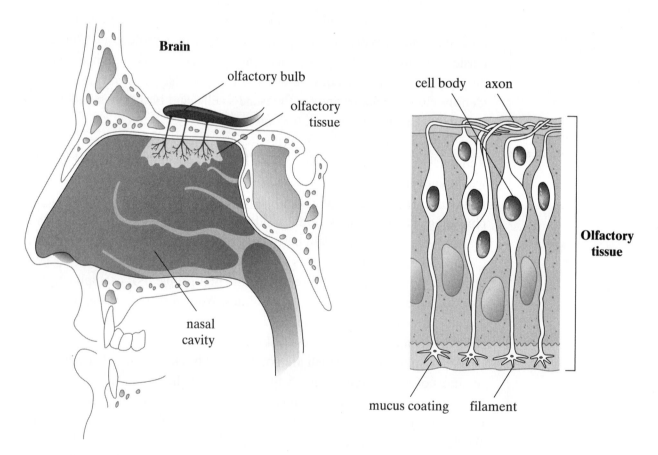

fiber: a long, thin thread-like piece of tissue

filament: a very thin fiber

impulse: a signal

protein: a compound that occurs in living things

tract: a system of connected parts

motor: refers to the parts of the brain that control movement

cortical: refers to the cortex, the part of the brain where conscious thought occurs

6   The smell receptors are located high inside the nasal cavity—one patch of mucus-coated olfactory tissue on each side. Each patch of tissue has an area of about 2.4 square centimeters and each consists of millions of receptor cells. Each receptor cell is a long fiber°, with a cell body resting in the olfactory tissue, a thread-like axon extending into the brain, and several long, hair-like filaments° extending out to the tissue surface. The molecules of chicken soup pass through the mucus coating and establish contact with the filaments, stimulating them to send a message (an electrical impulse°) along the nerve cell toward the brain.

7   The precise mechanism through which an odor, or chemical signal, reaches the brain remains a mystery. We know that individual odors trigger more than one receptor, and that proteins° play a role in the activation of a receptor and in the translation of an odor into an electrochemical nerve impulse. We also know that the encoded "smell picture" goes first to the olfactory bulb, or "nose brain," as it is called, where the first step in processing the information takes place. The olfactory bulb then transmits the message by secondary nerve tracts° to motor° and cortical° areas of the brain. Some of these areas govern automatic body responses to smells; others govern emotional responses. Still other nerve tracts carry the message to association areas of the cortex, where olfactory information is combined with input from all other senses and may be enriched by recollections of past experience stored in memory areas. While we understand the basic process of olfaction, much remains to be learned about the details of this sequence of events.

8   Our olfactory sense helps to guide and often to warn us of unseen hazards, and contributes to many of our sensations of pleasure. The flexibility and adaptability of our sense of smell allows us to explore the environment. Unlike insects, which have receptors programmed to detect only a few specific odors for identification of particular food plants, mates, and other necessities, we have cells that delight or annoy us with a near-infinite variety of input as we search the environment for suitable foods, both familiar and novel, reject toxic substances, and enjoy the multitude of floral, fruity, earthy, wonderful smells that fill the air.

About the Author

Susan Gordon Thomas, Ph.D., is a researcher at the Batelle Marine Sciences Lab in Washington State, where she is developing techniques using living fungus to find and eradicate pollution and to convert waste to valuable products. In addition to her research, Dr. Gordon Thomas writes, speaks, teaches, and develops educational materials in the field of science.

Understanding the Reading

With a partner or a small group, discuss the following questions.

1. While reading "How Do You Smell?" you probably found both familiar and new information. List three pieces of information from this reading that were familiar to you and three pieces of information that were new to you.

2. In paragraph 2, Gordon Thomas writes, "To perhaps a more than usual degree, I am acutely aware of smells. I recognize people and places by their distinctive odors, notice subtle changes in friends' scents when their moods change. . . ." Science writers seldom refer to themselves in their writing. Why do you think Gordon Thomas chose to mention herself in this article?

3. In paragraphs 4, 5, and 6, Gordon Thomas used an example about chicken soup. Why do you think she chose this example?

4. In writing this article, Gordon Thomas used the rhetorical strategies you are familiar with. Locate the strategies listed below, and write the number of the paragraph or paragraphs where you find it.

   a. description _____   d. comparison/contrast _____

   b. example _____   e. logical division/classification _____

   c. cause and effect _____

5. Writers use quotation marks to show that certain words were spoken or written by someone. They also use quotation marks to show (1) that they believe there is something wrong with or strange about a word or its usage; (2) that a word is not being used in its usual sense or that it has been assigned a new meaning; or (3) that a word has recently been invented, perhaps by the author himself or herself. Refer back to the text, and explain why Gordon Thomas put quotation marks around the following words.

   a. "smell-blind" (paragraph 3)   c. "smell picture" (paragraph 7)

   b. "pure" (paragraph 4)   d. "nose brain" (paragraph 7)

6. In scientific writing, definitions of terminology are often necessary. Gordon Thomas provides several brief definitions in this text. A brief definition can be a single word, a phrase, or a clause. Brief definitions can be placed in parentheses ( ) or introduced with the phrase *that is* or the conjunction *or*. Find and underline the definitions in the text of the following terms.

   a. "Nose"   d. soluble

   b. anosmic   e. lipid

   c. volatile   f. olfactory bulb

Vocabulary Expansion

The vocabulary of science. Science has many branches, and college and university students can choose from a wide variety of science courses. The following exercise lists some of the courses that you might find in a college catalogue.

Exercise 1

A. Look at the chart. Column **A** gives the names of several fields of science. Column **B** gives definitions of those fields of science. Column **C** gives information about the importance of each field of science in today's world. For each item in Column **A**, find the correct definition in **B** and an appropriate phrase in **C**. Next to each field of science, write the letter of the definition and the number of the phrase.

A: Field of Science	B: Definition	C: How Important
1. astronomy __c__ __ii__ 2. botany ____ ____ 3. genetics ____ ____ 4. geology ____ ____ 5. microbiology ____ ____ 6. nutrition science ____ ____ 7. oceanography ____ ____ 8. pharmacology ____ ____ 9. physics ____ ____ 10. zoology ____ ____	a. the study of drugs and their effects on the body b. the study of very small living things c. the study of stars and planets d. the study of animals and their behavior e. the study of Earth f. the study of the components of foods and how they help the body g. the study of plants h. the study of matter, motion, and energy i. the study of oceans j. the study of how the traits of an organism are passed on to its offspring	i. may tell us how hereditary diseases can be prevented ii. may help us understand the history of the universe iii. may tell us about the origin of human language iv. may help us understand the effects of the dietary change that is occurring in many countries v. may help us protect the fish stocks that feed people all over the world vi. may help us understand how to control the spread of bacteria and viruses in the environment that cause disease vii. may help us predict earthquakes viii. may help us develop new foods or medicines from rare plants that live in the rain forest ix. may help us understand how new man-made building materials can be used safely x. may help us develop new medicines for people who have adverse reactions to medicines that are used today

B. Combine the information you matched from Columns **A**, **B**, and **C**. Make statements that (1) contain adjective-clause or noun-phrase definitions and (2) give information about the importance of the field today. Do this exercise either orally or in writing.

For more on adjective clauses, see Appendix IA, page 261.

Astronomy, which is the study of stars and planets, may help us understand the history of the universe.

OR

Astronomy, the study of stars and planets, may help us understand the history of the universe.

WRITING

Assignment

In this chapter, you are going to write a definition paragraph or essay. (If you like, you can begin by writing a paragraph and later expand your definition to essay-length.) Choose one of the following topics, and then write a paragraph or essay-length definition.

1. Define a healthy lifestyle, physical fitness, or proper nutrition. Or define a health problem, such as a disease.

2. Write a scientific definition of an aspect of human physiology and/or experience such as eyesight, hearing, taste, touch, respiration, laughter, singing, headaches, or the common cold.

3. Write a scientific definition of a piece of technology that affects your daily life such as the gasoline engine, the microwave oven, or the type of heating system used in your home.

4. Write a definition of a plant or animal that lives in your native country.

What Definition Is and Why It Is Important

The verb *to define* originally meant *to set a boundary* as someone would draw a line on a map to indicate where his or her property ends. Therefore, to define a word is to tell what the meaning of that term includes and does not include.

A definition may be long or short. We use short, one- or two-sentence definitions in essays and articles to make sure that readers understand new or difficult terms. Sometimes we use extended (paragraph- or essay-length) definitions to explore the meaning of a new term such as *hydrogen fuel cell* or to develop a better understanding of a familiar idea such as *sunlight*. Definitions are important in writing because, in order to communicate well with others, we must establish a common understanding of what words and ideas mean.

The one-sentence definition. There are various ways to write brief definitions, including use of **synonyms**, **negation**, and **comparison**.

SYNONYM: The larynx, <u>or voice box</u>, produces the vowel sounds in human speech.

NEGATION: The voice box <u>is not an actual box</u>, but a tube that can be partly or completely closed by the vocal cords.

COMPARISON: The vocal cords <u>are like guitar strings</u> in that they produce sound waves when they vibrate.

The classification-type definition. One more way to write a one-sentence definition is to use classification. Classification-type definitions are effective because they tell you two things: (1) the broader category that the thing belongs to and (2) the distinguishing characteristics that separate the thing from other members of its category or class. Look at the following examples.

    TERM   CATEGORY   DISTINGUISHING CHARACTERISTICS
The stomach is the organ that digests food.

    TERM   CATEGORY   DISTINGUISHING CHARACTERISTICS
Carbon dioxide is a gas (that is) released when we exhale.

In classification-type definitions, the distinguishing characteristics are usually expressed in adjective clauses. However, sometimes an adjective clause can be reduced to an adjective phrase, as you see in the second example above.

Exercise 2

Choose one of the following pairs of words and, on a piece of paper, write a one-sentence, classification-type definition for each of the terms. Use a dictionary if you need to.

1. a. adrenaline   b. endorphins

    a. Adrenaline is a hormone that is produced by our bodies when we are feeling stress.

    b. Endorphins are chemicals produced by the brain that reduce the feeling of pain and can affect the emotions.

2. a. reptile   b. amphibian

3. a. star   b. planet

4. a. the liver   b. the kidneys

5. a. malaria   b. typhoid

The extended definition. Because all types of information can go into definitions, there are many ways to write them. You can give the **origin of the word** or include its **dictionary definition**. You can use **negation** (that is, tell what the word does *not* mean). You also can employ any of the following **rhetorical strategies** alone or in combination.

Rhetorical Strategies

1. **Description:** Specific details that tell how something looks, sounds, feels, smells, or tastes. For example, you could define *hurricane* by describing its powerful winds and heavy rain.

2. **Narration:** A story or anecdote. For example, you could define *radium* by narrating its discovery by Marie Curie.

3. **Example:** A reference to a specific person, thing, or event that represents the more general idea that you want to define. For instance, you could define *crustacean* by referring to crabs and shrimp.

4. **Logical division:** An analysis of the parts or aspects of the thing you want to describe. For example, you could define *cell* by naming its parts (cell wall, nucleus, and chromosomes).

5. **Classification:** A discussion of something in terms of either (1) the category that it belongs to or (2) the categories it contains. For example, you could define *pepper* as a kind of spice and then identify the different kinds of pepper (black, white, and red).

6. **Cause and effect:** An explanation of the conditions that lead to an event or the results of an event. For example, you could define *earthquake* in terms of its effects on roads, bridges, and buildings.

7. **Comparison/contrast:** A discussion of the differences (or similarities) between two things. For example, to explain what a *virus* is, you could explain how a virus is similar to and different from a bacterium.

8. **Process:** The series of steps to take in order to do or make something. For example, you could define *photosynthesis* by explaining, step by step, how the cells in a green leaf turn sunlight into food.

Exercise 3

The following one-paragraph extended definitions were written with a variety of strategies. Read each extended definition, and mark it to show where each strategy is used. Choose from the following strategies.

origin of the word	narration	logical division *or* classification
dictionary definition	example	comparison/contrast
negation	process	

1.

The Photocopy Machine

Narration

Negation

The photocopy machine was first developed by a physicist named Chester Carlson in the 1930s. Carlson's invention uses no liquid inks. Instead, it uses electricity to reproduce images. The first step is to put an electrical charge on a surface covered with a chemical that is sensitive to

Process

light. When that surface is exposed to light reflecting from the document to be copied, the chemical causes the electric charge to disappear from the lighted areas but to remain where dark letters or images are. The surface is then dusted with another chemical called *toner*, which is attracted to the electric charge in the dark areas. Finally, the toner is melted onto a sheet of paper. Carlson sold his patent for the photocopy machine to a company

Narration

which adopted the name The Xerox Corporation and began selling his invention in the 1960s.

Bunce, N., & Hunt, J. (1984). How the photocopier works. *The science corner*. Retrieved August 19, 2003, from http://physics.uoguelph.ca/summer/scor/articles/scor54.htm

Science and Technology Department of the Carnegie Library of Pittsburgh. (1994). *The handy science answer book* (1st ed.) (p. 441). Detroit, MI: Visible Ink.

2.

Corn

Corn is an old English word that means *grain*, but the corn plant is native to the Americas. There are many types of corn. Some kinds produce kernels that are high in starch, while others are high in sugar. In Mexico and Central America, where corn is a staple of the diet, a type of corn that is high in starch is used to make flat cakes called *tortillas*. Sweet corn, which is cultivated worldwide, is a variety that can be eaten directly off the cob after being roasted or steamed. Other varieties of corn are used to produce corn oil and corn syrup, the sweetener used in candies and soft drinks. One type of corn is fed to cattle and chickens and thus is important in meat production. Corn is an extremely valuable food plant.

McGee, H. (1984). *On food and cooking: The science and lore of the kitchen* (pp. 240–242). New York: Scribner's.

Salvador, R. J. (2004). Corn. *World Book online reference center*. Retrieved June 5, 2004, from http://www.worldbookonline.marinet.lib.ca.us:80/wb/Article?id=ar134160

3.

Regeneration

According to *Webster's New World College Dictionary,* in the biological sciences *regeneration* means "the renewal or replacement of any lost part." Plants can regenerate, or grow back, branches that are cut off. Some animals, such as crayfish, starfish, salamanders, and frogs can regenerate lost limbs, and some lizards can grow new tails. Certain parts of some plants and some animals have the capacity to grow an entirely new organism. For example, just one cell in the tip of a carrot can grow an entirely new plant. A small piece of a sponge, which is one of the most basic animals, can develop into a new sponge. In human beings and the higher animals, regeneration is much more limited. In humans, skin and liver cells regenerate, and there is evidence that some nerve cells of the brain and nervous system can regrow. Future research in regeneration may help people with brain and spinal cord injuries.

Barclay, L. (2000). New research may aid future treatments for spinal cord injury. *WebMD medical news archive.* Retrieved June 6, 2004, from http://my.webmd.com/content/Article/23/1728_56998.htm

Kimball, J. W. (2003). Regeneration. *Kimball's biology pages.* Retrieved June 6, 2004, from http://users.rcn.com/jkimball.ma.ultranet/BiologyPages/R/Regeneration.html

Webster's new world college dictionary (4th ed.). (2001). Foster City, CA: IDG.

4.   **The Eye**

In some ways the eye is similar to a camera, but in other ways it is different. The dark pupil in the center of the eye is an opening that can widen or narrow to control the amount of light that comes into the eye, just as an adjustable shutter that opens and closes allows light rays to enter a camera. In both the eye and the camera, light passes through a lens that bends or focuses it on a light-sensitive area where it causes a chemical reaction to take place. But here the similarities end. The light-sensitive cells at the back of the eye that convert the light energy to electrical impulses are far different from the plastic film covered with a chemical emulsion in the back of a camera. And of course the eye is made of living cells that regenerate, while the camera is manufactured of plastic parts. But the greatest difference between the eye and the camera is the eye-brain partnership that develops throughout life.

Cole, K. C. (1985, Spring). Vision: In the eye of the beholder. *Exploratorium Magazine, 9*(1), 1–4.

Meyer, D. B. (2002). Eye. In *McGraw-Hill encyclopedia of science and technology* (9th ed.) (Vol. 6) (pp. 779–787). New York: McGraw-Hill.

White, L. R. (2002). Camera. In *McGraw-Hill encyclopedia of science and technology* (Vol. 3) (pp. 414–418). New York: McGraw-Hill.

Prewriting

To prepare to write your extended definition, follow the prewriting steps. You will see how Amin, a student from Iran, prepared to write a paper defining the human hand.

Important: You will probably do some research to complete this writing assignment. When you use dictionaries, encyclopedias, books, or online sources, you must avoid plagiarism. When you take notes, be sure to use quotations and paraphrasing so that you will not accidentally plagiarize when you write your paragraph or essay.

STEP **1** | Write a **one-sentence, classification-type definition**. Use a dictionary if you need to.

Amin wrote the following sentence.

The hand is a part of the body that is designed for movement and sensation.

STEP 2 | Make a **list of things you know** about your topic and a **list of questions** you would like to find answers for.

Amin made the lists below.

Things I Know about Hands

Human hands can write, draw, use tools, and even communicate with gestures.

Only primates (humans, apes, and monkeys) can pick things up with their hands.

The hand has many bones and muscles.

Things I Would Like to Know about Hands

How many bones, muscles, and nerve endings are there inside our hands?

How do we move our hands?

What role did the hand play in human evolution?

Note that although you may not be able to find answers to all the questions you write down, they will help you direct your research.

STEP 3 | Do some **research** and **take notes**.

For more on citing sources and note taking, see Appendix IC, page 320.

Amin consulted an online encyclopedia, a magazine, and two books. He took notes from each. Below you see his notes from one of the books. Notice how Amin put complete bibliographical information about the book at the top of the page and wrote page numbers in the margin on the left for each paraphrase or quotation so that he could re-check his information if necessary and he could include accurate citations in his paper.

Amin put complete information about the author, title, and publisher on the top of the page.

The page numbers where Amin found the information in the sources are noted in the margin.

This note is a paraphrase.

This note is a direct quote.

Wilson, F. R. (1998). The hand: How its use shapes the brain, language, and human culture. New York: Pantheon

136 | In human evolution, two changes had to occur in the thumb in order for the hand to function as it does today. First, the thumb had to become longer, and second, it had to be able to rotate. That way, the soft, sensitive pads on the thumb and forefinger could face each other and grasp things.

138 | "The thumb is the only digit in the hand that has the freedom to rotate or swivel..."

STEP 4 Review (1) the **list of things you know**, (2) the **list of questions** you wrote, and (3) your **notes**, and check (✓) the items that you want to include in your paragraph or essay. Make a **brief outline**, putting the most essential information first and the least essential last.

Note that definitions are organized differently from other kinds of paragraphs or essays. In a definition, you should provide the most basic or essential information first.

Amin selected the following topics from his notes and made this brief outline.

1. the anatomy of the hand

2. how the hand works

3. the role of the hand in human evolution

STEP 5 If you need more information before you can make a **complete outline**, discuss your topic with your classmates, or do some additional **research**.

At this point, Amin had enough information to make the following outline.

The hand is a versatile body part that has many internal structures and remarkable functions, and it has played a critical role in human evolution.

I. The hand has many internal structures.
   A. bones
   B. muscles
   C. tendons and ligaments
   D. blood vessels
   E. nerves

II. The hand has remarkable functions.
   A. Motor nerves control movement by signaling muscles to contract.
   B. Sensory nerves detect pressure, heat, cold, and pain and relay messages to the brain.

III. The hand has played a critical role in human evolution.
   A. thumb rotation
   B. tool use
   C. development of advanced brain, social life, and communication

With his outline complete, Amin was ready to write a first draft. He began by writing a paragraph. After revising, he produced the following paragraph.

The Hand

The hand is a versatile body part that has many internal structures and remarkable functions, and it has probably played a critical role in human evolution. In spite of its small size, the hand contains twenty bones, twenty muscles, many tendons (which connect muscles to bones) and ligaments (which connect bones to each other), numerous branching blood vessels, and thousands of nerve endings. Motor nerves deep in the hand signal muscles to contract. Sensory nerve endings close to the skin detect pressure, heat, cold, and pain. The greatest number of nerve endings is found in the tips of the index finger and thumb. Scientists say that the fact that the thumb can rotate so that the index finger and thumb can face each other and hold things between them has made a great deal of difference in human history. Without this capacity, early humans might not have been able to make and use tools, and without tools they might not have developed an advanced brain, social life, and language.

After writing this paragraph, Amin returned to his research materials and notes. He decided that he would like to include more information and expand his definition paragraph to an essay. He drafted an essay and, after several revisions, completed the draft that follows. Note that the citations you see at the end of Amin's draft and throughout this chapter are in the APA style.

The Hand

The hand, with its detailed structures, has made many human achievements possible. I use my hands to play basketball, fix cars, write essays, and play a Middle Eastern stringed instrument known as the "oud." Other people use their hands to dance, communicate in sign language, and perform surgery. How our hands do so many things remains, in some ways, a mystery to science, but it is clear that the hand has a very complicated anatomy and that its many parts function together in complex ways. It has also been suggested that the hand has played a crucial role in human evolution.

The anatomy of the hand is very intricate. In spite of its small size, each hand has twenty bones, twenty muscles, tendons and ligaments to connect the muscles and bone, numerous branching blood vessels, and twenty kinds of nerve endings, which can detect heat, cold, pain, pressure, and vibration. But according to Mandayam Srinivasam, who runs a laboratory that investigates the tactile capacity of the hand at the Massachusetts Institute of Technology, naming the structures within the hand itself does not adequately describe it. Srinivasam points out that additional muscles, tendons, and ligaments in the arm control the hand and that "nerves from the hand go all the way to the brain. So the hand really ends at the brain" (Wolkomir, 2000, p. 42).

Any activity of the hand, therefore, is a result of coordination between the brain, the muscles, tendons, and ligaments of the arm, and the many parts of the hand itself. When I play the oud, my brain is sending electrochemical signals to motor nerves deep in my hands and forearms, which in turn are transmitting messages to my muscles to contract so that my right hand can grasp the pick and move it against the strings and the fingers of my left hand can depress the strings on the neck. Nerves in my hand are sending messages back to inform my brain that my muscles are contracting and that my fingers are bent, and nerves close to my skin are relaying signals about the pressure of the pick in my hand and the vibrations of the strings under my fingers. My brain analyzes the incoming sensory input, determines the location of my hand and position of my fingers, and sends motor signals to my hands to make their

214 | Chapter 8

next movements. All this happens in seconds without my ever looking at my hands or even thinking much about them. Exactly how the brain analyzes sensory information and directs the hands is not understood, but as everybody knows, practice makes the brain and hand work together better.

Hand specialists Frank R. Wilson (1998) and John Napier (1980) maintain that the hand is not only remarkable for what it can do today, but that it has played a key role in human evolution. Analysis of the hand bones of the Australopithecine skeleton nicknamed Lucy shows that 3.2 million years ago early humans had the ability to pick up and use stone tools. This movement became possible because a joint at the bottom of the thumb allowed the thumb to rotate. According to Wilson and Napier, without this capacity, early humans might not have been able to make and use tools, and without tools they might not have developed an advanced brain, social life, and language.

The human hand is truly extraordinary in its physiology and functions and most likely very important in human evolution as well. So the next time you write your name, make a sandwich, or sew a button on your shirt, remember that you are using one of nature's marvels—your hand.

Napier, J. (1980). *Hands*. New York: Pantheon.

Opgrande, D. J. (2003). Hand. *World Book online reference center*. Retrieved August 7, 2003, from http://0-www.worldbookonline.com.marinet.lib.ca.us: 80/ar?/na/ar/co/ar244700.htm

Wilson, F. R. (1998). *The hand: How its use shapes the brain, language, and human culture*. New York: Pantheon.

Wolkomir, R. (2000, June). Charting the terrain of touch. *Smithsonian, 31*(3), 38–48.

Exercise 4

With a partner or a small group, discuss the following questions about Amin's essay.

1. How did Amin catch the reader's interest in his introduction? What is his thesis statement?

2. What are the topics of Amin's body paragraphs? Why did Amin order his body paragraphs in this way?

3. Underline all the supporting information that Amin added to the text when he expanded the paragraph to an essay. Do you think he developed the definition in a balanced way? If so, explain.

4. How did Amin conclude the essay?

5. Is the essay cohesive? Find one example of cohesion between the thesis statement and the topic sentences of the body paragraphs (see Chapter 6, pages 156–158) and one example of cohesion within a body paragraph (see Chapter 7, page 185).

6. How many outside sources did Amin cite within his essay? How many did he list at the end of the essay? Why are there more citations at the end than within the essay?

7. Notice the form of Amin's citations at the end of the essay. How do the book citation, magazine citation, and Web site citation differ?

First Draft

Once you have completed an outline, write your first draft. Then share it with a classmate or friend, asking the reader to tell you if there are any information gaps. If your first draft is a paragraph, you could use your reader's questions to expand the definition to an essay.

REVISING

As you proceed through the lessons and exercises in this section of the chapter, review your draft regularly, and follow the advice in the Review and Revise boxes.

Composition Focus

Cohesion and redundancy. You have learned that you can use pronouns and repeated words to create cohesion between sentences in paragraphs. While this is true, using too many pronouns or repeated words creates **redundancy**, or excess repetition. Use the following guidelines to learn how to use pronouns and avoid redundancy.

Guidelines for Using Pronouns

1. When there is a second reference to a noun in a single sentence, a pronoun is almost always used for the second reference.

   The lungs remove oxygen from the air and transfer *it* to the blood.

2. When a noun appears in one sentence and there is a second reference to that noun in the following sentence, a pronoun is usually used in the second sentence. However, if the pronoun could refer back to two different nouns and thus cause confusion, the pronoun cannot be used.

   Respiration is a process carried on by living things. *They* must carry on this process in order to survive.

   The heart
   The heart and the lungs together carry out respiration. ~~It~~ pumps the oxygen-rich blood through the body.

3. Pronouns can be used more than once to refer to a single noun. However, after two or three pronouns, writers usually use the noun again.

   When <u>babies</u> are born, *they* begin to cry. As *they* cry, *they* have to take great gulps of air into *their* lungs. In this way, <u>babies</u> survive the first few minutes of life.

To review pronouns and possessive adjectives, see Appendix IA, page 292.

Exercise 5

In the following passage, decide whether to fill in each blank with a pronoun or with the noun or noun phrase you see below the line.

The Telephone System

A telephone has the power to overcome the problem of distance by bringing people closer. When Ivan calls his girlfriend Tatiana back home, the telephone carries ____his____ voice to _____ ear by transforming
1. Ivan's   2. Tatiana's

sound waves and routing _____ through miles of wire and cable. When
3. the sound waves

_____ says *Hello* to _____, the microphone in _____
4. Ivan   5. Tatiana   6. Ivan's

phone changes the sound waves of _____ voice into electrical signals.
7. Ivan's

_____ are sent through the telephone wire to a digital switch in
8. The signals

_____ area where _____ become digitalized. _____ are
9. Ivan's   10. the signals   11. The signals

then sent by copper wires or fiber optic cables to a conversion station in the

town where _____ lives. Because _____ uses a cell phone,
12. Tatiana   13. Tatiana

_____ call is then routed to _____ cellular telephone company
14. Ivan's   15. Tatiana's

office, which sends _____ to the nearby telephone towers. _____
16. the call signal   17. The towers

beam a signal out to all the cell phones in _____ area. When
18. Tatiana's

_____ phone detects _____, one of the towers then transmits the
19. Tatiana's   20. the signal

call in the form of radio waves. Just seconds after _____ says *Hello*,
21. Ivan

_____ replies. _____ voice sounds as though _____ were
22. Tatiana   23. Tatiana's   24. Tatiana

next to _____. The telephone system makes distance much less
25. Ivan

troublesome and brings friends together.

Davis, J. H. (1997). Telephone service. In *McGraw-Hill encyclopedia of science and technology* (8th ed.) (Vol. 18) (pp. 189–197). New York: McGraw-Hill.

Skurzynski, G. (1992). *Get the message: Telecommunications in your high-tech world.* New York: Bradbury.

With your teacher and classmates, review the changes you made. In some situations, either a noun or pronoun may be used. When you find differences in your answers, discuss why you would prefer either a noun or a pronoun.

> **Review and Revise 1: Using Pronouns**
> Check your draft to see if you have used pronouns correctly. If you need to make changes in your use of pronouns, make them now.

Guidelines for Avoiding Redundancy

1. When you are defining a word, do not repeat that word or use any form of it in the definition.

   make it easy to comb
   A conditioner is a product that people put on their hair to ~~condition it~~.

2. Make sure every sentence gives some new information. If a sentence does not contain sufficient new information, delete it, add information to it, or combine it with another sentence.

   Removing the oil leaves negative electrical charges in hair. ~~There are negative electrical charges in hair after it is shampooed~~. Conditioner puts positive electrical charges back into the hair.

   cells that produce the hair are located
   Hair grows from the roots. The roots are where the ~~hair growth takes place~~.

   Fortunately, hair grows five inches a year, so a bad haircut grows out quickly.
   ~~Hair grows five inches a year. That is fortunate. A bad haircut grows out quickly~~.

3. To avoid repeating a noun or noun phrase, use a demonstrative adjective (*this, that, these,* and *those*) with a synonym or related word.

   This substance
   Hair color is determined by the amount of melanin it contains. ~~Melanin~~ also determines skin color.

4. Use conjunctions to combine short sentences, show logical relationships, and avoid repeating subjects and verbs.

   Shampoo contains foaming agents, fragrance, and color.
   ~~Shampoo contains foaming agents. It contains fragrance. It contains color~~.

   Shampoo doesn't contain ordinary soap but detergents.
   ~~Shampoo doesn't contain ordinary soap. Shampoo contains detergents~~.

In the examples in Guideline 4, the subjects and the verbs were omitted from the added clauses when the sentences were combined. Omitting repeated words and phrases is known as **ellipsis**. We use ellipsis with the coordinating conjunctions *and, but, or,* and *nor.* Here are some more examples:

Dark-haired people have about 200,000 hairs on their heads, but redheads have only about 170,000 ~~hairs on their heads~~.

When you brush ~~your hair~~ or ~~when you~~ comb your hair, you remove positive electrical charges.

For more on ellipsis, see Appendix IA, page 286.

Bleaches and dyes are not good for hair, nor are permanents ~~good for hair~~.

Exercise 6

The following essay has some inappropriate repetition. Cross out the unnecessary words, phrases, or sentences. When needed, complete the revision by replacing them with pronouns or synonyms or by combining sentences.

Germs

1   [1]The majority of living things on Earth are too small to see without a microscope. [2]They are called *microorganisms*, which means small ~~organisms~~ living things. [3]Countless tiny single-celled creatures are in the ground. [4]They are in the water. [5]They are in the air. [6]There are one trillion of them in our bodies and on our bodies. [7]For the most part, they do not cause us any trouble, and some are even beneficial to us. [8]But a few microorganisms can make us sick, and we call the microorganisms that make us sick *germs*.

2   [9]The term *germ* actually refers to many different kinds of microorganisms, but bacteria and viruses are the most common. [10]In fact, there are many other types. [11]Scientists have classified germs a number of ways, but for the average person, the most practical way to categorize germs is according to how germs spread from person to person and transmit disease. [12]Germs can be transmitted several ways.

3   [13]Many germs are transmitted by person-to-person contact. [14]According to microbiologist Dr. Philip Tierno (2001), 80 percent of all infectious diseases are transmitted by touch (p. 13). [15]This happens if we have contact with someone who is carrying germs or if we handle something that an infected person has touched. [16]Dr. Tierno (2001) writes, "Common cold, flu, and stomach viruses, for example, can live on the fingertips for hours, and they can survive on the surfaces of objects for days" (p. 89). [17]Fortunately, there are some precautions we can take to prevent catching illnesses this way. [18]If we are near someone who is sick, we should clean any surfaces that might have germs on them, such as telephones, doorknobs, or tabletops, and wash our hands frequently. [19]Hand washing, above all, is necessary.

4   [20]Germs are also spread through the air when an infected person sneezes, coughs, or talks. [21]Cold viruses can survive in the air for hours. [22]Flu viruses can survive in the air for hours. [23]In intemperate climates, people get sick more often in winter because people spend most of their time indoors with their windows closed. [24]We can prevent contracting air-borne germs by remembering the following precautions. [25]If someone in the household is ill, we should open the windows and ventilate the home. [26]We can remind people who have a cold or the flu to cover their mouths and noses when they sneeze or when they cough.

5   [27]Another way that germs can be spread is by insects. [28]Mosquitoes, ticks, and fleas can carry germs. [29]Mosquitoes carry yellow fever, encephalitis, and malaria. [30]Ticks can carry Lyme disease, and fleas can transmit plague. [31]To protect ourselves against insect-borne diseases, we need to find out which insects in our area may transmit a disease, what the symptoms of the disease are, and how to prevent insect bites.

6   [32]Water can also carry infectious diseases. [33]The most serious problems occur where there is standing water, such as in air-conditioning systems, or where water is contaminated by sewage. [34]When people drink sewage-contaminated water, they are exposed to various water-borne germs that cause diarrhea. [35]Diarrhea can be fatal. [36]If you think your water may be contaminated, have your water tested. [37]In addition, you should boil water that you are not sure is safe. [38]Or you can chemically treat it.

7   [39]Food is another potential source of germs. [40]The *salmonella bacterium*, which occurs in raw eggs and chicken, and *E. coli*, which can be present in beef and unpasteurized milk, can cause stomach and intestinal problems. [41]To protect yourself against stomach and intestinal problems, store food properly; cook eggs, poultry, and meat thoroughly; and wash utensils and cutting boards that come in contact with raw eggs, chicken, and meat with hot, soapy water.

8 [42]Germs have been on the planet over 3.5 billion years, and they are not going to go away. [43]We will never remove them from our bodies or our homes. [44]Our best defense against the diseases germs can cause is to learn where the microorganisms occur and how to prevent infection. [45]That way, we can protect ourselves and our families.

Bakalar, N. (2003). *Where the germs are: A scientific safari*. New York: Wiley.

Tierno, P. (2001). *The secret life of germs: Observations and lessons from a microbe hunter*. New York: Pocket Books, Simon and Schuster.

Stolar, M. W. (2002). Disease. *The World Book encyclopedia* (Vol. 5) (pp. 225–234).

Discuss the revisions you have made with your classmates and teacher.

Review and Revise 2: Avoiding Redundancy
Look at the repeated words and phrases in your paragraph or essay, distinguishing between the necessary repetition that improves cohesion and any unnecessary repetition. If you find any redundancy, remove it and revise.

Language Focus

Using outside sources as support. You have learned that using the words and ideas of other people in your writing without giving them credit is plagiarism, and plagiarism is considered dishonest and is not tolerated in academic and professional writing. Therefore, when you use source material to support the points you want to make, you have to decide how to present it. Here are the rules you have to follow.

1. Use quotations or paraphrase and cite the author in the text when the information contains the author's own ideas and opinions, little-known facts that do not appear in other sources, or statistics. (Paraphrase the language that introduces the statistics. Do not change the facts or numbers.)

2. Use paraphrase but no citation when the information contains general knowledge or information that is available in other books.

3. Avoid long quotations of more than two or three sentences and using too many quotes. Quotes should make up no more than 10 percent of your paper and should not be used in your thesis statement or the topic sentences of your body paragraphs.

Exercise 7

Read these statements from outside sources. Write *citation* or *no citation (general knowledge)* after each statement, following the previous rules. Then compare your answers with a partner's. Discuss the reason for each answer with your classmates and teacher.

1. Yeast is a single-celled organism that bakers put into dough to make it rise (Ashe, 2004).

   <u>no citation (general knowledge)</u>

2. Both bread and wine are made by yeasts (Kohn, 1969).

   _____

3. Yeast not only leavens dough but gives it a characteristic flavor (McGee, 1984).

   _____

4. Yeast fungi lack chlorophyll, the green matter that green plants use to make their own food. Therefore, yeasts must rely on other sources for food. They feed on sugar from a variety of natural sources, including fruit, grain, and nectar, and also from molasses (Ashe, 2004).

   _____

5. Starch is by far the major component of flour, accounting for about 70 percent of its weight (McGee, 1984).

   _____

6. And in yeast-raised breads, damaged starch granules—from 10 to 35 percent of the total—are attacked by starch-breaking malt enzymes, which convert them into sugars that the yeast cells can use as food (McGee, 1984).

   _____

7. The ideal water temperature for yeast growth is between 105° and 110° F, just a little warmer than body temperature (Dackman, 1983/1984).

   _____

8. Bread dough is very hard to mix. You have to knead it instead (Kohn, 1969).

   _____

9. Although domestic bread-making techniques have changed very little over the centuries, the proportion of bread baked in the home has fallen off drastically (McGee, 1984).

Ashe, A. J., III. (2004). Yeast. *World Book online reference center*. Retrieved June 5, 2004, from http://0-www.worldbookonline.com.marinet.lib.ca.us:80/wb/Article?id=ar613160.

Dackman, L. (1983/1984, Winter). On the rise. *The Exploratorium Magazine: Cooking*, 7(4), 19–21.

Kohn, B. (1969). *Our tiny servants: Molds and yeasts*. Englewood Cliffs, NJ: Prentice-Hall.

McGee, H. (1984). *On food and cooking: The science and lore of the kitchen*. New York: Scribner's.

Paraphrasing strategies. Paraphrasing means changing the vocabulary and grammar of a statement while keeping the original meaning. A good paraphrase is usually about as long as the original sentence.

Remember that to paraphrase successfully, you need to change a sentence as many ways as possible. Therefore, the following seven examples, which show only one type of change, are not good paraphrases. In fact, they are examples of plagiarism.

As a first step to learning how to paraphrase well, study the seven following strategies one by one. Then, do Exercise 8, which will show you good paraphrases, ones that have more than one change.

1. Use synonyms or synonymous phrases.

    ORIGINAL: Germs are everywhere.

    PARTIAL PARAPHRASE: Potentially harmful microorganisms are everywhere.

2. Change the form of words.

    ORIGINAL: Storing food properly is important.

    PARTIAL PARAPHRASE: Proper food storage is important.

3. Change the grammar. This often means changing the order of parts of the sentence. For example, the subject can be moved, and phrases and clauses can be shifted. It can also mean changing from singular to plural.

    ORIGINAL: Bacteria, molds, and yeast cause food spoilage.

    PARTIAL PARAPHRASE: Food spoilage is caused by bacteria, molds, and yeast.

    ORIGINAL: When food is frozen, most microorganisms in it die.

    PARTIAL PARAPHRASE: Most microorganisms in food die when it is frozen.

    ORIGINAL: Molds are able to grow under refrigeration.

    PARTIAL PARAPHRASE: A mold is able to grow under refrigeration.

4. Change the point of view. For example, if the subject of the sentence is *you*, change the subject to *we*, or use an impersonal subject such as *it* or *there*.

ORIGINAL: You can kill microorganisms in soup by boiling.

PARTIAL PARAPHRASE: We can kill microorganisms in soup by boiling.

PARTIAL PARAPHRASE: It is possible to kill microorganisms in soup by boiling.

5. Omit any unnecessary words or phrases that do not contribute to the meaning.

ORIGINAL: The earliest method of food preservation was drying, which means removing up to 99 percent of the moisture in food.

PARTIAL PARAPHRASE: The earliest method of food preservation was drying.

6. Change conjunctions and transition words.

ORIGINAL: Refrigeration slows the growth of microorganisms. However, it does not kill them.

PARTIAL PARAPHRASE: Refrigeration slows the growth of microorganisms, but it does not kill them.

7. Divide long sentences, or combine short sentences. Combining sentences may involve omitting unnecessary words or phrases.

ORIGINAL: Sometimes we cannot detect dangerous bacteria in food, so we should discard food that has passed its expiration date or is no longer fresh. For example, *Clostridium botulinum*, which causes the disease called botulism, may be present without changing the appearance, smell, or taste of food.

PARTIAL PARAPHRASE: Sometimes we cannot detect dangerous bacteria in food such as *Clostridium botulinum*, which causes the disease called botulism, so we should discard food that has passed its expiration date or is no longer fresh.

Exercise 8

Study the following paraphrases and identify the strategy or strategies used from the preceding paraphrasing strategies list.

Source Material

Paraphrase

1. The common kitchen measurement we call temperature is an indicator of molecular motion: The higher the temperature, the faster the food molecules are moving, and the more likely they are to be changed when they collide with each other (McGee, 1984).

   Temperature indicates the motion of molecules: The hotter food is, the more rapidly its molecules are moving, and the more rapidly the molecules move, the more likely they are to undergo change when they bump into each other (McGee, 1984).

   Paraphrasing strategy/strategies: _The writer omitted unnecessary words (the common kitchen measurement); used a different word form (indicator→indicate); and used four synonyms (molecular motion→ the motion of molecules; higher temperature→hotter; faster→more rapidly; to be changed→to undergo change; and collide with→bump into)._

2. Radiation, convection, and conduction are the three principal means of transferring heat from a hotter object to a colder one (Hillman, 1981).

   The three main ways of moving heat from a hotter object to a cooler one are radiation, convection, and conduction (Hillman, 1981).

   Paraphrasing strategy/strategies: _____
   _____
   _____
   _____

3. Most cooking simultaneously involves two, or all three, of these processes (Hillman, 1981).

   Cooking usually includes more than one of these processes (Hillman, 1981).

   Paraphrasing strategy/strategies: _____
   _____
   _____
   _____

4. Radiant heat is transferred in the form of electromagnetic waves or particles from a hot object, such as the heating element of your broiler or toaster, to food (Hillman, 1981).

   In radiation, heat moves as electromagnetic waves or particles from something that is hot, like the heat source in a broiler or toaster, to food (Hillman, 1981).

Paraphrasing strategy/strategies: _____

_____

_____

_____

5. Convection is the transfer of heat by the movement of a heated material (Cezairliyan, 2003).

Transferring heat by the movement of a heated material is called *convection* (Cezairliyan, 2003).

Paraphrasing strategy/strategies: _____

_____

_____

_____

6. For example, convection currents will form in a pan of cold water on a hot stove. As the water near the bottom of the pan warms up and expands, it becomes lighter than the cold water near the top of the pan. This cold water sinks and forces the heated water to the top (Cezairliyan, 2003).

There are convection currents in a pan of cold water heating over a stove. When the water near the bottom of the pan is heated and expands, it becomes lighter than the cooler water near the top. Thus, the cooler water sinks, pushing the heated water to the top (Cezairliyan, 2003).

Paraphrasing strategy/strategies: _____

_____

_____

_____

_____

_____

7. In the technique called baking, we surround the food with a hot enclosure, the oven, and rely on a combination of radiation from the walls and, to a lesser extent, air convection to heat the food (McGee, 1984).

When food is baked, it is warmed by heat that is radiated from the sides of the oven and, to a lesser degree, air convection (McGee, 1984).

Paraphrasing strategy/strategies: _____

_____

_____

_____

8. Conduction is the movement of heat through a material (Cezairliyan, 2003).

When heat moves through a material, the process is called conduction (Cezairliyan, 2003).

Paraphrasing strategy/strategies: _____

_____

_____

9. Pan-frying a fish exemplifies this principle. The heat of the flame is transferred—on a molecule-to-molecule basis—first through the pan, then through the thin oil layer, and finally through the fish (Hillman, 1981).

In pan-frying a fish—an example of conduction—the heat of the flame moves directly through the pan and the oil in it and finally through the fish (Hillman, 1981).

Paraphrasing strategy/strategies: _____

_____

_____

_____

_____

Cezairliyan, A. (2003). Heat. *World Book online reference center*. Retrieved August 31, 2003, from http://0 www.worldbookonline.com.marinet.lib.ca.us:80/ar?/na/ar/co/ar250080.htm

Hillman, H., with Loring, L. (1981). *Kitchen science: A compendium of essential information for every cook*. Boston: Houghton Mifflin.

McGee, H. (1984). *On food and cooking: The science and lore of the kitchen*. New York: Scribner's.

Exercise 9

With a partner or a small group, paraphrase the following sentences on another piece of paper, using the strategies listed on pages 222–223.

1. Because nutrition is a matter of finding and ingesting particular chemical compounds, the sense of taste has been a necessity from the very beginnings of life (McGee, 1984).

   To get proper nutrition, people must find and eat certain chemical compounds, so the ability to taste has been vital throughout history (McGee, 1984).

2. It appears that almost all of our preferences and aversions in the area of food are learned: That is, we must find out by experience what constitutes acceptable food (McGee, 1984).

3. The taste buds on our tongues can detect the presence of a few basic tastes, including sweet, sour, bitter, and *umami* (Schlosser, 2001).

4. *Umami* is a taste discovered by Japanese researchers—the savory flavor of meat, shellfish, soy sauce, and mushrooms (Schlosser, 2001).

5. The taste buds on the tongue offer a limited means of detection, however, compared with the human olfactory system, which can perceive thousands of different chemical aromas (Schlosser, 2001).

6. The aroma of a food can be responsible for as much as 90 percent of its taste (Schlosser, 2001).

7. The flavor industry emerged in the mid-nineteenth century, as processed foods began to be manufactured, but did not assume its key role in the food economy until the mid-twentieth century, when fast-food restaurants caught on with the public (Schlosser, 2001).

8. The canning, freezing, and dehydrating techniques used in processing destroy most of food's flavor—and so a vast industry has arisen to make processed food palatable (Schlosser, 2001).

9. Complex aromas, such as those of coffee and roasted meat, are composed of volatile gases from nearly 1,000 different chemicals (Schlosser, 2001).

10. Flavor compounds often contain more ingredients than the foods to which they give taste (Schlosser, 2001).

11. Artificial strawberry flavor, for example, contains about forty-four ingredients (Schlosser, 2001).

12. In addition, flavor compounds can mask flavors that are undesirable or give the perception of fat on the tongue in low-fat or non-fat foods (United).

Adapted from H. McGee. (1984). *On food and cooking: The science and lore of the kitchen.* pp. 561–562. New York: Scribner's.

Adapted from E. Schlosser. (2001, January). Why McDonald's fries taste so good. *Atlantic Monthly,* 50–56.

Adapted from United Soybean Board. Panel Discussion in Talksoy.com with Robert Nelson, Senior Food Scientist, Flavors of North America. Retrieved June 21, 2004, from http://www.talksoy.com/Health/t98Symposium4.htm

Paraphrasing and plagiarism. You have no doubt found that paraphrasing is hard work. Paraphrasing scientific writing is especially challenging. There are no synonyms for some scientific terms such as *atom* and *molecule.* Furthermore, scientific writing is very precise, and therefore, when you paraphrase, you must be especially careful not to change the original meaning.

Exercise 10

On the left is an original paragraph, and on the right is a paraphrase of it which contains five instances of plagiarism. Find and underline the plagiarism, and then eliminate it by paraphrasing. Paraphrasing someone else's whole paragraph in your own work is not a good practice. When you use someone else's ideas without acknowledging your source, you are plagiarizing.

Original Paragraph

[1]If there were no water on Earth, there would be no life. [2]Scientists now believe that life originated in the water of the oceans, and the bodies of all living things are made up mainly of water. [3]It is because of the extraordinary properties of water that our planet has been able to sustain life. [4]To better understand this, we must look at the molecular characteristics of water. [5]The water molecule is shaped like a V, with a single hydrogen atom in the center and a pair of oxygen atoms attached to it. [6]Because the hydrogen atom has a positive electrical charge and the two oxygen atoms have a negative electrical charge, there is a strong attraction between water molecules. [7]Consequently, water does not become a gas too quickly when the temperature increases, and it can move through the bodies of living things. [8]Another consequence of water's unique balance of positive and negative charges is that it can

Paraphrase Containing Some Plagiarism

[1]Life would not be possible on Earth without water. [2]According to scientists, life ~~originated in the water of the oceans~~, and the bodies of all living things consist largely of water. [3]Life on this planet has continued to exist because of the extraordinary properties of water. [4]This becomes clear when one considers the molecular traits of water. [5]The V-shaped water molecule has one hydrogen atom in the middle with two oxygen atoms attached to it. [6]The hydrogen atom is positively charged and the two oxygen atoms are negatively charged, so there is a strong attraction between water molecules. [7]Therefore, water does not vaporize too quickly when the temperature increases, and it can move around inside living organisms. [8]A second effect of water's special arrangement of positive and negative charges is that almost anything can dissolve in it. [9]To

started in the seas

dissolve almost anything. [9]For example, the positively charged sodium atoms in salt are attracted to the negatively charged oxygen atoms in water. [10]Therefore, salt remains suspended in water. [11]This is why ocean water is salty. [12]Because water has this capacity to dissolve things, all the substances in the bodies of living things float in it. [13]The chemical transformations of life are possible due to water.

illustrate, there is an attraction between salt's positively charged sodium atoms and water's negatively charged oxygen atoms. [10]Therefore, salt remains suspended in water. [11]This is why the oceans are salty. [12]Water's ability to dissolve things means that every substance in the body of a living organism can hang suspended in it. [13]Water makes possible the chemistry of life.

Cole, K. C. (1982, Summer). The incredible everyday physics of water. *Exploratorium Magazine,* 6(2), 8–15.

Kalumuck, K. E. (2001, Summer). Water: The liquid of life. *Exploratorium Magazine,* 25(2), 8–24.

Compare your paraphrases with a partner's. If you have questions about your paraphrases, discuss them with your teacher and classmates.

> **Review and Revise 3: Use of Outside Sources as Support**
> If you included information from outside sources in your extended definition, check your writing to make sure that you have not plagiarized. If you are not sure, write your teacher a note on your paper. Make sure that you have used correct in-text and end-of-text citations. If you did not make use of outside sources, make sure that your paper is adequately developed. If you feel that your paper is underdeveloped, you may want to do some research now.

PEER REVIEW AND FINAL DRAFT

Now it is time to share your composition with readers. Exchange papers with one or two classmates. Read each other's papers carefully. Turn to page 339 in Appendix II, and fill out the Peer Review form.

After considering your classmates' suggestions, prepare a final draft of your composition to hand in to your teacher. Before handing your paper in, proofread it carefully for spelling, grammar, punctuation, and cohesion.

CHAPTER REVIEW

Look back at what you have accomplished in Chapter 8. Check (✓) what you have learned and what you have used as you have written and revised your essay.

Chapter 8 Topics	I understand this	I have used this
writing a one-sentence, classification-type definition (page 207)		
writing an extended definition using dictionary definitions, word origins, negation, and various rhetorical strategies (description, narration, example, cause and effect, comparison/contrast, and process) (pages 207–208)		
using pronouns correctly (page 215)		
distinguishing between necessary repetition that improves cohesion and redundancy; omitting redundancy (pages 217–218)		
knowing when to cite a source and how to paraphrase (pages 220 and 222–223)		

From School to Work

◆ **Writing an Argumentative Essay**

When young people start to work, they assume the role of adults. Preparation for this important step is critical for both youth and their society. In this chapter, we will look at some of the choices people face as they proceed from school to work and ask what society should do for them to make their transition successful.

This chapter will help you

- plan and write an argumentative essay.
- limit, define, and analyze your topic.
- present and respond to opposing points of view.
- use qualifiers to avoid overgeneralizing.

READING FOR WRITING

Before You Read

A. You are going to read two argumentative essays about high school education. First, reflect on your own opinions about what high schools should do to prepare youth for the future. Mark each opinion statement *A* (agree) or *D* (disagree). Then follow the directions for a group discussion.

_____ 1. All high school students should have an opportunity to prepare for college if they choose to make that their goal.

_____ 2. High schools should give extra help to students who have been disadvantaged by poverty or racial discrimination so that they can better compete with students who have had more advantages.

_____ 3. High schools should respond to the needs of the economy and train students for the kinds of jobs that will be available to them.

With a small group of classmates, choose one of the statements above, and discuss what it means. All of you should then express your opinions about the statement and explain why you have that point of view.

B. Each of the following two argumentative essays contains a description of a program developed for high school students, a main argument about that program, and supporting arguments (reasons why readers should accept the main argument). As you read each essay, look for the main and the supporting arguments. After you finish each reading, write the arguments on the lines that follow.

sorcery: magic

apprenticeship: a job an employee takes, usually at low pay, in order to learn an occupation

The Sorcery° of Apprenticeship°

By Wilfried Prewo

1   In order to succeed in today's global economy, a nation must have an educated labor force and must help its young people make a smooth transition from school to work. The German economy today is productive despite high taxes and high labor costs largely because of one outstanding factor: a highly skilled labor force. That labor force is largely the product of systematic youth training: Some 65% of the employed persons in Germany are certified graduates of the nation's youth training system. Currently, German teenagers leaving school may choose among apprenticeship programs that will prepare them for a solid future in some 350 occupations.

2   An advantage of the German apprenticeship system—and the key to its success—is that training is based in the workplace. The 67% of German teenagers who enter apprenticeship programs spend four days a week at their training company and one day in public vocational school. This means that changes in workplace technology are included in the training immediately. The system is organized and operated by city and regional chambers of industry and commerce in partnership with private companies. Apart from states funding schools and federal law setting broad guidelines, government is not involved. The chambers of industry and commerce register the apprenticeship contracts, certify training companies, regulate and supervise the program, settle disputes, establish examination boards staffed by volunteers, organize midterm and final exams (88% pass), and issue certificates recognized all over Germany and, increasingly, across Europe.

3   A second advantage of the German apprenticeship program is that it offers a smooth transition from school to training to work. Many teenagers have strong doubts about the relevance of high-school classroom work. In the workplace, young apprentices discover the pleasure of accomplishing something, and, no less important, they are among adult workers, so they have models to imitate. The reward for their successful work is a clear one—after certification, a quadrupling° of their paychecks. Contrast this with the directionless wandering from minimum-wage job to minimum-wage job of many American high-school graduates. At age 25, Americans who have not attended college often find themselves no higher up the job ladder than they were at age 18. Their German counterparts, by contrast, usually hold well-paying skilled jobs.

quadrupling: increasing by a factor of four

4   An additional benefit of the program is that money is not wasted on unnecessary training. Americans, by comparison, have traditionally wanted a college education for their children. An important factor in the German success, though, is recognizing that college is not always the answer. Many jobs, in fact, do not call for a costly college education. The American pro-college bent often yields over-qualified and directionless people: For example, an individual trained as a biologist may work as a chemistry lab assistant. In Germany, a lab assistant is a person trained as such. There's no wasteful academic detour°. The German system, however, does not close the door on education. In their late 20s, many of the apprentices enroll in further training to advance in their fields. In 2000, 54,331 Germans passed exams to become supervisors. The cream of the alumni° crop° then trains the apprentices in the workplace.

detour: an alternate route that is longer than the usual route

alumni (pl.): people who have finished a school or training program

the cream of the crop: the best people in the group

5   Another positive outcome of the system is that it strengthens the tradition of internal advancement. Hillmar Kopper, the former chief executive of Deutsche Bank, the largest in Germany, does not have a university degree.

He joined his bank after high school as an apprentice. Juergen Schrempp, the current chief executive of DaimlerChrysler, started there as a mechanics apprentice.

6   Finally, youth training is good unemployment insurance. In Germany, youth unemployment is below the general jobless rate, a relationship that is the reverse in most other countries. In 2002, unemployment among those with occupational training was 1.4% below the general unemployment rate.

7   Training does, however, cost dearly. In 2000, German companies spent some 28 billion Euro (about $32 billion U.S.) to train apprentices. Subtracting the contribution of the apprentices to an output of 13 billion Euro ($15 billion U.S.), the net cost was 15 billion Euro ($17 billion U.S.) or 8,700 Euro ($10,000 U.S.) per apprentice. But for industry, this is a worthwhile investment because it promises lower turnover°.

8   Germany, of course, is not the only mass model; Denmark, Austria, and Switzerland also have good systems. While not every detail of these systems can be transposed to America, a country whose companies would probably require a substantial tax credit to be persuaded to undertake° training in significant numbers, the U.S. administration should set a national framework, offer tax credits and, on the state or local level, provide vocational schools.

turnover: the number of employees who leave a company and need to be replaced

undertake: to start to do a piece of work

About the Author

Wilfried Prewo is chief executive of the Chamber of Industry and Commerce in the city of Hanover, Germany. In this position, he oversees a large apprenticeship program. Dr. Prewo, who grew up in Germany, received an M.A. and a Ph.D. in economics at Johns Hopkins University in Baltimore, Maryland.

Outline

Main Argument: _____

_____

Supporting Argument 1: _____

_____

Supporting Argument 2: _____

_____

Supporting Argument 3: _____

_____

Supporting Argument 4: _____

_____

Supporting Argument 5: _____

_____

McDonald's or IBM?

By Damien Jackson

1 Education policies have been changing in the United States in response to an increasingly competitive global marketplace. In the state of North Carolina, educational reform has led to harsh new policies which have had harmful effects on many students.

2 North Carolina recently implemented° a new policy asking eighth graders to choose one of four high school "pathways." The courses they take in one of the pathways will prepare them either to attend a four-year college or university, to enter a community or technical college, or directly to enter the job market upon graduation. The fourth is a program for disabled students. Once students select their pathways, they must fulfill their particular requirements to receive a high school diploma. A parent's signature is required on the selection form.

3 The pathways program and similar policies are the latest in a series of events in a reform movement begun two decades ago when a national commission° concluded that education in the United States was in crisis. The commission declared that there was "a rising tide of mediocrity°" in public education that threatened the future of the nation. It also suggested that business-minded experts who understood the demands of the competitive marketplace could make useful recommendations to improve education. North Carolina's pathways program was created by the state's Education Standard and Accountability Commission, which is largely composed of corporate leaders. The problem with the pathways program and others like it is that it focuses on creating employees, not on educating human beings.

4 A major problem with the pathways program is the age at which students are required to make decisions about their future. For most students, eighth grade is an awkward and uncertain time of physical and emotional change. Few eighth-grade students are mature enough to recognize their individual talents or plan their futures. "I cannot see how this will not be a disaster," says Dr. Charles Payne, a professor of African-American Studies and History at Duke University who studies urban educational policy. "You're asking kids in eighth grade to make a decision that's going to greatly impact the remainder of their lives," he adds, one they "cannot possibly understand the consequences of." Given that college students change majors several times before graduating and that adults change occupations almost as frequently, isn't it too much to ask adolescents to make a life-defining decision at the age of thirteen or fourteen?

5 Also of concern is the effect on kids who have aspirations° to attend a four-year college but who are not in good academic standing in middle school. Mary Phillips High School in Raleigh, N.C., specializes in teaching

---

implement: to make a plan or policy happen

commission: a group of people with the official responsibility to perform a certain task

mediocrity: the quality of being no better than average

aspiration: a hope to achieve something

instrumental: important in making something happen

to be hit hard: to be very negatively affected

implicit: suggested without being stated directly

marginalize: to make a group of people unimportant or powerless

kids with family or emotional problems who didn't perform well in elementary or middle school. "It's going to have a big impact on our kids," says Loretha Peacock, a guidance counselor at Phillips. The students at Phillips are usually behind in credits when they arrive, making it unlikely that they will be able to complete the requirements of the university preparation course of study in four years. "I'm hoping that guidance counselors will steer kids towards college," says Rukiya Dillahunt, an assistant principal at Phillips High, but she fears that many won't.

6   Dr. June Atkinson, Director of Instructional Services for the North Carolina Department of Public Instruction, who was instrumental° in writing the new policy, also says guidance counselors should encourage students to take the most challenging courses they can, and then, if necessary, switch to a less demanding course of study later. However, it is not easy to transfer from one pathway to another. For example, a student who fails to meet the requirements of the university preparatory pathway and transfers to the two-year college course of study will have to make up four credits in a career/technical field that the university prep pathway does not include.

7   Many people feel that minority populations will be hit especially hard° by the new policy. "African-American and Latino kids are commonly tracked into lower level math classes," says Daniella Cook, who analyzes education policy for the Common Sense Foundation in Raleigh, North Carolina. The former teacher says this is because minority students' schools often have fewer resources, and less qualified teachers, and these students face language barriers and discrimination. Cook is concerned that the new policy "will lock out a whole generation of Black and Latino kids from four-year colleges." Ms. Peacock predicts that the new policy will cause more minority students to drop out of high school in a state where the dropout rate for minority students is already high. Idola Scimeca, the mother of a 16-year-old junior at Durham's Jordan High, wonders about the implicit° message of the pathways program. She feels that these measures are being used to marginalize° minority students. She says, "It's like they're categorizing these kids by eighth grade and telling some, 'you're going to work at IBM, and you're going to work at McDonald's.'"

About the Author

Damien Jackson writes for *The Independent Weekly,* a newspaper in Durham, North Carolina. In his columns, he writes about race and poverty in the United States including issues in education that affect minority students, such as testing and tracking (grouping students according to ability level). Mr. Jackson wrote "McDonald's or IBM?" as a fellow (a journalist awarded special financial and professional support) of the Independent Press Association. This story was produced under the George Washington Williams fellowship, a project sponsored by the Independent Press Association. "McDonald's or IBM?" originally appeared in the Winter 2002/2003 issue of *Rethinking Schools.*

Outline

Main Argument: _____

_____

Supporting Argument 1: _____

_____

Supporting Argument 2: _____

_____

Supporting Argument 3: _____

_____

Supporting Argument 4: _____

_____

Understanding the Readings

With a partner or a small group, discuss the following questions.

1. Mark the paragraphs in Prewo's essay that describe the apprenticeship program in Germany and the paragraphs in Jackson's essay that describe the pathways program in North Carolina.

2. Review the main and supporting arguments of each essay. Discuss which individual supporting arguments you think are strong and which you think are weak. (A strong argument is a **persuasive**, or believable, argument—you do not have to agree with it to see that it is strong.) Discuss which essay has a stronger set of arguments *overall*.

3. Note what kind of development the authors have used for each supporting argument. In the margin next to the sentences that develop each supporting argument, write *facts, explanation, example, cause-and-effect reasoning, comparison,* or *citing an authority*. (An **authority** is a knowledgeable person whose ideas can be quoted or paraphrased as a means of support.) What kind of development does each author favor? What kind of development do you think makes an argument strongest?

4. Do Prewo and Jackson include opposing points of view or criticisms of their argument in these essays? If so, write *opposing view* in the margin where the opposing views appear, and write *response* next to the author's reply. Then discuss whether you think the author's response is persuasive.

5. Arguments often contain **implicit** (suggested, but not clearly stated) opinions or beliefs. Which of the following opinions are implicit in Prewo's essay, and which are implicit in Jackson's essay? Mark them *P* or *J*.

_____ a. The purpose of education is not to enrich people intellectually or spiritually, but to prepare them for work.

_____ b. Schools should help individual students create the best possible future for themselves rather than help the business community train workers for certain types of jobs.

_____ c. Workers care more about income and job security than the status associated with a job or the pleasure they get from doing it.

_____ d. Schools should try to increase equality in society and should not do anything that will cause a wider gap between people who already have advantages and people who are disadvantaged.

_____ e. Business's need for workers with certain specific skills should not influence the development of high school programs.

_____ f. Healthy competition assures that the most gifted go to college. Those who are less gifted should not be encouraged to aim for higher education.

6. Do you agree fully or in part with either essay? Which main and supporting arguments do you agree with, and why? Which of the implicit arguments do you agree with?

Vocabulary Expansion

Words with a positive or negative meaning. In an argumentative essay, words that have a positive or negative meaning can express the writer's attitude. For example, Prewo tells us that the German labor force is an *outstanding* factor in the country's productivity (*positive judgment*), and Jackson tells us that education reform in North Carolina has been *harsh* (*negative judgment*). Many such words are adjectives, but nouns such as *advantage,* verbs such as *fail,* and adverbs such as *remarkably* also convey positive or negative attitude.

Negative prefixes. Many positive words can be made negative by adding prefixes that have a negative meaning. For example, *dis-* can be added to *agreement* to make a word that has the opposite meaning, *disagreement.* Some negative prefixes are shown in the following chart.

For more on prefixes, see Appendix IA, page 310.

Prefix	Meaning	Comes Before	Example
dis-	the opposite of, not	consonants and vowels	disadvantage
il-	not	l	illogical
im-	not	b, m, or p	immature
in-	not	consonants and vowels	inability
ir-	not	r	irrational
mal-	bad, badly	consonants and vowels	maladjustment
mis-	wrongly	consonants and vowels	misuse
un-	not	consonants and vowels (add only to adjectives, including participial adjectives)	unskilled

Exercise 1

Choose the appropriate forms of the words from the list in each box to complete each paragraph. For each word you choose, decide whether to use a negative prefix, and decide which suffix to use. (If you are not sure of the part of speech of a suffix, check your dictionary.) In some cases, more than one answer may be possible.

A.

> (dis)respect, -ful, -fully   (mal)function
>
> (im)patient, -ce, -ly   (un)selective, -ly, -ity
>
> (in)adequate, -ly

I think the hardest job I ever had was at the bicycle factory. The supervisor spoke (1) ___disrespectfully___ to the employees. He said, "Hey, you!" instead of calling us by name. When we didn't know what to do, he never showed us. If someone asked him a question, he responded (2) _____, "I can't spend all day holding your hand!" The owners didn't manage the factory very well either. They failed to maintain the equipment, so the machines would often (3) _____. They purchased inexpensive tools which were (4) _____ to do the job. From this experience, I learned to be more (5) _____ when I accept a job.

B.

(in)attentive, -ly, -ness	(mis)behavior
(in)sensitive, -ly, -ity	(mis)trust, -ful, -fully
(ir)responsible, -bly -bility	

My job in the child-care center was challenging. I was assigned to take care of sixteen energetic three-year-olds, and I had a lot to learn. At first I found them (6) _____ and unmanageable. They would not stop what they were doing and listen to me. But afterward I discovered that they would respond to me once they had learned to (7) _____ me. I also had to become skilled at handling (8) _____ so that I could prevent fights and accidents. Although this job was difficult, it taught me to be (9) _____ to children's feelings and assume (10) _____ for others.

C.

(dis)incentive	(un)predictable, -bly, -bility
(un)committed	(un)rewarding
(un)disciplined	

I think being a police officer is the perfect job for me. I love being part of an organization that is (11) _____ to public service and public safety. I respect my fellow officers. They are very highly trained and very (12) _____: Even in difficult, dangerous situations with (13) _____ people, they follow the procedures they have been taught. Finally, there are opportunities to advance in the ranks, so there is an (14) _____ for working hard. Overall, the job is very (15) _____.

WRITING

Before you select a topic for your argumentative essay, you do not need to have an opinion—you can formulate an opinion as you analyze your topic during prewriting. Be sure, however, that you can develop at least two persuasive supporting arguments to back up your opinion.

Assignment

1. Should high schools and two-year colleges offer vocational education?

2. Should schools provide moral education for youth, or should instruction in values be left to parents?

3. In college and university admissions procedures, should admissions officers consider whether applicants are disadvantaged by race or poverty when they decide whom to admit?

4. Should all public schools receive the same level of funding from the government?

5. Should young people be required to do community service?

What Argumentation Is and Why It Is Important

In previous writing assignments, your primary goal has been to give your audience information. However, in writing an argumentative essay you have to *persuade your audience to consider your point of view*, even if they may disagree with it. This requires some care and skill: You need to show respect for opposing points of view, you must choose vocabulary carefully, and, above all, you must write clearly and logically.

To prepare to write a logical argument, begin by defining and limiting the topic. Then explore opposing points of view and their supporting reasons before drafting your thesis statement.

Define the topic. Some topics require definition. For example, if your topic is *Should schools provide moral education?* you will have to explain what *moral education* means. You may find that some people define *moral education* as teaching students about values such as *honesty, kindness,* and *loyalty,* while others define it as teaching students how to make moral decisions. As a writer, you have to decide how *you* want to define a term. Check a dictionary or other sources to see how the term has been defined before, and then draft your own definition. Remember that you can change your definition as you write your paper. Be sure to record your sources because, if you use all or part of a published definition in your paper, you must include a citation.

Put a definition of an important term in the introduction of your essay if it will help readers understand your thesis. A definition can be any length—a phrase or clause, a single sentence, or several sentences.

Limit the topic. Some argumentative topics require limiting. For example, if your topic is *letter grades* and your thesis says *Teachers should not use letter grades,* readers may wonder whether you mean *all teachers at all levels from kindergarten through college* or *just certain teachers* should not use them. They may also wonder whether you would allow teachers to use letter grades if students or parents requested them. You can respond to such questions by adding limiting phrases to your thesis statement. The revised thesis, *Elementary school teachers should not* *assign letter grades to student work unless parents make a special request*, limits the topic to *elementary school* and states a condition, *unless parents make a special request*.

You will learn more about how to limit thesis statements and supporting arguments in the section on qualifiers in the Language Focus section of this chapter.

Analyze the topic. Before you decide upon a point of view, you should analyze the issue thoroughly. Most argumentative topics have two points of view, *for* and *against*, and can be stated as a yes/no question, such as *Should high school students work during the school year?* You can discuss a topic such as this with your classmates and friends to find out how those who answer yes support their opinion and how those who answer no support theirs. You can also research the topic on the Internet or in the library. Afterward, write down the two opinions, and list the reasons that support each one, as in the following examples.

OPINION: *High school students should work during the school year.*

> They can save for college.
> They can make new friends.
> They can learn responsibility.
> They may discover a career for themselves.

OPINION: *High school students should not work during the school year.*

> They can get better grades if they don't work.
> They can participate in extracurricular activities.

Before making a final decision about your *own* point of view about the topic, it is a good idea to evaluate the strength of the supporting reasons you have listed. A strong reason is one that is believable, relevant, and important. To test each reason on your lists, ask yourself these questions: *Is it true? Is it clearly connected to my topic? Does it matter, or does it have real consequences?* You should be able to answer *yes* to all three questions. (You can agree that a reason is strong without agreeing with the position it supports.) As you choose a point of view and write your thesis, make sure that your point of view can be supported by strong reasons. Strong reasons will make your essay persuasive.

Write a thesis statement. The thesis statement of an argumentative essay must contain an opinion. Opinions are usually expressed with the modal verb *should* or evaluative words such as *good* and *bad*.

Teenagers *should* have part-time jobs.

Part-time work is *good* for teenagers.

A complete thesis statement also contains reasons, or supporting arguments.

```
┌──────────── OPINION ────────────┐ ┌──────── REASON 1 ────────┐ ┌── REASON 2 ──┐
```
Employers should hire teenagers because they are eager to work, they are flexible,

```
┌──────────────────── REASON 3 ────────────────────┐
```
and they have the knowledge and skills required to do many entry-level jobs.

A thesis statement may also contain an opposing view.

```
┌──────────────────── OPPOSING VIEW ────────────────────┐
```
While some people say that teenagers do not have a good work ethic,

```
┌──────────── OPINION ────────────┐ ┌──────── REASON 1 ────────┐ ┌── REASON 2 ──┐
```
employers should hire teenagers because they are eager to work, they are flexible,

```
┌──────────────────── REASON 3 ────────────────────┐
```
and they have the knowledge and skills required to do many entry-level jobs.

An opposing view in a thesis statement is usually introduced by the subordinating conjunctions of comparison/contrast *while* or *although*.

Exercise 2

List the elements that each statement contains (*opinion, supporting reasons, opposing view, definition, limiting statement*).

1. Although some people say that tracking (placing students in certain classes according to their ability level) unfairly reduces some students' chances of going to college, tracking makes sense for both teachers and students because it decreases the likelihood of the fastest learners becoming bored. Further, the slowest learners become less frustrated, and grading becomes more fair for all students.

   opposing view, definition, opinion, supporting reasons

2. High schools should encourage young people to volunteer three or four hours of their time every week to help others in their society.

   _____

3. The pass/not pass grading policy at Green Hills College allows students to request that, for a particular class, they be given a grade of P for satisfactory work or NP for unsatisfactory or incomplete work. The P/NP grades replace the traditional letter grades of A, B, C, D, and F. This policy should be discontinued because it has led to a higher failure rate and a lowering of standards.

   _____

4. Schools should provide age-appropriate character education to elementary school students.

_____

5. Some people say that they want their tax money to go to their neighborhood schools rather than to all public schools. However, this leads to lower funding for schools in poor neighborhoods, which is unfair. The rate of public funding for education, that is, the amount of money the government gives to a school for each hour a student attends, should be the same for all schools because all students are equal under the law and all schools are required by law to provide the same basic education.

_____

Prewriting

As you read through the prewriting steps, you will see how Alina, a student from the Philippines, developed an argument and prepared to write an essay on the question _Should young people be required to do community service?_

STEP 1 | Explore a potential topic by discussing it with your classmates or by doing a brief Internet search. After choosing a topic, write questions and answers that you need to (1) **define key terms** and (2) determine how you will **limit the topic**.

Alina wrote the following questions and answers.

Defining
What does "community service" mean?
—Community service is any work done to help people in one's neighborhood or city who need assistance. Some examples are helping elderly people maintain their homes, teaching children to read, repairing or maintaining historic buildings, guiding visitors in a museum, and picking up garbage on beaches or in city parks.

Limiting
Isn't community service usually voluntary?
—Community service is usually voluntary, but some countries have compulsory community service. For example, in the Philippines, college students and young men who choose not to do military service are required to do community service.

Limiting

Isn't community service usually unpaid?

—Community service is usually unpaid, but sometimes compensation is offered. For example, in the United States, the AmeriCorps program compensates participants with vouchers for college tuition.

Limiting

If community service is to be required, how much work would youths be expected to do?

—I think everyone should have to perform the same number of hours, and the amount should not be excessive—perhaps about fifty hours. Young people could work up to twenty-five hours a week during vacations or as little as an hour a week during the school year, so the term of service would vary.

STEP 2 Identify two **opposing opinions**, and list as many reasons as you can to support each one. To do this, you may need to discuss the topic further with friends or do some research.

After discussing the topic with her classmates, Alina listed the arguments for and against community service.

For

Community service is beneficial.

—Community service provides chances for young people to meet others.

—It teaches youth compassion, responsibility, and how to relate to all kinds of people.

—It benefits society.

—It teaches young people about the world outside their home, school, and neighborhood.

—It gives youth work experience they can use when applying for jobs in the future.

—It gives young people a chance to apply what they have learned in school.

Against

Community service is not beneficial.

—Community service takes time young people could spend on their studies.

—Community service programs would be expensive to administer.

—Some teenagers need paying jobs so they can help their families. They cannot afford the time to do volunteer work.

STEP 3 Select the reasons on your lists that you think are most important or most persuasive, and decide on the opinion you wish to present in your essay. Write a draft thesis statement and outline. If you wish, you can use order of importance (see pages 109–110) to organize your reasons.

Alina wrote the following thesis statement and outline.

Young people should be required to do community service because it benefits both the youth themselves and the society as a whole.

  I. Community service gives young people knowledge of the world.
     A. It helps them relate information in textbooks to the real world.

 II. Community service prepares youth for future employment.
     A. It helps them understand how organizations work.
     B. It provides opportunities to learn to work with all kinds of people.

III. Community service benefits the society because without it, many vital services would not be provided.
     A. Because of community service, more children get vaccinations.
     B. Because of community service, disaster relief is provided when it is needed.
     C. Because of community service, more poor people have adequate housing.
     D. Because of community service, children who need help in school get tutoring.

IV. Community service benefits the society in that it affects people's values in a positive way.
     A. It helps people become less self-centered.
     B. It makes people think about the concept of citizenship, and it gives participants a new understanding of citizenship.
        1. citizenship course at the University of the Philippines

After several drafts, Alina wrote the following draft. You will notice that in the process of writing and rewriting, she limited her thesis statement even more (by adding *about fifty hours of community service*) and added an additional body paragraph which is not represented on the outline above.

The Benefits of Community Service

1   Community service means committing one's time and efforts to serving individuals and organizations in one's own local area. The service can take many forms: It can be direct person-to-person assistance such as delivering meals to housebound elderly people or caring for children in after-school programs. Or it can involve working for organizations such as libraries, hospitals, museums, and charities. In my view, all young people between the ages of sixteen and twenty should be required to complete about fifty hours of community service because doing so will benefit both the participants themselves and their societies.

2   First of all, community service benefits young people by broadening their horizons. Many youths know little of the world beyond their homes, schools, and neighborhoods. Community service helps them understand who the people in their society are, what problems these people face, and how their lives can be improved. Young people who have performed community service find that it

enriches their learning in school because their service experience helps them relate information in their history, civics, and economics textbooks to the real world.

3   Community service also helps young people prepare for future employment. According to a U.S. Department of Labor report, in order to be ready to enter the labor force, a person must understand how organizations function and be able to work well with all kinds of people (U.S. Department of Labor, 15). Because it is not possible to learn these things at home or in school, a youth who has participated in a well-run community service program is better qualified for employment than a youth who has not had such an experience.

4   Community service not only rewards young participants but benefits the society as a whole by providing valuable assistance that would not otherwise be given. Without community service, children might not get vaccinations, the Red Cross/Red Crescent could not provide disaster relief, Habitat for Humanity could not build houses for the homeless, low-income children and adolescents would not get free tutoring in reading and math, and public museums and parks might close for lack of people to staff and maintain them.

5   Finally, community service benefits the society in a less tangible but very important way by shifting public values. In the modern world, the competition for schooling and jobs is encouraging people to be increasingly self-centered in their choice of goals. People have started to think of citizenship as a set of individual rights rather than rights and responsibilities that belong to people collectively. This trend can be reversed when young people are required to perform community service. When people get involved in service, they begin to reflect on the meaning of citizenship. In the Philippines, university students are required to perform community service, and at the University of the Philippines, students must take a citizenship course in conjunction with their service (Co, 191). Through the course and their service activities, students gain a deeper understanding of what citizenship means and how it can be applied through direct community action that improves people's lives.

6   Critics say that community service should be voluntary, not mandatory. They point out that young people in financial need cannot spare time to participate because they have to work to support themselves and their families. As a matter of fact, in the past, volunteer service was something the wealthy did for the poor, and thus it increased the social stigma of being poor. But, as Arthur Gilette, author and Director of UNESCO's Youth and Sports Activities Division, points out, if participation in community service is required of everyone, tolerance, equality, and cohesiveness will increase in society. Furthermore, because a well-run community service program will help all young people acquire knowledge and skills, it should be seen as part of every youth's education.

7   In conclusion, a well-administered community service program will have multiple benefits. It will expand youths' horizons and help them become ready

for the world of work. It will benefit the society as a whole by providing needed services and by reshaping the dominant values in a positive way. Therefore, governments should create community service programs and require young people's participation as an investment in everyone's future.

Co, Edna A. "Developing Citizenship through Service: A Philippines Initiative." *Service Enquiry: Service in the 21st Century*. Ed. Helene Perold, Susan Stroud, and Michael Sherraden. Global Service Institute and Volunteer and Service Enquiry Southern Africa. Sept. 2003. 23 Nov. 2003 <http://www.service-enquiry.org.za>

Gilette, Arthur. "Taking People out of Boxes and Categories: Voluntary Service and Social Cohesion." *Service Enquiry: Service in the 21st Century*. Ed. Helene Perold, Susan Stroud, and Michael Sherraden. Global Service Institute and Volunteer and Service Enquiry Southern Africa. Sept. 2003. 23 Nov. 2003 <http://www.service-enquiry.org.za>

United States Dept. of Labor. *Secretary's Commission on Achieving Necessary Skills: Identifying and Describing the Skills Required by Work*. 4 June 2002. 6 Dec. 2003 <http://wdr.doleta.gov/SCANS/ idsrew/>

Exercise 3

With a partner or a small group, discuss the following questions.

1. Look at the introduction and find the defining and limiting phrases, clauses, and sentences. Circle the definition of *community service*. Explain why Alina placed the definition at the very beginning of the essay. Underline the limiting phrases in the thesis statement, and explain why they are important.

2. What is Alina's main argument and what are her supporting arguments? What transition signals did Alina use to link the supporting arguments?

3. Do you think the supporting arguments Alina chose are persuasive? Explain.

4. How did Alina develop each supporting argument? What strategies (*the ideas of authorities, facts, explanation, examples, cause-and-effect reasoning, or comparison*) did she use in each of her body paragraphs?

5. The last body paragraph did not appear on Alina's outline. What does it discuss?

6. What strategies (*summary, prediction, recommendation*) did Alina use in her conclusion?

7. Alina's citations are in the MLA style. How many did she provide at the end of her essay? What kind of sources did she use?

Select a topic from the list on page 241 that you can form an opinion about and for which you can find strong reasons to support your opinion. Follow the prewriting steps that Alina used.

First Draft

Once you have completed an outline, write your first draft. As you write, focus on stating your thesis clearly and supporting it with well-developed reasons in your body paragraphs.

REVISING

As you go through the Revising section of this chapter, you will learn more about introductions, body paragraph development, and opposing points of view. Review your draft regularly, and follow the advice in the Review and Revise boxes.

Composition Focus

Introductions for argumentative essays. You learned in What Argumentation Is and Why It Is Important (page 241) that introductions to argumentative essays often contain definitions and limiting statements. Introductions to argumentative essays must also stimulate interest and lead readers to the thesis. To do this, you can use any of the strategies you learned in Chapter 5—*general statement, background,* and *anecdote* (see page 117). You can also include a quotation. In addition, the *turnabout,* a strategy which you learned about in Chapter 6 (page 150), can be very effective in argumentative essays. To use the turnabout, present an opposing view at the beginning of the introduction, and then respond to that view in your thesis statement.

Exercise 4

The following introduction, which begins with a general statement, is not very effective because it doesn't stimulate much interest or lead the reader smoothly to the thesis statement. With a partner or a small group, discuss which strategies (*background, anecdote, definition, quotation,* or *turnabout*) might be more effective with this topic. Then, on another piece of paper, revise the introduction, using another strategy or a combination of other strategies.

The Benefits of Homework

Students everywhere have homework, and most accept it as part of school. Doing homework benefits students because it helps them remember what they have been taught in school, it teaches them to study independently, and it allows them to learn more during the school year.

Share your revised introduction with other students and listen to theirs, noticing the effect of different strategies.

Review and Revise 1: Introductions
Review your introduction. Make sure that it defines and limits your topic, if necessary. Ask yourself if it stimulates readers' interest and leads them to your thesis statement. Finally, consider whether using a different strategy or adding a strategy would make your introduction more effective. If you can improve your introduction, revise it now.

Support. Support is the most essential part of an argumentative essay because it is what persuades readers to consider your point of view. If you select reasons to support your opinion that are believable, relevant, and important and develop them fully in your body paragraphs, your argument will be effective.

Each supporting argument in your essay should be presented and developed in a body paragraph. The topic sentence of each body paragraph should state the supporting argument and should contain a transition to show how that supporting argument relates to the other supporting arguments. You may use cause-and-effect transitions such as *one reason* and *another reason* (see Chapter 5, page 121).

Developing body paragraphs. As you learned on page 237, support in argumentative essays includes facts, explanation, examples, cause-and-effect reasoning, comparison, and the ideas of authorities. Whichever strategies you use in the supporting sentences of a body paragraph, you must make sure that each sentence is logically related to the topic sentence. In addition, you need to use the signals of cohesion (*repeated words, synonyms, transitions*) to link the supporting sentences to the topic sentence.

Exercise 5

The five supporting arguments and the ten developing sentences that follow are from an essay written in support of vocational education. Match each supporting argument with the appropriate developing sentences. Then label each developing sentence with the development strategy or strategies it represents (*facts, examples, the ideas of authorities, cause-and-effect reasoning, or comparison*).

THESIS: Vocational education can benefit some high school and community college students by making their learning more meaningful and preparing them for a better future.

Supporting Arguments

a. Many high school students do not see the relevance of their studies to their future employment.

b. A majority of high school and two-year college students are already working. Most of them hold jobs that have no future and do not relate to their course of study.

c. High school and community college vocational programs can introduce students to careers they would never have imagined for themselves.

d. Most of the jobs that are currently available do not require four-year college degrees.

e. Vocational classes can lead to a significant increase in a person's earning potential.

Developing Sentences

1. A glance at the classified section of your local newspaper will reveal that there are more openings for dental technicians, computer software salespersons, and automobile mechanics than there are for jobs which require a bachelor's degree.

   Development for supporting argument: ___*d*___

   Type of development: _*examples*_____

2. The California Community College Chancellor reports that a vocational certificate awarded after only a year and a half of study can increase a person's salary by 28 percent (Leovy, 6).

   Development for supporting argument: _____

   Type of development: _____

3. According to Jill Leovy (6), almost 20 percent of people who graduate from four-year colleges do not find the type of employment they were educated for.

   Development for supporting argument: _____

   Type of development: _____

4. In addition, vocational programs offer field trips to businesses that are likely to take on apprentices or hire young people. My cousin Silvia took a field trip to a computer graphics company with her vocational program. Intrigued by what she saw there, she decided to take some art and computer classes, and she now works for an animation company.

   Development for supporting argument: _____

   Type of development: _____

5. If a vocational program is well designed, it can make students understand how psychology relates to management skills, how physics relates to factory assembly, and how English composition relates to business correspondence.

   Development for supporting argument: _____

   Type of development: _____

6. Because careers are so specialized today, it is impossible for anyone to know about all the kinds of jobs available. Therefore, vocational counselors are a valuable resource because they spend much of their time talking to employers and learning about employment opportunities in their local areas.

   Development for supporting argument: _____

   Type of development: _____

7. But if students enroll in a vocational program, they accumulate work experience that will help them advance to better jobs.

   Development for supporting argument: _____

   Type of development: _____

8. Barbara Schneider and David Stevenson, authors of *The Ambitious Generation: America's Teenagers, Motivated but Directionless,* claim that too many young people mistakenly believe that college will lead them to a professional career.

   Development for supporting argument: _____

   Type of development: _____

9. A technical degree can lead to, for example, a job in construction that pays $33,700 or in computer and office machine technology that pays $32,000 (Leovy, 6).

   Development for supporting argument: _____

   Type of development: _____

10. Compared to students enrolled in a regular high school or community college program, vocational students have a greater sense of purpose and more confidence about their future.

    Development for supporting argument: _____

    Type of development: _____

Leovy, Jill. "Vocational School Values: The Right Choice Can Put Money in Your Pocket." *The Los Angeles Times* 23 May 1999, "Education Times" 6.

Schneider, Barbara and David Stevenson. *The Ambitious Generation: America's Teenagers, Motivated but Directionless.* New Haven: Yale, 1999.

Review and Revise 2: Developing Arguments
Ask yourself if each of your reasons or supporting arguments is well developed. Review the six strategies (*facts, explanation, examples, the ideas of authorities, cause-and-effect reasoning,* and *comparison*), count how many you have used, and ask yourself if you can add more. Make sure that your body paragraphs are both balanced (equally well developed) and cohesive. Finally, if you have used outside sources, make sure that you have identified them with correct in-text and end-of-text citations.

Opposing points of view. You have seen that opposing points of view can be included in introductions (page 249), thesis statements (pages 242–243), and body paragraphs (page 250). While it is not always necessary to present an opposing view in an argumentative essay, it is a good idea to include another view when you think that your readers are likely to be aware of it. By including an opposing view, you show readers that you know your topic thoroughly, and by **refuting** the opposing view (proving it to be incorrect by presenting a stronger supporting argument), you strengthen your argument overall. If you decide to include an opposing view, consider the following questions.

1. Where should I put the opposing view?

If the opposing view relates to one of your supporting arguments, put it in the body paragraph where that supporting argument is presented. If the opposing view relates to your thesis, you can put it in the introduction, in the body of the essay, or in the conclusion. (If you are writing on a computer, you can easily move the opposing view around to evaluate its effect in various parts of your paper.) If your topic is very controversial, it is a good idea to present and refute the opposing view early in your paper so that readers can focus on your argument. Here, for example, are the first two sentences of the introduction to an essay about affirmative action.

> Some people object to affirmative action policies in college admissions, which give special consideration to racial minorities or disadvantaged applicants. They say that such affirmative action policies may benefit underqualified people and exclude qualified applicants.

2. Should I **concede** (agree in part) with the opposing view?

If you feel that the opposing view contains some truth, you should say so. Readers will appreciate your showing them which part of the opposing view you think is correct and which part is not. Notice how the **concession statement** from the same introduction admits that *part* of the opposing view is correct.

> Some people object to affirmative action policies in college admissions, which give special consideration to racial minorities or disadvantaged applicants. They say that such affirmative action policies may benefit underqualified people and exclude qualified applicants. <u>Indeed, it is true that affirmative action can lead to the exclusion of a few individuals who would otherwise be admitted on the basis of their qualifications.</u>

3. How should I respond to the opposing view?

You must **refute** it, or say clearly that you disagree with the opposing view and give one or more strong reasons for your disagreement. The fact that the opposing view appears in your essay without supporting reasons and your refutation appears with reasons strengthens your argument. Look at the refutation in the same introductory paragraph about affirmative action.

Some people object to affirmative action policies in college admissions, which give special consideration to racial minorities or disadvantaged applicants. They say that such affirmative action policies may benefit underqualified people and exclude qualified applicants. Indeed, it is true that affirmative action can lead to the exclusion of a few individuals who would otherwise be admitted on the basis of their qualifications. <u>However, affirmative action addresses a much larger issue, a problem of historical injustice: Minority individuals have been denied access to institutions of higher education in the past, and this has led to their exclusion from positions of power in society. In order to ensure that minorities will be represented at the highest levels in business and government, colleges and universities must implement affirmative action policies for a limited period of time.</u>

The following examples show you how to present and respond to opposing views.

┌──────────────────── OPPOSING VIEW ────────────────────┐
Some people say that teenage boys and girls should study in separate classes.

┌──────────────── REFUTATION ────────────────┐
However, such a separation creates an unnatural situation.

┌──────────────────── OPPOSING VIEW ────────────────────
Proponents of creating separate classes for teenage boys and girls claim that it

─────────────────────────────────┐ ┌──────────── CONCESSION ────────────
improves the students' behavior. Granted, all-boy or all-girl classes are easier

─────────────────────────┐ ┌──────────────── REFUTATION ────────────────
for teachers to control. Yet the separation is unnatural, and when boys and

──┐
girls are separated, they do not learn how to get along with each other.

Here are the signals you can use with opposing views, concessions, and refutations.

To Introduce an Opposing View	To Signal a Concession	To Signal a Refutation
Some people say that Proponents of . . . claim that Critics of . . . maintain that It is sometimes/often argued that	Granted, Indeed, It is a fact/true that	However, But (in fact/as a matter of fact/it is a fact that) Yet (in fact/as a matter of fact/it is a fact that) Nevertheless,

Exercise 6

The following thesis statement and body paragraphs are from an essay on the topic *Should teenagers work?* In the box are three opposing views that readers would likely be aware of. On a piece of paper, revise the body paragraphs. Begin each body paragraph with an opposing view, and make sure a refutation follows it. (Some of the refutations are in the essay already.) When appropriate, add a concession before the refutation.

Opposing views

- By working, youth can help their families financially.
- Youth gain valuable experience by working.
- Work teaches youth how the real world operates.

The Effects of Work on Teenagers

1THESIS: Except in cases of real economic need, high school students should not work for several reasons: Having additional pocket money encourages them to be materialistic, part-time jobs cause them to forfeit valuable extracurricular activities, and work has a negative impact on their performance in school.

2 Work encourages teenagers to become materialistic. Very few young workers actually give their earnings to their parents or save for their own future, but instead spend their earnings on themselves—on cars, clothes, music, and electronic gadgets. Earning and spending money on material possessions distracts teens from much more important matters such as figuring out what their goals in life are and how they will reach those goals. The teenage years should be a time when young people acquire a sense of themselves and learn how to get along in society, not a time for acquiring material possessions.

3 Working students do not have time for extracurricular activities, and if they miss the many programs and clubs that high schools offer, they will never have a second chance to take advantage of them. A student can participate in sports, orchestra, student government, speech club, drama, and many other activities. These extracurricular programs give young people a chance to make friends, learn to cooperate with others, and acquire confidence. A low-level part-time job such as one in a fast-food restaurant does not give teenagers the same quality of learning experience or sense of accomplishment as the extracurricular activities available in high school.

4 The most important problem associated with high school students working is that jobs take time away from study. A high school curriculum is challenging. High school teachers give complex long-term projects which require doing research, writing papers or delivering speeches, and sometimes creating posters or models. Teachers often assign these projects to groups of students who may have to meet after school to complete their assignments. The working student isn't able to collaborate with classmates after school and often cannot manage to complete even short homework assignments on his own. After four or five hours at an after-school job, he returns home too tired to study well. If he tries to do his homework, he loses valuable sleep and will not be able to concentrate in class the next morning. As a result, his grades are likely to drop, threatening his chances of getting admitted to a good college later on.

After you revise the paragraphs, compare your concessions and refutations with your classmates'. Discuss how adding refutations has changed the effect of this essay.

> **Review and Revise 3: Opposing Points of View**
> Review your essay, asking yourself whether including an opposing view would strengthen your essay. If you have not included an opposing view, but think adding one will improve your essay, add one now. If you have included an opposing view, evaluate its placement and your response to it.

Conclusions. The final paragraph in an argumentative essay is like other essay conclusions: It summarizes the main points of the essay, and it may make predictions about the future. However, more often than other essay conclusions, it asks the audience to do something—to consider a new point of view or to take action. For example, Prewo's essay, "The Sorcery of Apprenticeship," concluded by recommending that the U.S. government set up a national youth employment training program.

Exercise 7
Write a conclusion for the essay on page 255 about working teens, and then share it with your classmates. As you listen to the conclusions your classmates have written, comment on how they have incorporated summary, predictions, or recommendations to consider a new point of view or take action.

> **Review and Revise 4: Conclusions**
> Review the conclusion of your own essay, checking to see that it contains a brief summary of your main points. If your conclusion does not also include a prediction or recommendation, ask yourself if it would be improved by adding either one. Make any revisions that are needed.

Language Focus

Qualifiers. When you write argumentative essays, you want your readers to have confidence in you as a writer and be persuaded by what you say. If you exaggerate or overgeneralize, you will lose readers' confidence. You can avoid overgeneralizing by using qualifiers in your thesis and supporting arguments.

In Chapter 7, you learned that you can use qualifiers such as the verb *tend* and the adverb *usually* to modify general statements (see page 180). English has a number of other qualifiers, as you can see in the following box.

For more on expressions of quantity like *many* and *most*, see Appendix IA, page 291.

For more on *can, may,* and other modal verbs, see Appendix IA, page 305.

Qualifiers Used in General Statements

Teenagers **tend** to hold low-paying jobs.

Teenagers **usually/often** hold low-skilled jobs.

Most/The majority of/Many teens hold dead-end jobs.

These jobs **seem/appear** to be **somewhat/rather** undesirable.

Qualifiers Used to Predict Results

Work **can** affect a teen's grades negatively.

If teens work more than fifteen hours a week, they are **likely** to be sleep-deprived.

If teens work more than fifteen hours a week, they are **unlikely** to do all their homework.

If teens work more than fifteen hours a week, they **will probably/may** fail some of their classes in school.

Reducing the number of hours spent on a part-time job will **help** a student succeed in school.

To see how qualifiers affect the meaning of sentences, remove the qualifiers from the previous sentences. When the qualifiers are removed, you have broad statements that express absolute certainty and are too difficult to defend in an argumentative essay.

Exercise 8

With a partner, add qualifiers to limit or modify the following general statements and predictions. There is more than one way to modify each statement.

1. *The majority of adolescents* ~~Adolescents~~ are too immature to make lifetime career decisions.

2. Tracking has a negative impact on the motivation of students.

3. Learning a new skill increases a teenager's self-esteem.

4. If businesses set up apprenticeship programs with schools, participating students will move into well-paying jobs rapidly.

5. Although teenagers say that they dislike schoolwork, they are happier when they are accomplishing something.

6. Everyone agrees that responsibility, respect, honesty, and care for others are values that all young people should learn.

7. If young people are required to perform community service, they will develop social awareness.

8. Teenagers have a poor work ethic.

9. If an employer treats teenagers respectfully and acknowledges their effort, the teens will accept working for lower wages than they could get elsewhere.

10. Affirmative action will create a level playing field.

> **Review and Revise 5: Qualifiers**
> Review your essay, focusing on general statements and predictions. If you find any overgeneralizations, revise them by adding qualifiers.

PEER REVIEW AND FINAL DRAFT

Now it is time to share your composition with readers. Exchange papers with one or two classmates. Read each other's papers carefully. Turn to page 340 in Appendix II, and fill out the Peer Review form.

After considering your classmates' suggestions, prepare a final draft of your composition to hand in to your teacher. Before handing in your paper, proofread it for spelling, grammar, punctuation errors, and cohesion.

CHAPTER REVIEW

Look back at what you have accomplished in Chapter 9. Check (✓) what you have learned and what you have used as you have written and revised your essay.

Chapter 9 Topics	I understand this	I have used this
defining, limiting, and analyzing an argumentative topic before writing (pages 241–242)		
writing introductions and thesis statements for argumentative essays that include necessary definitions of key terms and limiting statements (pages 241–243)		
presenting supporting arguments in the topic sentences of body paragraphs with transitions (page 250)		
using various strategies to develop supporting arguments including citing the ideas of authorities and using facts, explanation, examples, comparison, and cause-and-effect reasoning (page 250)		
including opposing views and responding to them with concessions, when appropriate, and refutations (pages 252–254)		
writing conclusions for argumentative essays using summary, prediction, or recommendation (page 256)		
using qualifiers to modify general statements and predictions (page 257)		

Appendix 1A: Grammar

1. Adjective Clauses

When writing, you can use adjective clauses to describe or define nouns and to create longer, more sophisticated sentences. An adjective clause begins with a **relative pronoun** (*who, which, that, whose, where,* or *when*). The relative pronoun refers back to the noun or pronoun that the clause modifies.

I have a friend ***who** can play the drums.*

This is the highway ***that** goes to New York.*

Who, which, and that. Use the relative pronouns **who** to refer to people and **which** to refer to things. Use **that** to refer to either people or things.

I know a man ***who/that** speaks Russian.*
I photographed a building ***which/that** is 500 years old.*

Sometimes the relative pronoun is the subject (s) of the adjective clause.

You know the people ***who** are coming to visit.*

I own a car ***that** can carry five passengers.*

Sometimes the relative pronoun is the direct object (o) of the verb in the adjective clause.

The people ***who** I called are coming to visit.*

The car ***that** I own can carry five passengers.*

Whom. Use **whom** to refer to people. *Whom* is always in the object position in an adjective clause. *Whom* is formal, so it is most often used in writing.

The people ***whom** I called are coming to visit.*

In less formal English, no pronoun (**Ø**) is often used when the relative pronoun is an object in the adjective clause.

The people (**Ø**) *I called are coming to visit.*

The car (**Ø**) *I own can carry five passengers.*

All of the adjective clauses discussed so far can be formed more than one way. However, **which** is seldom used as the object of the verb in the adjective clause.

SUBJECT CLAUSE MODIFYING A PERSON
The boy ***who/that** won the prize* was delighted.

SUBJECT CLAUSE MODIFYING A THING
The plane ***which/that** arrived at 5:00* was full.

OBJECT CLAUSE MODIFYING A PERSON
The teacher *who/**that**/Ø I wanted to see* was busy.

OBJECT CLAUSE MODIFYING A THING
The dictionary ***that**/Ø/(which) I bought* is useful.

The relative pronoun (**who, which,** etc.) can also be the object of a preposition (OP) in the adjective clause.

This is the friend *who/**that**/Ø I eat lunch* **with**. [OP] [PREP]

When a preposition comes at the beginning of the adjective clause, you must use **whom** or **which**.

This is the friend ***with whom** I eat lunch.* [PREP] [OP]

Here is the address ***to which** you should send the letter.* [PREP] [OP]

When a preposition is at the end of the adjective clause, you can omit the relative pronoun (**Ø**).

I contacted the customer *who/whom/**that**/Ø you told me about.* [OP] [PREP]

Here is the address ***that**/Ø/(which) you should send the package to.* [OP] [PREP]

Whose. The relative pronoun **whose** is a possessive in an adjective clause. *Whose* can represent *his, her, its, their, Mario's, the company's,* etc. *Whose* follows a noun that refers to either a person or a thing.

This is the girl. ~~Her~~ *whose mother brought the cake.*

A building *whose rooms are bright* is pleasant to be in. ~~Its rooms are bright.~~

Where and when. In adjective clauses, **where** and **when** represent adverbs. Use **where** to replace a prepositional phrase of location (*in that building, at the corner*) or the adverbs *there* or *here*.

That is the building. ~~I work in that building.~~ *where I work.*

I went to a park. ~~Lots~~ *where lots of children were playing* ~~there~~.

Use **when** to replace a prepositional phrase of time (*on that day, at the moment, in the nineteenth century*) or the adverb *then*.

Can you remember the day? ~~You~~ *when you were interviewed?* ~~on that day.~~

Where and **when** can be replaced by **that** or Ø. If **that** or Ø replaces **where**, a preposition must be in the adjective clause.

This is the building ***that/Ø*** *I work* ***in***.
Can you remember the day ***that/Ø*** *you were interviewed*?

1a. Position of Adjective Clauses

An adjective clause should come as close as possible to the noun it modifies. In most cases, it immediately follows the noun.

The books ***that*** *the school is giving away* are in the library storeroom.

However, sometimes a prepositional phrase comes between the noun and the adjective clause that modifies it.

The boxes of books ***that*** *the school is giving away* are in the library storeroom.

1b. Use of Commas with Adjective Clauses

Rule 1 Some adjective clauses have commas, and others do not. An adjective clause that provides information which is *essential* to define the noun or pronoun does not have commas. It is called a **restrictive clause**.

The man *who always wears green neckties* is a banker.

An adjective clause that provides *additional* information which is not essential to define the noun or pronoun has commas. It is called a **non-restrictive clause**.

Antonio**,** *who always wears green neckties,* is a banker.
My wife**,** *who is an artist,* has three paintings in that art gallery.

An adjective clause that modifies either a proper noun (*Antonio*) or a noun that refers to someone or something that is unique (*my wife*) is always non-restrictive and always has commas.

Rule 2 Adjective clauses after indefinite pronouns (*no one, anyone, something*) do not have commas.

The police are looking for someone *who saw the accident.*
I could not find anything *that I wanted to eat* on the menu.

Rule 3 Adjective clauses made with expressions of quantity (*one of, some of, all of*) always have commas and use only the relative pronouns **whom**, **which**, or **whose**.

The bride and groom greeted the guests, ***several of whom*** *had traveled long distances to come to the wedding.*
Last year the organization received a sum of money, ***much of which*** *has already been spent.*

Other nouns can be combined with **of which** to introduce an adjective clause.

> I brought the contract, ***the last page of which*** *you must sign.*
> The instructor gave us a homework assignment, ***the purpose of which*** *was to review verb tense.*

1c. Common Errors in Adjective Clauses

Avoid the following common errors made with adjective clauses.

ERROR 1 **The verb in the adjective clause does not agree in number with the noun in the main clause.** This problem can only occur when the pronoun is the subject of the adjective clause, and it is most likely to occur when there is a prepositional phrase between the noun and the adjective clause.

> We have contacted the manufacturers of this product who ~~is~~ ^{are} sending us a new catalogue.

ERROR 2 **There is incorrect repetition of a pronoun, a preposition, or other words in an adjective clause.**

> The groups of people that the advertising consultant has talked to ~~them~~ agree that the product is very useful.
> The chapter of the math textbook with which I had the most difficulty ~~with~~ was the one about graphs.
> The pronunciation class is at 8:00 A.M. in the morning when I'm too sleepy. ~~at 8:00 A.M.~~

ERROR 3 **The relative pronoun *where* is used incorrectly.** *Where* can only be used to introduce an adjective clause after a noun that refers to a location.

> That is the episode of the TV show ~~where~~ ^{in which} Harry Lam appears.
> Computer hacking is the kind of crime ~~where~~ ^{for which} it is difficult to prepare a legal case.

ERROR 4 **Commas are used incorrectly.** Sometimes commas are not placed where they are needed. In the sentence below, the adjective clause is non-restrictive because the noun phrase, *my oldest brother,* is unique.

> My oldest brother, who is 33, has two children.

Sometimes commas are placed where they are not needed. In the sentence below, the adjective clause *who looks like me* is restrictive because it is needed to identify the noun *child*.

> The child who looks like me is the older one.

EXERCISE 1

As you read the following passage, find and correct the twelve adjective clauses containing the four problems listed in the previous section. The first one has been done for you.

Fireflies, which ~~is~~ *are* actually not flies but beetles, are known for their unusual ability to produce flashing lights. Fireflies have light-producing organs in their bodies in which a chemical reaction takes place in them. This process is so energy efficient that almost 100 percent of the chemical energy, the firefly produces, is converted to light.

Adult fireflies produce light to attract mates. Each species of firefly can be distinguished by the color, brightness, length, and duration of its flashing lights. In addition, in most species, males produce a brighter light than females. When a female sees the particular kind of flashing that are produced by a male of her species, she flashes back in response. The pair will continue their dialogue of flashes until they locate each other and mate.

In some species of fireflies, the males gather in groups where they all flash simultaneously. A group may gather in a single tree which lights up with their rhythmically flashing signals. A female is attracted to a male whose his light is the brightest in the group. Biologist John Buck who studied synchronous flashing in fireflies for over 40 years found that in order to flash synchronously, male fireflies must be close enough to one another to see each other. A male firefly looks for another male where is close to him, registers the rhythm at which that male is flashing at, and begins flashing synchronously.

Of the more than 2,000 known species of fireflies in the world, fewer than 100 flash synchronously, and most of those inhabit swamps which has dense vegetation. Scientists think that synchronous flashing must give a firefly species an advantage in this type of environment. They think that a female firefly is more likely to find a mate if she can locate him easily, and the flashing of a synchronized group is easier to find than the light of a lone male.

1d. Reducing Adjective Clauses to Adjective Phrases

Adjective clauses that begin with *who, which,* or *that* and a form of the verb *to be* can be reduced, or shortened. By reducing adjective clauses to adjective phrases, you can make your writing more concise. That is, you can present more information in fewer words.

The money ~~*that is*~~ *on the table* is mine.

An adjective clause that contains a progressive verb can be reduced to an *-ing* participial phrase.

The companies ~~*that are*~~ *selling software* are doing well.

An adjective clause that contains a passive verb can be reduced to an -*ed* participial phrase.

The songs ~~that have been~~ *recorded in the last five years* are frequently played on the radio.

When reduction of an adjective clause leaves a single adjective, the adjective moves in front of the noun it modifies.

The dictionary ~~which is~~ (red) is José's.

When an adjective clause has commas, its reduced form also has commas.

Genghis Kahn, ~~who was~~ *a Mongol emperor from 1206 to 1227*, conquered most of Asia.

Subject-type adjective clauses containing other verbs other than *be* can sometimes be reduced to -*ing* participial phrases.

The teacher told us to refer to the chart ~~that shows~~ *showing* the chemical elements.

Adjective clauses containing the verb *have* can be changed to phrases containing the preposition *with*.

The man ~~who has~~ *with* a moustache is the finance minister.

EXERCISE 2

The following passage contains 16 adjective clauses, 15 of which can be reduced to adjective phrases. Change the adjective clauses that allow reduction, and notice the effect on the passage. The first one has been done for you.

Calcium, ~~which is~~ a soft, whitish chemical element, is the fifth most abundant element in the Earth's crust. Calcium does not occur by itself in nature, but in compounds with other elements. Calcium's most common compounds, which are calcium carbonate, calcium sulfate, and calcium fluoride, are found in limestone, gypsum, and other rocks and minerals. These compounds have many uses which are important.

Classroom chalk, which is a very soft, fine-grained white limestone, is pure calcium carbonate. It is also an ingredient that is in toothpastes and some stomach medicines, as well as in rubber and paint.

Harder varieties of limestone are used as cut stone in building construction and in the manufacture of mortar and cement. When limestone is heated, it becomes lime, or calcium oxide. Lime is used as a fertilizer, and it has many industrial applications, which include the production of steel, leather tanning, and petroleum refining.

The mineral gypsum, which is soft and whitish-yellow, can be processed to yield calcium sulfate, which is a compound which is used in making cement and plaster. When gypsum is heated, it becomes plaster of Paris, which is a material which is used for all kinds of molds as well as casts which are for broken arms and legs. Plaster of Paris is named for a gypsum mine which is in France. Calcium sulfate is also used in a wide variety of products which range from fertilizer to candy.

Fluorite, which is a mineral that occurs in veins in granite and other rocks, consists of calcium fluoride. Calcium fluoride is important in the production of aluminum, steel, and glass. It is also added to water supplies in small amounts to prevent tooth decay.

Although we don't see calcium in the world around us, it is present in many of the things that we use every day.

2. Adjectives and Noun Modifiers

Adjectives are words such as *big* or *expensive* that describe nouns. By selecting and using appropriate adjectives, you can make your writing more descriptive and informative. Adjectives are placed either before a noun or after the verb *be* or a linking verb like *appear* or *seem*. When adjectives are placed before a noun, they must be in the order shown in the following chart.

A noun can have the same function as an adjective. That is, it can modify another noun. A noun that modifies another noun is called a **noun modifier**. A noun modifier, as you see in the chart, is placed directly before the noun it modifies.

Article, Number, Quantity, or Possessive Noun	General	Size	Shape	Age	Color	Nationality	Participial Adjective	Noun Modifier	Noun
an	excellent	pocket-sized						college	dictionary
three/some	unusual		square		green	Turkish			rugs
Mrs. Lee's	elegant, expensive			antique			carved	wood	furniture

Note that when two general adjectives are placed before a noun, either a comma or the conjunction *and* may be placed between them.

Mrs. Lee has some elegant**,** expensive antique carved wood furniture.
Mrs. Lee has some elegant **and** expensive antique carved wood furniture.

EXERCISE 3

As you read the paragraph, find and correct 11 errors in the order of the adjectives and noun modifiers. Use the chart on page 267 as a guide. The first one has been done for you.

As you step through the doorway, you notice the peacefulness of this quiet, dark reading room. Each wall is covered with shelves that hold hundreds of books. A red wool ~~soft~~ ^soft^ carpet covers the floor. Two glass wide doors bring in bright sunlight and give a view of a garden where beautiful pink large roses and blue tiny forget-me-nots are in bloom. In the middle of the reading room are two upholstered comfortable chairs and a wood polished round table that holds a glass fine green lamp. Two thick volumes—a Russian nineteenth-century novel and a history of the War of 1812—are on one side of the table. On the other side are a Mexican twentieth-century well-known novel and a history of Mexico. A yellow tiger-striped big cat sleeps in one of the chairs and a skinny black little cat sleeps in the other. The reading room is a calm, restful place to escape from the busy world outside.

2a. Participial Adjectives

Present participles and past participles are often used as adjectives. The meaning of present and past participles is different.

RULE 1 The present participial adjective (-*ing*) refers to an action in progress, an action that occurs regularly, or an action that can occur any time. The past participial adjective (-*ed*) refers to an action that is complete.

Growing children (children under 18 who are in the process of growing) need a lot of help from their parents.
Grown children (children over 18 who have finished growing) can help their parents.
The police caught the **escaping** prisoner as he climbed over the fence. (The prisoner was in the process of escaping.)
The police caught the **escaped** prisoner, who had been hiding in the woods for several weeks. (The prisoner had completed his escape.)
I keep my **writing** supplies (the pen and paper that I use every time I write) in this drawer.
I turn in all my **written** work (the work that I have finished writing) to my teacher on time.

RULE 2 Pairs of participial adjectives like *bored/boring* or *interested/interesting* can describe people's reactions to things and the effect of things on people. The present participial adjective (-*ing*) modifies something (or someone) that affects someone.

The video game was	amazing boring disappointing exciting fascinating uninteresting	to/for the boys.

The past participial adjective (-*ed*) modifies the people who are affected by that thing (or person).

The boys were	amazed by bored with disappointed by/with excited about/by fascinated by/with uninterested in	the video game.

Check your dictionary to find out which preposition follows a participial adjective.

EXERCISE 4
As you read the paragraph, find and correct the seven errors in participial adjectives like this.

The ~~dined~~ *dining* room was empty.

The ~~polishing~~ *polished* silverware was shining in the candlelight.

At 5:00 P.M. the restaurant kitchen was quiet. The chefs and their helpers were taking a break as they waited for the orders of the first diners. Everything was ready for a busy night. Hundreds of washing plates were ready on the shelves. Clean carving knives, served spoons, and fried pans hung from the wall. A mountain of slicing bread sat near the door, ready for hungry customers. Freshly iced cakes and appealing fruit tarts waited on a side table. Chopping vegetables and carefully trimmed pieces of meat and fish were chilling in the refrigerator. A warming oven was keeping bowls of cooked rice and mashing potatoes hot and ready to serve. A large pot of steaming soup sat over a low fire on the stove, and its appetized smell mixed with the aroma of freshly ground coffee. The staff appreciated these few quiet moments before the first customers arrived because they would not rest again for six hours.

3. Adverb Clauses

Adverb clauses are dependent clauses that are joined to sentences by subordinating conjunctions. You can use **adverb clauses** to show relationships between ideas. The subordinating conjunction you choose tells what kind of relationship an adverb clause has to a sentence.

Relationship	Subordinating Conjunctions
comparison	as*, just as
concession	although, even though, though
condition	if, in case, unless
contrast	whereas, while
purpose	so that
reason	as*, because, now that**, since*
result	so/such . . . that
time	after, as*, as long as, as soon as, before, by the time, every time, once, since*, the first/next/last time, until, when, whenever, while

*The subordinators *since* and *as* have more than one meaning. When you use one of these subordinators, you have to make sure that the meaning you want to express is clear.

> Enrico has been good at math **since** he was in elementary school. (time)
> Enrico is majoring in math **since** he likes numbers. (reason)

> Enrico's interest in math increased **as** he was taking algebra in high school. (time)
> Enrico got straight *As* in algebra **as** he found it easy. (reason)
> Mathematics requires practice with different kinds of problems, **as** playing a musical instrument requires practice with different types of music. (comparison)

**The subordinator *now that* combines two meanings: *now* and *because*.

> Enrico has been able to study advanced math **now that** he is in college. (time and reason)

3a. Adverb Clauses and Verb Tense

Sentences with adverb clauses have at least two verbs, one in the main part of the sentence and one in the adverb clause. The tenses of those verbs must make sense together. To choose the correct tense for a verb in a sentence with an adverbial clause, you must consider

1. the meaning of each verb in the sentence

2. the time relationship between the clauses in the sentence

3. the two rules that follow

Rule 1 In sentences about the future, make sure that the verb in the adverb clause is always in the simple present or present perfect tense.

When we **graduate**, we will have a party.
As soon as the party **has finished**, we will return home.

Rule 2 Use the subordinating conjunctions *since* and *by the time* only with certain verb tenses.

PRESENT PERFECT OR
PRESENT PERFECT PROGRESSIVE   SIMPLE PAST
He **has lived/has been living** in this house *since* he **moved** into town.

     PRESENT   SIMPLE
     PERFECT   PRESENT
The sun **has** usually **set** *by the time* we **arrive**.

    FUTURE PERFECT   SIMPLE PRESENT
The sun **will have set** *by the time* we **arrive**.

    PAST PERFECT   SIMPLE PAST
The sun **had set** *by the time* we **arrived**.

EXERCISE 5
As you read the paragraph, underline the adverb clauses, and find and correct the ten verb tense errors. The first one has been done for you.

I love to visit New York City. <u>Every time I travel there</u>, I ~~had~~ *have* new experiences and come away with new impressions. The first time I went, I climb to the top of the Statue of Liberty. When I have reached the top of the spiral staircase and was looking out over New York Harbor, I was thinking about the many immigrants from all over the world who come to the city since Dutch colonists settled the area in 1625. Before the Dutch came, Native Americans have been living in the area. It is astonishing to think that the Colonists were paying the Native American tribe only $24 for the Island of Manhattan. Now trillions of dollars change hands at the New York Stock Exchange every day. On my last trip, I visited the United Nations. As I was touring the U.N., I have been listening to the knowledgeable guide explain how the U.N. works. By the time the tour has finished, I had learned quite a lot. When I left the U.N., I had dinner in a Czech restaurant. New York seems to have as many kinds of ethnic restaurants as there are countries at the U.N. I have tried Puerto Rican, Cuban, Korean, and Indonesian food, and the next time I am going, I plan to eat in Chinatown. I am sure that I will keep visiting New York as long as I will be able to. There will always be more to see!

3b. Reducing Adverb Clauses

Some adverb clauses of time and reason can be reduced to participial phrases, as shown below. Reducing adverb clauses allows you to write more concisely, that is, to put more information in fewer words, as in this example.

> ~~Because Sara had~~ ^{Having} brought her lunch to school, ^{Sara} ~~she~~ looked for a table to sit down and eat.

3b.1. Reducing Time Clauses   Follow these rules.

RULE 1 You can only reduce an adverb clause when the subject of the adverb clause and the subject of the main clause are the same.

> While Sara ate/was eating her lunch, she read the newspaper.
> *While eating* her lunch, Sara read the newspaper.
> *Eating* her lunch, Sara read the newspaper.

RULE 2 When you reduce an adverb clause at the beginning of a sentence, you often need to change the subject of the main clause from a pronoun to a noun.

> *While reading* the newspaper, ^{Sara} ~~she~~ ate her lunch.

RULE 3 An *-ing* participial phrase in a sentence indicates actions that are happening at the same time (*Reading* the newspaper, Sara ate her lunch.). To indicate that the action expressed in the phrase occurred at an earlier time, use *after* + (verb + *-ing*) or *having* + (verb + *-ed*).

> After Sara had finished lunch, she started to do her homework.
> *After finishing* lunch, Sara started to do her homework.
> *Having finished* lunch, Sara started to do her homework.

RULE 4 You can reduce time clauses with *after, before, since,* and *while* to participial phrases, but only *after* and *while* can be deleted from reduced adverb clauses.

> *Before starting* her essay, Sara read her textbook.
> *(While) reading* her textbook, Sara took notes.

3b.2. Reducing Reason Clauses   Reduced adverb clauses of reason do not contain *because*. Because reduced adverb clauses that begin with **verb** + *-ing* or *having* + (**verb** + *-ed*) can express either a time relationship or a reason, you must make sure the meaning of a participial phrase is clear. If reducing an adverb clause will make the meaning of a sentence unclear, do not reduce it.

> Because Sara needed to write an essay, she started brainstorming.
> *Needing* to write an essay, Sara started brainstorming.

> Because Sara had thought about her topic beforehand, she found it easy to brainstorm.
> *Having thought* about her topic beforehand, Sara found it easy to brainstorm.

Because Sara made lists in order to brainstorm for all of her assignments, she began to write down her ideas for this assignment one after the other. (In this case, the adverb clause should not be reduced because reducing it would produce a confusing sentence.)

EXERCISE 6

Find the eight adverb clauses in the passage that may be reduced to adverb phrases. Reduce them, changing the subject of the sentence to a noun or noun phrase when necessary. The first one has been done for you.

Jose Martí was a political activist as well as a lawyer, journalist, teacher, and poet who was born in Cuba in 1853, when Cuba was under Spanish rule. Martí opposed the occupation of Cuba, so he spent much of his life outside his native country.

As a teenager, Martí published a pamphlet protesting the Spanish occupation, for which the Spanish authorities sentenced him to prison for six years. After his release, he was deported to Spain. ~~While Martí was living~~ <ins>While living</ins> in Spain, ~~he~~ <ins>Martí</ins> studied law and literature at the University of Zaragoza.

In 1875, Martí went to Mexico City, where he lived and published a journal for two years. Then he moved to Guatemala, where he taught literature for a short time. Because he wanted to practice law in Cuba, Martí returned to his native country in 1878. However, the Spanish authorities did not allow Martí to be a lawyer but instead arrested him for political conspiracy and again deported him to Spain.

After Martí left Spain, he went to Venezuela. He had planned to settle in Venezuela permanently. However, because he found himself in conflict with the Venezuelan government, Martí had to move again.

After Martí had left Venezuela, he moved to New York, where he stayed from 1881 to 1895. While Martí was living in New York, he published a book of poetry called *Ismaelillo* and wrote articles for the Buenos Aires newspaper, *La Nación*. In 1893, Martí organized Cuban exiles in the United States against the Spanish occupation of Cuba. Because the U.S. government supported his efforts against Spain, it appointed Martí to various consular posts. However, Martí was opposed to not only Spanish but also U.S. interests in Cuba. He wanted to see his country independent. Martí resigned from the consular positions and began to organize a revolt against Spanish rule in Cuba.

In 1895, Martí returned to Cuba to lead the insurrection. There, while Martí was fighting against Spanish occupation, he was killed. Martí is remembered both as a national hero in Cuba and as a journalist and poet.

3c. Conditional Sentences

As a writer, you sometimes need to discuss things that are possible. Conditional sentences allow you to do that. Most conditional sentences contain the subordinating conjunction *if*. Conditional sentences are classified according to time (present, future, or past) and according to whether they represent a **real** situation or an **unreal** situation.

Real Conditional Sentences

PRESENT

If (when) I **have** extra money at the end of every month, I always **deposit** it in the bank.

FUTURE

If I **have** extra money at the end of next month, I **will deposit** it in the bank.

PAST

Five years ago, if (when) I **had** extra money at the end of a month, I always **deposited** it in the bank.

Note that in the main clause of real future conditional sentences, you can also use *be going to* (*I am going to deposit*) and various modal verbs (*I might/may/can/ should deposit*).

Unreal Conditional Sentences

PRESENT

If I **owned** a car now, I **would travel**. (I don't own a car.)

PAST

Five years ago, if I **had owned** a car, I **would have traveled**. (I didn't own a car.)

Note that in the main clause of present and past unreal conditional sentences, you can also use these modals: *might* (*I might travel/might have traveled*) and *could* (*I could travel/could have traveled*).

EXERCISE 7

As you read the passage, find the eight errors in conditional sentences and correct them. The first one has been done for you.

Weather has a major effect on people, so accurate weather prediction can save lives. For example, if residents are warned in advance of an approaching typhoon or hurricane, they ~~could~~ ^{can} evacuate to a safe place, or if fishermen knew a storm is coming, they can delay going out to sea.

Forty or fifty years ago, the only way to predict weather was to use statistics. For example, if it rained the first week of March ten times over a 40-year period, one can say that there is a 25-percent chance of rain the first week of March. If one averaged all the recorded temperatures for one day, say September 2, over a 30-year period, one will be able to predict the September 2 temperature for this year quite accurately.

Since 1960, when the first weather satellite was sent into space, weather prediction has become even more accurate. Without satellite images, weather forecasters could not predict weather affected by atmospheric events over the ocean. For example, the people of the Hawaiian Islands would have had no warning of Hurricane Iwa in 1982 if there are no satellite images. Satellites now send data twice a day to a number of weather centers located around the world. Forecasters can make certain predictions just by looking at the pictures. For instance, if they see an area with a piece of clear sky surrounded by clouds in the morning, they knew that thunderstorms may hit that area later in the day. In addition, computers can analyze satellite images along with information about air pressure, temperature, and wind speed to create simulations that can predict weather weeks—even months—into the future.

Weather prediction is an example of successful international cooperation. If forecasters on one side of the globe see that potentially dangerous weather events are going to affect people on the other side of the globe, they would have issued advisories to protect those people right away. If everyone could follow this model of cooperation and share other kinds of information as openly as weather information is shared, many people will benefit.

4. Adverbs

Adverbs add various kinds of information to sentences. Some adverbs modify entire sentences, a few adverbs modify adjectives, and many adverbs modify verbs.

Kinds of Adverbs					
Modifying Sentences		Modifying Adjectives or Other Adverbs	Modifying Verbs		
Sentence	Transitions	Degree	Place	Manner	Time
fortunately generally	however nevertheless	very, quite, rather, especially	here next door	carefully happily	yesterday usually

4a. Adverb Placement

English has several rules that govern where you can put adverbs in a sentence.

RULE 1 The various types of adverbs have different positions in a sentence. The chart below shows the usual placement of most adverbs and adverb phrases.

Placement of Adverbs and Adverb Phrases			
Beginning of a Sentence	**Middle of a Sentence**		**End of a Sentence**
Sentences and Transitions	**Frequency (*always, often, never*, etc.)**	**Other Mid-sentence Adverbs (*already, also, just, probably, recently, still*, etc.)**	**Place + Manner + Time**
Generally, the spring months are warm. *However*, this spring was cool.	The boys are *usually* in school. The boys *never* come to school on time.	She has *already* taken the test. Her test has *probably* been corrected.	We set the gifts *here carefully yesterday*. The children came *into the room happily this morning*.

RULE 2 **Middle-of-sentence adverbs** are one-word adverbs. They should be placed (1) after the *be* verb (The boys are ***usually*** in school.), (2) after the first auxiliary verb (Her test has ***probably*** been corrected.), and (3) before simple present or simple past tense verbs (The boys ***usually*** come/came to school on time.).

RULE 3 End-of-sentence adverbs must be in the order **place + manner + time**.

$$\overbrace{\text{PLACE}} \quad \overbrace{\text{MANNER}} \quad \overbrace{\text{TIME}}$$
The singer walked off the stage confidently at the end of his performance.

RULE 4 Do not put an adverb between a verb and its direct object.

carefully
We set ~~carefully~~ the gifts here.
∧

RULE 5 **Adverbs of degree** are placed directly before the words they modify.

Although the food was **especially** salty, the diners complimented the cook **very** politely.

EXERCISE 8

As you read the paragraph, find the nine misplaced adverbs and adverb phrases. Move them to the correct positions. The first one has been done for you.

Three quarters of a century after Charlie Chaplin made his silent films, ~~still~~
still
he is remembered fondly because he created a character that was both funny
∧
and sympathetic. Chaplin's character was a poor little tramp, a bum who tried

to look like a gentleman in clothes that fit poorly him. The tramp was not a real gentleman, but he maintained his dignity always while he struggled to survive in difficult situations. In *Gold Rush* (1925), the tramp has gone to Alaska. In the cold, snowy wilderness, he finds shelter in a cabin with a stranger. Both men are starving. The stranger considers eating the tramp, so the tramp tries to run away, but the wind is blowing so hard that the poor fellow cannot escape. To relieve their hunger, the tramp cooks his own shoe for dinner. He carves it as though it were roast turkey and eats delicately it with great enjoyment. He goes later into town and sees at a dancehall a beautiful girl. She smiles in his direction and he smiles back. Then he discovers that she at someone else is smiling. Though Chaplin's character faced danger and humiliation again and again, he endured. He overcame difficulty always with optimism and dignity.

4b. Subject-Verb Inversion Following Certain Adverbs at the Beginning of a Sentence

Sometimes subjects and verbs are inverted; that is, the *be* verb or an auxiliary verb comes before the subject of a sentence. By inverting subjects and verbs, you can avoid repetitive sentence beginnings and add variety to your sentences.

RULE 1 When a sentence begins with an adverb or adverb phrase of place, the subject and verb can be inverted.

$$\text{\textbf{In the corner of the room}} \overset{\text{V}}{was} \text{ a comfortable } \overset{\text{S}}{\text{armchair.}}$$

RULE 2 When a sentence begins with a negative adverb such as *never*, *seldom*, or *not only* or an adverb or adverb phrase of place, you must invert the subject and verb.

Hardly ever *does* the bus *come* on time.
Not only *did* Father *sing* well, but both my parents played the violin.

RULE 3 When a sentence begins with *only* and an adverb, you must invert the subject and verb.

Only recently *has* he *spoken* in class.

5. Articles

English has two **articles**, *a* and *the*. Sometimes no article (Ø) is used. When you use articles correctly in your writing, you are telling your readers which nouns represent new information and which nouns represent old information. You are also telling them whether or not singular nouns are countable.

Use the **indefinite article *a*** before singular count nouns that are indefinite or represent new information. Use ***an*** before words that begin with a vowel sound, as in ***an*** *overcoat* or ***an*** *hour*.

I am looking for **a** raincoat and **an** umbrella.

Use the **definite article** *the* before singular count nouns, plural nouns, and uncountable nouns that represent old or known information.

The television, **the** dishes, and **the** furniture you gave us are wonderful.

Use **no article (Ø)** before plural nouns and uncountable nouns that are not definite.

Ø Homeless people need Ø money, Ø food, and Ø clothing as well as Ø housing.

5a. Definite Nouns

If something is *definite*, it is known to the speaker or writer as well as the listener or reader. A noun can become definite in the following five ways.

1. The noun is followed by a clause or phrase which makes it definite.

    the house you can see in the distance
    the mayor of our town

2. The noun represents something that is unique.

    the sun
    the moon
    the tallest student in the class

3. The noun represents something that the speaker/writer and the listener/reader are familiar with.

    the library
    the post office

4. The noun has been mentioned in the conversation or text earlier.

    I saw a car. **The** car was traveling too fast.

5. The noun is associated with the topic of the conversation or text.

    I saw a building. **The** roof was bright green.

5b. General Statements

General statements are not definite, so they are usually made with plural count nouns or uncountable nouns.

Computers give people access to knowledge.
Knowledge improves people's lives.

Exception: General statements about animals, human inventions, and the organs of the body can be made with *the* and a singular noun, as in the following examples.

The horse provided transportation for people before **the** automobile was invented. (= Horses provided transportation for people before automobiles were invented.)
The diaphragm and **the** lungs make it possible for us to breathe.

5c. Expressions of Quantity

Expressions of quantity are usually indefinite (*a* cup of Ø sugar, *some* Ø salt), but the material to be measured may be definite (a cup of *the* sugar in the cabinet, some of *the* salt on the table).

EXERCISE 9

As you read the paragraph, find and correct the 15 errors in article usage. The first one has been done for you.

You know that the coins in your pocket and the bills in your wallet have ~~the~~ value. But why are they valuable? Metal your coins are made of and paper your bills are printed on are not worth much themselves. The money is valued because people in societies all over world have agreed to give it value. If you give someone handful of the dollars, yen, pesos, rubles, dinars, or euros, you expect to get something in return. Long ago, people used the things like beads or the seashells as money. Then they discovered a gold or silver and used it as currency. Bag of gold bullion or gold coins represented wealth of the owner. Today person's wealth is represented by numbers that are stored in the computers. Imagine! Without the electricity, you would not be able to find out how much money you own.

5d. Special Uses of *the* and Ø

Many uses of *the* and Ø do not have rules, and you just need to memorize them. Many of these uses are shown in the following chart.

the	Ø
Time	
in *the* morning, *the* afternoon, *the* evening	at night
the 1980s, *the* nineties	
the nineteenth century, *the* twentieth century	
the past, *the* present, *the* future	
Numbers	
the first, *the* second, *the* third (ordinal numbers)	Chapter 1, section 2, page three (cardinal numbers)

Location	
the front, *the* middle, *the* back	
Some Geographic Names	
(mountain ranges) *the* Ural Mountains	(single mountains) Mount Fuji
(oceans, seas) *the* Pacific Ocean, *the* Mediterranean Sea	(lakes) Lake Geneva
(rivers) *the* Yangtze River	
(deserts) *the* Gobi Desert	
Groups of People	
(nationalities or ethnic groups) *the* Chinese, (*the*) Iranians	(ethnic, racial, or religious groups) Hispanics, whites, Buddhists

6. Comparatives and Superlatives

English has various ways to express **comparative** and **superlative** relationships using adjectives, adverbs, and expressions of quantity.

COMPARATIVE WITH AN ADJECTIVE
Networking is hard**er** to learn **than** web-page development.
Web-page development is easi**er** to learn **than** networking.
Networking is **not as** easy to learn **as** web-page development.

COMPARATIVE WITH AN ADVERB
Today's software operates **more** efficiently **than** the software of the past.
The software of the past did **not** operate **as** efficiently **as** today's software does.
The software of the past operated **less** efficiently **than** today's software.

Note in the above examples that one-syllable adjectives and adverbs and two-syllable adjectives that end in *-y* form the comparative with *-er*. All other adjectives and adverbs form the comparative with *more*. In addition, note that some adjectives and adverbs, such as *bad, good,* and *far* have irregular comparative and superlative forms. To find irregular comparative and superlative forms of adjectives and adverbs, check your dictionary.

COMPARATIVE WITH AN EXPRESSION OF QUANTITY
There is **more/less** activity on campus in the morning **than** in the afternoon.
(There is **not as much** . . . **as** . . .)
There are **more/fewer** people on campus in the morning **than** in the afternoon. (There are **not as many** . . . **as** . . .)

Use *less* and *not as much* before uncountable nouns. Use *fewer* and *not as many* before countable nouns.

SUPERLATIVE WITH AN ADJECTIVE

Of all the buildings on campus, the science center is **the most used**.

The science center is **the most used** building on campus.

SUPERLATIVE WITH AN ADVERB

Of all the courses, computer science classes are the ones that students choose **most frequently**.

Computer science classes are the ones that students choose **most frequently** of all the classes.

SUPERLATIVE WITH AN EXPRESSION OF QUANTITY

Of all the instructors, Dr. Tong demands the **most/least** effort from his students.

Note that one-syllable adjectives and adverbs and two-syllable adjectives that end in *-y* form the superlative with *-est*. All other adjectives and adverbs form the superlative with *most*. Note also that *the* precedes superlative adjectives and expressions of quantity but not superlative adverbs.

6a. Modifying Comparative Statements

The meaning of comparative statements can be changed slightly by adding these adverbs: *a lot, a few, a little, many, much, quite a bit, quite a few,* or *quite a lot.*

BEFORE A COMPARATIVE ADJECTIVE

The automobile repair program is **a little/quite a bit/quite a lot/much/a lot** more challenging than Saleem thought.

BEFORE A COMPARATIVE ADVERB

Saleem is working **a little/quite a bit/quite a lot/much/a lot** harder this semester than he did last semester.

BEFORE A COMPARATIVE EXPRESSION OF QUANTITY

Saleem has done **a little/quite a bit/much/a lot** more studying this semester than last.

Saleem has taken **a few/quite a few/quite a lot/many/a lot** more tests this semester than last semester.

6b. Ellipsis in Comparative Statements

In comparative statements, you should omit repeated words after **than**. This is called using **ellipsis**. Using ellipsis means omitting all but the essential information in order to make your writing concise. (See Ellipsis, page 286.)

Saleem's grades are higher this semester than ~~they were~~ last ~~semester~~.

Students in the automobile repair program today study harder than ~~students~~ they

~~in the automobile repair program studied~~ did ten years ago.

7. Coordination

Coordination is the linking of words, phrases, or clauses that are equally important with coordinating or correlative conjunctions. You can use coordination to connect ideas and avoid unnecessary repetition.

7a. Coordinating Conjunctions

English has seven **coordinating conjunctions**:

and	for	or	yet
but	nor	so	

All of them can join independent clauses.

INDEPENDENT CLAUSE   INDEPENDENT CLAUSE
Here the weather is hot, **or** we have tropical storms.

INDEPENDENT CLAUSE   INDEPENDENT CLAUSE
We do not have enough jobs, **nor** is there enough food.

INDEPENDENT CLAUSE   INDEPENDENT CLAUSE
People move to the city to find jobs, **for** the factories are in the urban centers.

You must invert the subject and verb after the negative coordinating conjunction *nor*. That means that you must place a form of the *be* verb or an auxiliary verb (*does, has, will*, etc.) before the subject.

We do not have enough jobs, nor **do** we have enough food.

In addition to joining independent clauses, the coordinating conjunctions *and, or, but*, and *yet* can also link words, phrases, and dependent clauses within sentences.

The *courthouse, library,* **and** *museum* are beautiful buildings. (nouns)
To reward **or** *to punish* children's behavior is to teach them the difference between right and wrong. (infinitives)
The apartment is *small* **but/yet** *comfortable.* (adjectives)
Boris hopes to *marry soon, have several children,* **and** *enjoy family life.* (verb phrases)
My mother says *that it is economical to buy a used car* **but** (*that*) *it involves risk.* (noun clauses)
A politician *who can communicate ideas simply, who understands people's fears,* **and** *who can give them hope* gains popularity. (adjective clauses)

EXERCISE **10**

This passage does not have any coordinating conjunctions. On another piece of paper, rewrite the passage using coordinating conjunctions to combine sentences and link words, phrases, and clauses. Omit unnecessary repetition. Check your finished paragraph for subject-verb agreement. (See Appendix IA, section 14f, page 299.) The first paragraph has been done for you.

Choosing a career is a very important step. You will spend a good part of your life working. The career you choose can determine who your friends are. It can determine where you live. It can determine how much money you make.

Choosing a career is a very important step, for you will spend a good part of your life working. The career you choose can determine who your friends are, where you live, and how much money you make.

People differ in their abilities. They differ in their interests. They differ in their temperaments. A job may be perfect for one person. It may be a nightmare for someone else. For instance, Patricia is very good at working with abstract ideas. Gina is very good at working with abstract ideas. Patricia likes to solve problems. Gina likes to solve problems. They are both considering computer programming as a career. Only one of them, Gina, is able to work quietly alone for long periods of time. Only Gina should consider going into programming. Consider two other people, Alexi and Etien. Alexi is thinking about becoming a graphic designer. Etien is thinking about becoming a graphic designer. One of these men should not choose graphic design as a career. Alexi is creative. Etien is creative. Alexi is very patient. Etien is not very patient. Etien does not like to do precise work. Etien does not have the patience to redo flawed projects. Etien has artistic talent. He would not make a good graphic designer.

A career can make you happy. A career can make you unhappy. Before choosing a career, get to know yourself well. Learn what kind of jobs are available. Ask your relatives for advice. Ask your teachers for advice. Ask your friends for advice. Making the right career choice can have a big influence on your future well being.

7b. Parallel Structure

When two or more words, phrases, or dependent clauses are linked by a conjunction (*and, or, but,* or *yet*), make sure the items are in the same grammatical form. This is called **parallel structure**.

In the following example, *sunny* is an adjective, and *wind* is a noun. To make these words parallel, change *wind* to an adjective.

The day was sunny but ~~wind~~ windy.

In the next example, *drove to the city* and *visited our relatives* are verb phrases, and *to the movie theater* is a prepositional phrase. To make these phrases parallel, put a verb before *to the movie theater.*

We drove to the city, visited our relatives, and went to the movie theater.

In the following example, *to get health information* and *to check the prices of products* are infinitive phrases, and *on-line games* is a noun phrase. To make these phrases parallel, put an infinitive before *on-line games*.

I usually use the Internet to get health information, to check the prices of
products, or ⟨to play⟩ on-line games.

In this final example, *who is able to speak effectively* is a dependent clause, and *a good listener* is a noun phrase. To make these sentence parts parallel, change the noun phrase to a dependent clause.

For the position of manager, we need someone who is able to speak
effectively yet ⟨who is⟩ a good listener.

EXERCISE 11

As you read this paragraph, find and correct the 11 errors in parallel structure. The first one has been done for you.

Adaptation is a characteristic of an individual plant or animal that allows it to survive and ~~reproducing~~ *reproduce* in its environment. Adaptation allows a plant or animal to get the water and nutrients it needs to survive, avoid being eaten, adjustment to climatic conditions, and reproduce. For example, most plants produce tens of thousands of seeds because so few seeds will actually germinate and growth. Some pine trees are adapted to reproduce only when there is a forest fire. The heat of the flames causes the pine cones to open and scattering seeds. Animals show various adaptations as well. Many animals have camouflage—the ability to blend into their environment so that they are not seen by predators. Small animals can call out or running away fast when they are threatened, while larger predatory animals have keen senses of smell, hearing, and vision in order to locate prey. In regions where the winters are harsh, animals grow thicker fur in the fall to prepare for cold weather and then loss of that extra hair in the spring. In the heat of the desert, reptiles maintain a constant body temperature by moving back and forth between sunny and shade. Mammals in the desert are inactive in the heat of the day and activity at night. For the purpose of mating, male and female animals and birds look different. Male animals are often larger, and the colorful feathers of male birds. Adaptation is so important that unless a plant or animal is successfully adapted, it will have little chance of survival and reproducing.

7c. Correlative Conjunctions

Correlative conjunctions work in pairs to join items in sentences.

both . . . and   neither . . . nor
either . . . or   not only . . . but

Correlative conjunctions give you a way to draw attention to parallel items. Notice in the following examples that some correlatives can be replaced by coordinating conjunctions, but using correlative conjunctions adds emphasis.

Rafael can play **both** the saxophone **and** the piano. (Rafael can play the saxophone *and* the piano.)

Either Sylvain **or** Marie will lead the group. (Sylvain *or* Marie will lead the group.)

The furniture was **neither** attractive **nor** well made. (The furniture was not attractive, *and* it was not well made, either./The furniture was not attractive, *nor* was it well made.)

Ali **not only** speaks three languages **but also** has a Master's degree in history. (Ali speaks three languages, *and*, in addition to that, he has a Master's degree in history.)

The first three pairs of correlative conjunctions (*both . . . and, either . . . or, neither . . . nor*), emphasize both items in the correlative phrase equally. However, *not only . . . but also* puts greater emphasis on the second item in the correlative phrase. Look at these examples.

He excels in **both** sports **and** academic work. (In this example, *sports* and *academic work* are equally important.)

He excels in **not only** sports **but also** academic work. (In this example, *academic work* is more important than *sports*.)

In sentences with *not only . . . but, as well* and *too* may replace *also*.

He excels in **not only** sports but academic work **as well**.
He excels in **not only** sports but academic work **too**.

The items in correlative phrases must follow the rule of **parallel structure**. In the following example, *work in his father's company* is a verb phrase and *college* is a noun. To make these sentence parts parallel, place a verb before *college*.

After high school, José will either work in his father's company or ^attend^ college.

In the following example, *the basic subjects such as math and reading* is a noun phrase, and *they need art and music* is a clause. To make these sentence parts parallel, omit the subject and verb.

Students need not only the basic subjects such as math and reading but ~~they need~~ art and music as well.

8. Ellipsis

Repeated words and phrases in a sentence can distract us from new information, so it is usually best to omit them. Omitting repeated words and phrases is called **ellipsis**. Notice in the following examples that auxiliary verbs are repeated but other parts of the verb phrase are not. (Words in parentheses may or may not be omitted.)

ELLIPSIS WITH COORDINATING CONJUNCTIONS
Tomiko will major in architecture, and Hanh **will** ~~major in architecture~~ too.

ELLIPSIS WITH SUBORDINATING CONJUNCTIONS
Alex is studying engineering, (just) as his father ~~studied engineering~~ **did**.

ELLIPSIS WITH COMPARATIVE STATEMENTS
The engineering program has been in existence longer than (the) materials science (program) **has** ~~been in existence~~.

9. Gerunds and Infinitives

Two verb forms, the **gerund** (*-ing*) form and the **infinitive** (*to* + simple form), act as nouns in sentences.

A gerund can be the subject of a verb, the direct object of a verb, or the object of a preposition.

Jogging is good exercise.
He enjoys **jogging**.
This path is a good place for **jogging**.

An infinitive can be the subject of a verb or the direct object of a verb.

To exercise is important.
He needs **to exercise**.

Infinitives are only used in the subject position to make general statements.

9a. Gerunds and Infinitives after Verbs

Some verbs, such as *enjoy*, can have a gerund as a direct object, and other verbs, such as *need*, can have an infinitive as a direct object. A number of verbs, such as *like*, can have either a gerund or an infinitive as a direct object, but sometimes the meaning changes, as with the verb *stop*.

I **stopped buying** milk at the corner grocery store. (I no longer buy milk there.)
I **stopped to buy** milk at the corner grocery store. (I bought milk there while I was going somewhere else.)

To find out if you can use a gerund, an infinitive, or either one after a certain verb, consult your dictionary.

9b. Expanding a Gerund or Infinitive Phrase

You can expand gerund phrases to include more information in your sentences. A gerund or infinitive phrase may include a noun object (Making **cookies** is fun.), a prepositional phrase (I plan to swim **in the ocean**.), or an adverb (She decided to exercise **more often**.). Negative infinitives are common (We promised **not** to forget.), but negative gerunds are rare (Instead of *I enjoy **not** working*, use *I enjoy relaxing*.).

9c. Gerund and Infinitive Forms: Active, Passive, Simple, and Past

This chart shows all possible forms of gerunds and infinitives.

		Active Forms	**Passive Forms**
Gerunds	**Simple Form**	I love **driving**.	I love **being driven**.
	Past Form	I regret **having spent** all my money.	I appreciate **having been given** a gift.
Infinitives	**Simple Form**	I expect **to attend** college.	I expect **to be admitted** to that college.
	Past Form	I expected **to have received** the letter by now.	I expected **to have been sent** the money by now.

10. Noun Clauses

A **noun clause** allows you to place a statement and or a question inside a sentence. A noun clause occupies a position in a sentence that is usually occupied by a noun. It can be the subject of a sentence, the direct object of a verb, or the object of a preposition.

> **That Juan is friendly** is easy to see. (subject)
> Everyone knows **that Juan is friendly**. (direct object)
> Juan differs from his sister in **that he is friendly**. (object of a preposition)

Many noun clauses are the direct objects of verbs such as *know, believe, think*, or *say*. When a noun clause is the object of the verb, you can omit *that*.

> Everyone knows **Juan is friendly**.

That can join a noun clause to a sentence. A question word (*who, which*, etc.), an *-ever* word (*whoever, whichever*), or *whether* or *if* can also connect a noun clause to a sentence. Some clauses are introduced by a phrase like *the fact that* or *the idea that*.

> **That** *some people steal* is upsetting.
> **Who** *stole the purse* is **what** *we want to know*.
> **Whoever** *took it* should be punished.
> The police will find out **whether/if** *the purse was taken by a neighbor*.
> I am disturbed by **the idea that** *someone would steal something from me*.

10a. Reported Speech

You can use noun clauses to report statements and questions.

Reported Statements

When you change a quoted statement to a noun clause (reported speech), you may need to make two changes. Consider the following:

1. The point of view (pronoun) may change.

   He says, "I am right." → He says that **he** is right.
   He says, "You are right." → He says that **I am/we are** right.

2. Reported speech is introduced with a reporting verb such as *say* or *write*. If the reporting verb is past tense (*said* or *wrote*), the verb tense in the reported speech usually changes.

   She says, "The store sells coffee." → She **says** that the store **sells** coffee.
   She said, "The store sells coffee." → She **said** that the store **sold** coffee.

However, if you want to emphasize that the situation is continuing, you can use the present tense in the reported speech.

   She said, "The store sells coffee." → She **said** that the store **sells** coffee.

The following chart shows how verbs change after a past tense reporting verb like *said* or *wrote*.

Quoted Speech	Reported Speech
She said, "I exercise . . . ."	*She said she exercise*s*/exercise*d* . . . .
She said, "I am exercising . . . ."	She said she *was* exercising . . . .
She said, "I have exercised . . . ."	She said she *had* exercised . . . .
She said, "I exercised . . . ."	She said she *had* exercised . . . .
She said, "I was exercising . . . ."	She said she *had been* exercising . . . .
She said, "I had exercised . . . ."	**She said she had exercised . . . .
She said, "I was going to exercise . . . ."	She said she *had been* going to exercise . . . .
She said, "I will exercise . . . ."	She said she *would* exercise . . . .
She said, "I am going to exercise . . . ."	She said she *was* going to exercise . . . .
She said, "I can exercise . . . ."	She said she *could* exercise . . . .
She said, "I have to exercise . . . ."	She said she *had* to exercise . . . .
She said, "I may exercise . . . ."	She said she *might* exercise . . . .
She said, "I must exercise . . . ."	**She said she must exercise . . . .
She said, "I should exercise . . . ."	**She said she should exercise . . . .
She said, "I might exercise . . . ."	**She said she might exercise . . . .

*Statements in the simple present tense often do not change in reported speech because they refer to the past, present, and future.

**Statements in the past perfect tense (*had* + past participle) and verbs containing the modals *must, should,* and *might* do not change in reported speech.

Reported Questions

A noun clause can also report a question. Reported questions do not contain auxiliary verbs such as *do*, and so reported questions have the same word order and the same verb form as statements, subject + verb.

> He asked me, "Where do you work?"
> He asked me where I worked.

Introduce reported *yes/no* questions with *if, whether,* or *whether or not.*

> He asked me, "Have you worked there very long?"
> He asked me **if/whether/whether or not** I had worked there very long.

EXERCISE 12

Read the dialogue and the report of the dialogue that follows. As you read the report, find and correct the nine errors in reported speech. The first two have been done for you.

Note that in a passage of reported speech, you should be consistent. If the verbs at the beginning of the passage shift to the past, all of the verbs in the passage usually shift to the past.

Dialogue

Julio: Where are you from?

Claude: I came from Haiti. I miss my country.

Julio: What do you miss about it?

Claude: I have a lot of friends and relatives there, and we had a good time together. When I was in Haiti, every Saturday someone hosted a party, called a *samboche*.

Julio: I heard that your country has a lot of political unrest.

Claude: Yes, there have been many coups in Haiti's history. And unemployment is 50 percent. But in spite of the conflict and poverty, the Haitian people still enjoy life, especially during Carnival.

Julio: Is Haiti's Carnival like Carnival in Brazil?

Claude: It's similar, but not exactly the same. The music at a Haitian Carnival celebration is called *ra-ra* rock. It's a mixture of traditional Haitian rhythms and techno-rock. People wear traditional Haitian costumes.

Julio: Are you going to go back to Haiti sometime?

Claude: I've been saving money, and if possible, I will go next year for Carnival.

Report of Dialogue

Julio asked Claude where ~~was~~ was he from. Claude told him that he had come from Haiti and he missed his country. Julio asked Claude what he ~~misses~~ missed about Haiti. Claude told him that he had a lot friends and relatives there and that they had had a good time together. He mentioned that when he had been in Haiti, every Saturday someone hosted a party, called a *samboche*. Julio said that he had heard that Haiti had a lot of political unrest. Claude confirmed that. He said that there had been many coups in Haiti's history and that unemployment was 50 percent, but in spite of the conflict and poverty, the Haitian people still enjoyed life, especially during Carnival. Julio asked if Haiti's Carnival was like Carnival in Brazil. Claude replied that it was similar, but not exactly the same. He told Julio about *ra-ra* rock, a mixture of traditional Haitian rhythms and techno-rock. He added that people wore traditional costumes. Julio asked Claude if was he going to go back to Haiti sometime, and Claude replied that he has been saving money and, if possible, he will go next year for Carnival.

11. Nouns

Nouns identify persons, places, objects, or ideas.

11a. Irregular Nouns

Some nouns have irregular plural forms.

> child, children
> man, men
> woman, women

Some nouns have special endings in both the singular and the plural.

> crisis, crises
> medium, media
> phenomenon, phenomena

Some nouns have only a plural form.

> belongings
> clothes
> manners

When you are unsure about the form of a noun, check your dictionary.

11b. Countable and Uncountable Nouns

Countable nouns can be made plural: *one statistic, two statistics*. Uncountable nouns are always singular. Generally speaking, English has three types of uncountable nouns:

MASS ITEMS
air, aluminum, oxygen, sand, water

GENERAL TERMS THAT REPRESENT CATEGORIES OF THINGS
equipment, furniture, jewelry, mail, transportation

ABSTRACT IDEAS
education, freedom, honesty, strength, wealth

Many nouns are both countable and uncountable. The choice of form depends on the meaning of the noun in a particular sentence.

I ordered **two coffees** in the restaurant. **Coffee is** getting expensive.

When you are unsure about whether a noun is countable, uncountable, or both, check your dictionary.

11b.1. Expressions of Quantity with Countable and Uncountable Nouns

Some expressions of quantity are used only with uncountable nouns. Some are used only with countable nouns. Others are used with both.

USED WITH UNCOUNTABLE NOUNS
a little humor
quite a bit of traffic
not **much** time

USED WITH COUNTABLE NOUNS
a story
a few jokes
several ideas
quite a few vehicles
not **many** minutes

USED WITH BOTH COUNTABLE AND UNCOUNTABLE NOUNS
some plants, **some** vegetation
a lot of/a great deal of facts, **a lot of/a great deal of** information

You can use all of the expressions above—except the indefinite article *a*—with *of the* if the noun is definite (some *of the* plants, some *of the* vegetation).

12. Prepositions

Prepositions are words that come before nouns, pronouns, and gerunds. Most prepositions refer to time (***at** ten o'clock*, ***in** the morning*) or place (***by** the library*, ***on** the street*). A few prepositions express logical relationships.

Because of/Due to/As a result of the weather, the party was held indoors. (reason)
In spite of/Despite the late hour, the guests did not seem ready to leave. (surprising result)
Like the children, the adults enjoyed themselves. (similarity)
Unlike the adults, the children did not get up and dance. (difference or contrast)
The guests ate some food, **such as** sandwiches and chips. (example)
According to my uncle, everyone had a good time. (citation)

Some prepositions (*as a result of, according to*, etc.) are more than one word.

A preposition always has a noun or pronoun object. A preposition, together with its object and any modifiers of that object, is called a **prepositional phrase**. Prepositional phrases can occur anywhere in a sentence and can modify nouns, verbs, or complete sentences. You can use prepositional phrases to add information to your sentences and make your writing more precise.

When you are not sure about the meaning or use of a preposition, look it up in your dictionary. If you are not sure which preposition should follow a particular verb, adjective, or noun, look up the verb, adjective, or noun in your dictionary.

13. Pronouns

Pronouns replace nouns and noun phrases. You can use pronouns to avoid repetition and to create links between sentences. English has four kinds of pronouns (subject, object, reflexive, and possessive) and possessive adjectives, which are similar to pronouns.

Subject Pronouns	Object Pronouns	Reflexive Pronouns	Possessive Pronouns	Possessive Adjectives
I	me	myself	mine	my
you	you	yourself, yourselves	yours	your
he	him	himself	his	his
she	her	herself	hers	her
it	it	itself	its	its
we	us	ourselves	ours	our
they	them	themselves	theirs	their

13a. Pronoun Agreement

Pronouns not only replace nouns and noun phrases but also refer back to them. That means pronouns make your writing cohesive (full of well-connected ideas). A pronoun usually refers to a noun in the same sentence or the preceding sentence.

> I took some pictures of the governor's old house. (It) is a two-story wooden structure.

Pronouns must agree in person and number with the nouns they refer to.

>   *They*   *them*
> I showed the photographs to Henri and Paul. ~~He~~ enjoyed ~~it~~.

They refers to *Henri and Paul,* and so must be plural. *Them,* which refers to *photographs,* must also be plural.

EXERCISE 13

As you read this paragraph, find and correct the eight errors in pronoun agreement. The first one has been done for you.

Ann Landers published a popular newspaper column in the United States
that helped people solve ~~his~~ *their* problems with relationships, health, and etiquette.
In the column, Landers printed people's letters and her responses to it.
Landers' replies were honest, sympathetic, and practical. For example, a
married woman wrote saying that she and her parents could not enjoy their
monthly visits because her husband did not get along with her parents.
Landers advised the woman to leave their husband home and "make everyone
happy." When a single woman wrote that, upon returning from vacation, she
had found that her steady boyfriend was dating someone else, Landers advised
them to "do some looking around herself." Because readers felt Landers'
advice made sense, he trusted her. Her column was so popular that they
continued for 46 years, 1,000 newspapers carried them, and many readers even
asked her local newspapers to continue printing it after Landers' death.

13b. Pronoun Reference

Every pronoun must refer to something. The first and second person pronouns
(*I, we, you*) refer to the writer and reader or the community of readers and
writers. The third person pronouns (*he, she, it, they*) refer back to a noun or
noun phrase mentioned earlier in the text. Two errors can occur with the third
person pronouns.

ERROR 1 A pronoun refers back to more than one noun.

INCORRECT: Paula told Karina the story. Then **she** told it to me.

Who does *she* refer to? It is not clear whether it refers to Paula or Karina.

CORRECT: Paula told Karina the story. Then ~~she~~ *Karina* told it to me.

ERROR 2 A pronoun does not refer back clearly to any one noun in the text.

INCORRECT: The school has a new rule. **They** say that students who are tardy
must go directly to the office.

Who does the pronoun *they* refer back to? The pronoun *they* has no referent, or
noun to refer back to.

CORRECT: The school has a new rule. ~~They say~~ *It says* that students who are late must
go directly to the office.

INCORRECT: Many violent crimes were committed in this city last year. The residents are concerned about **it**.

What does the pronoun *it* refer back to? To correct this problem, change *it* to a noun.

CORRECT: Many violent crimes were committed in this city last year. The residents are concerned about ~~it~~. *this situation*

In some cases, you can use the pronoun *it* as the subject of a sentence without a noun to refer back to.

It is cloudy today.
It is important to study for tests.
It is a well-known fact that eating too much salt is unhealthy.

EXERCISE 14

As you read this paragraph, underline all the pronouns and possessive adjectives. Then find and correct the four pronoun reference problems. The first three sentences have been done for you.

Louis Braille's development of a writing system for blind people was the result of a series of events—some of them unfortunate—in <u>his</u> life. At age four, Louis picked up a sharp tool called an awl that belonged to <u>his</u> father. ~~He~~ *Louis* injured one of <u>his</u> eyes with the awl. The eye became seriously infected. Then the infection spread to the other eye, and he lost sight in both eyes. In 1819, Louis's family sent him to a school for the blind, where the students were taught to read by running their fingers over embossed letters. It was very difficult to read this way. In 1821, a soldier visited the school and showed them a military code. It was called "night writing," and it consisted of a rather complicated arrangement of raised dots. He was 12 years old, and he was extremely interested in the code. He studied it and managed to simplify it, creating a system that would allow blind students to not only read but also write. Unfortunately, few people, even among the teachers at the school, recognized the value of his system. One teacher even prohibited them from using it. Nonetheless, Louis and the other students continued to use the code in secret. Years later, as an adult, Louis Braille became a teacher at the school. He taught his students how to read and write using the system he had developed, which came to be known as Braille.

13c. Pronouns that Play Special Roles in Cohesion

One and *another* and *this* and *these* play an important role in **cohesion**. These pronouns, which also function as adjectives, can help you draw readers' attention to your important ideas and create links between the key points in your paragraphs and essays.

13c.1. *One, Another, the Other*   To present items or ideas in a series, use the indefinite pronouns *one*, *another*, *some*, and *others*. If a series has a final item or items, use the definite pronouns *the other* or *the others*. This chart shows the pronouns and their corresponding adjectives.

	First in a Series	Following in the Series	Last in the Series
Singular Pronouns (and Adjectives)	First, here is **one** (*one* coin).	Next, here is **another** (*another* coin).	Finally, this is **the other** (*the other* coin).
Plural Pronouns (and Adjectives)	First, here are **some** (*some* coins).	Next, here are **others** (*other* coins).	Finally, these are **the others** (*the other* coins).

Note that the pronouns *others* and *the others* have a plural form, but the adjectives *other* and *the other* do not.

EXERCISE 15
As you read this paragraph, find and correct the five errors in the use of *another*, *other*, *the other*, *others*, and *the others*. The first one has been done for you.

A friend of mine collects musical instruments from all over the world. In his collection, he has three stringed, three wind, and seven percussion instruments. Two of the stringed instruments are lutes. One is a large oud from Syria with delicate inlaid decorations on its face. ~~Another~~ The other lute is a Chinese san xian, which has a long slender neck and only three strings. The third stringed instrument is a triangular balalaika from Russia. Like the san xian, it has only three strings, but unlike a lute, it has a flat back like a guitar. The wind instruments are also interesting. My friend has a set of panpipes from the Andes in Peru which makes a series of sweet, high sounds. The others wind instruments are two didgeridoos made by the Aborigines of Australia which produce haunting, vibrating sounds. One digeridoo is about a meter and a half long, and other is about a meter in length. Finally, there are the seven percussion instruments. Three are carved wooden drums from Africa that were made by hollowing out sections of tree trunks. The other is a steel pan from Jamaica which was made by pounding the top of a steel drum until it had the shape of a shallow bowl. Finally, other are three leather drums made by Native Americans. My friend's collection illustrates the wonderful variety of instrument forms in the world and the range of sounds that people can make with them.

13c.2. *This, That, These, Those*   To refer back to items or ideas that were mentioned previously in a text, use *this*, *that*, *these*, and *those*. These words are both adjectives and pronouns.

ADJ.

The teacher selected three students as reporters. **Those** students had to write down the main points presented by both sides in the debate.

ADJ.

The computer is fast, reliable, and moderately priced. **These** features have made it very popular.

The pronoun *this* often refers to an idea that has been expressed in a complete clause or sentence.

PRON.

We are cutting down the rain forests. **This** will lead to global climate change.

14. Sentences

To write correct, effective sentences, you need to be able to identify sentence parts and their functions.

14a. Parts of Speech

The parts of speech are identified in the following sections of Appendix IA.

Adjectives—section 2	Nouns—section 11
Adverbs—section 4	Prepositions—section 12
Articles—section 5	Pronouns—section 13
Conjunctions—sections 3, 7	Verbs—section 15

EXERCISE **16**

Identify the part of speech of each of the underlined words in these sentences as noun (**n.**), verb (**v.**), adjective (**adj.**), adverb (**adv.**), pronoun (**pron.**), preposition (**prep.**), or conjunction (**conj.**). The first one has been done for you.

(n.)
When <u>children</u> have normal contact <u>with</u> adults, they learn language in a fairly predictable way. Most babies say their <u>first</u> word, usually *Ma-ma* or *Da-da*, before they are one year old. At this time, <u>they</u> also respond appropriately to basic questions. If <u>someone</u> asks, *Where's the ball?* they will look for the ball. <u>When</u> they reach 18 months, they may begin to make two-word sentences <u>like</u> *Book here* or *Want milk*. They can <u>usually</u> answer simple questions, too. After children are two years old, they are <u>eager</u> to have <u>longer</u> conversations, although they frequently respond to questions with *No*. Until children reach age three, they don't use past tense verbs. <u>However</u>, three-year-olds can talk <u>about</u> where they went and what they did today. If someone tells them a story, they can remember <u>and</u> repeat it. Year by year, children's language <u>becomes</u> increasingly complex while they grow.

14b. Sentence Parts

Every sentence has a subject and a verb. Without both, you do not have a sentence.

Subjects

The subject is usually before the verb. The subject tells who or what the sentence is about. If the verb is an action verb, the subject also tells who or what performs the action.

Verbs

The verb describes an action or a condition. The verb of a sentence answers questions about the subject, such as *What did the subject do?* or *What is the state or condition of the subject?*

Transitive and Intransitive Verbs

Some action verbs require a direct object (*she said* **her name**), but others do not (*she spoke*). A dictionary can tell you whether a verb is **transitive** (requires a direct object) or **intransitive** (does not require a direct object) or whether it can be either.

Linking Verbs

English has two groups of verbs: **action verbs** such as *make* and *walk* and **linking verbs** such as *be, become, seem, appear, sound,* and *feel.* Action verbs are either transitive (*we made the dinner*) or intransitive (*we walked*), but linking verbs follow another pattern. Linking verbs are followed by nouns or adjectives that say something about the subject. These noun or adjective modifiers are called **complements.**

NOUN
COMPLEMENT
She is a translator.

ADJECTIVE
COMPLEMENT
She seems intelligent.

Sentences

The following examples show the basic sentence parts.

VERB
Listen. (The subject, *you*, is understood.)

SUBJECT   VERB
The music is playing.

SUBJECT   VERB   DIR. OBJ.
Margarita teaches jazz band.

SUBJECT   VERB   DIR. OBJ.   INDIR. OBJ.
Margarita teaches jazz band to high school students.

SUBJECT   VERB   COMPLEMENT   SUBJECT   VERB   COMPLEMENT
The concert will be very interesting. The music will be modern jazz.

In this paragraph, put <u>one line</u> under the subject(s) and <u>two lines</u> under the verb(s) in each sentence. The first one has been done for you.

<u>Stephane Grappelli</u> <u><u>was</u></u> a jazz violinist. Born in Paris in 1908, Grapelli lost his mother at three years old and spent his childhood in orphanages. At age 12, he and his father were reunited, and his father bought him his first violin. First, Grappelli studied classical violin, but he preferred jazz. He liked making up his own music as he played rather than playing from someone else's score. The sounds of the street musicians of Paris and of the jazz musicians from the United States, especially the jazz violinist Joe Venuti, appealed to him. In 1933, Grappelli helped to form the Quintet of the Hot Club of Paris. The Quintet made dozens of recordings, and Grappelli's career as a jazz musician lasted over 60 years. During his long career, Grappelli recorded music with many famous artists.

14c. Phrase or Clause

A **phrase** is a group of two or more words that does not contain both a subject and a verb. English has various kinds of phrases: adjective phrases, adverb phrases, noun phrases, prepositional phrases, and verb phrases.

> an unexpected telephone call (noun phrase)
> at 9:00 in the morning (prepositional phrase)
> was waiting to board the plane (verb phrase)

A **clause** is a group of words that contains a subject and a verb. A clause can be **independent** (a complete sentence) or **dependent** (not a complete sentence). English has three kinds of dependent clauses: **adjective clauses** (see section 1, page 261), **adverb clauses** (see section 3, page 270), and **noun clauses** (see section 10, page 287).

14d. Sentence Types

Three types of English sentences are simple, compound, and complex.
Simple sentences have **one independent clause** and no dependent clauses.

> Euclid invented geometry.

A simple sentence may have a compound subject and/or a compound verb.

> Alexander Fleming, Ernst Chain, and Howard Florey discovered, purified, and produced penicillin.

Compound sentences have **two or more independent clauses** and no dependent clauses.

INDEPENDENT CLAUSE   INDEPENDENT CLAUSE
Henry Ford did not invent the automobile, but he developed the assembly line.

Complex sentences have **one or more independent clauses** and **one or more dependent clauses**.

INDEPENDENT CLAUSE

Alexander Graham Bell is given credit for the invention of the telephone,

DEPENDENT CLAUSE

although Elisha Gray and Thomas Edison were also working on the telephone at the same time.

14e. Logical Connectors

Logical connectors show meaningful relationships (cause and effect, contrast, time, etc.) between sentence parts. English has four types of logical connectors.

- **Coordinating conjunctions** (*and*, *but*, *for*, *nor*, *or*, *so*, and *yet*) connect two or more independent clauses in compound sentences. (See Coordination, page 282.)
- **Subordinating conjunctions** (*after*, *because*, *while*, etc.) connect a subordinate clause to a main (independent) clause in a sentence. (See Adverb Clauses, page 270.)
- **The adverbs known as transitions** (*for example*, *however*, *therefore*, etc.) show logical relationships but do <u>not</u> connect clauses as coordinating and subordinating conjunctions do. (See Adverbs, page 275.)
- **Prepositions** (*because of*, *in spite of*, *such as*, etc.) show logical relationships within clauses. (See Prepositions, page 291.)

14f. Subject-Verb Agreement

A subject and verb must agree in number. Singular subjects require singular verbs, and plural subjects require plural verbs.

The student ask**s** questions.
The student**s** ask questions.

RULE 1 If a sentence begins with *There*, the *be* verb always agrees in number with the noun that follows it.

There **is** a **reception** in the hotel.

When a series of nouns follows the *be* verb, the verb agrees with the first noun in the series.

There **are photographers**, a newspaper reporter, and officials at the reception.
There **is** a **newspaper reporter**, photographers, and officials at the reception.

RULE 2 Phrases or clauses that come between the subject and verb do not affect subject-verb agreement.

> One **guest** at the reception for the employees of the consulate **is** a reporter.
> The **reporter**, as well as her husband and two daughters, **was** invited by a consular official.

RULE 3 A gerund subject is singular.

> News **reporting is** an exciting career.

RULE 4 When compound subjects are joined by the correlative conjunctions *either . . . or . . ., neither . . . nor . . .,* and *not only . . . but (also) . . .,* the verb agrees with the part of the subject that is closest to it.

> Neither the radio stations nor the television **station is** expected to be here.
> Not only the governor but also several **members** of his cabinet **are** attending the reception.

When compound subjects are joined by the correlative conjunctions *both . . . and . . .,* the verb is always plural.

> Both the **press** and the **guests are** going to enjoy themselves.

RULE 5 Some pronouns and adjectives are always singular.

> **One** of the cabinet members **is** late.
> **Every** member/**Every** one of the members **is** expected to attend the reception.
> **Everyone/Everybody is** expected to be there.
> **Each** person/**Each** of the people **has** been invited.
> Do you think **anyone/someone is** going to make a speech?
> **No one has** spoken yet.

EXERCISE 18

As you read this passage, find and correct 14 subject-verb agreement errors.

Every person ~~need~~ needs a certain amount of sleep every night, but individuals vary in the actual amount they requires. Some adults can get by on six hours, while others needs about nine. Sleep research indicate that the amount of sleep that an individual requires for good physical health cannot be changed.

Not only the body but also the brain benefit from a good night's sleep. Using an electroencephalograph to measure brain waves, scientists have studied the sleeping brain. They have found that sleep consist of two stages, REM and non-REM sleep. During REM (rapid eye movement) sleep, there is intense brain activity, and dreaming are more likely to occur than during non-REM sleep. Scientists believe that in REM sleep, the moving eyes follows the activity of the brain. They also think that REM sleep play an important role in consolidating memories. Perhaps that is why the person who stay up late the night before a test do not perform as well as the person who gets a good night's sleep.

Anyone who have trouble sleeping should maintain a regular sleep schedule. Getting enough physical exercise also help people sleep well. Sleep is vital for health and well being, so everyone need to make sure to get his or her share.

14g. Sentence Problems

Run-on sentences and fragments are sentence structure errors.

Run-on Sentences

A run-on sentence is a pair of sentences (two independent clauses) that are written as one sentence.

INCORRECT: Mario wants to buy a house in the future he is working at two jobs.

Adding a comma between the two sentences does not correct the problem.

INCORRECT: Mario wants to buy a house in the future, he is working at two jobs.

Three Ways to Correct Run-on Sentences

1. Use a period and a capital letter to mark the sentence boundary.

   Mario wants to buy a house in the future. Ĥe is working at two jobs.

2. Combine the sentences using a coordinating or a subordination conjunction.

   Mario wants to buy a house in the future, ŝo he is working at two jobs.

   B̂ecause Mario wants to buy a house in the future, he is working at two jobs.

3. Use a semicolon to mark the sentence boundary.

   Mario wants to buy a house in the future; he is working at two jobs.

   You can add a transition to make the logical relationship clear.

   Mario wants to buy a house in the future; *therefore*, he is working at two jobs.

EXERCISE 19

As you read this passage, find and correct eight run-on sentences, using all three correction strategies. The first one has been done for you.

Body language is the silent communication of gestures, facial expressions, eye behavior, and posture. ᵇody language communicates information about people's thoughts, feelings, identities, and relationships. Some body-language signals are learned these signals vary from culture to culture. Waving good-bye, nodding the head in agreement, and bowing to show respect are examples of culture-specific signals. Other body-language signals are universal. Smiling with happiness, tightening the fists with anger, and stiffening the shoulders in fear are examples of universal signals, people everywhere use these signals, often unconsciously.

When people are unaware of their body language, they may unintentionally send the wrong message for example, at a job interview, a nervous interviewee may unknowingly send signals that will hurt her chances of getting hired. Due to stress, the interviewee may appear stone-faced, not smiling even when she greets the interviewer. This could send the message that she cannot relate to people socially or that she may not fit in at the company. She may fidget, tapping her fingers or touching her jewelry, this could send the message that she is not really interested in the job. She may look at the floor she may fail to make sufficient eye contact with the interviewer. In the business culture of the United States, this could send the message that the interviewee does not respect the interviewer it might even be interpreted as a sign of dishonesty.

Anyone can become more aware of nonverbal communication by studying other people in conversation in particular, one should observe how people adapt their body language to specific situations, such as the job interview. By learning about body language, people can improve their communication with others.

Fragments

A fragment is an incomplete sentence. There are four kinds of fragments.

1. A dependent clause

   INCORRECT: When the boss was in the office.

2. A participial phrase (an *-ing* or *-ed* phrase)

   INCORRECT: Running into the office at 9:15.

3. An infinitive phrase (*to* + verb)

   INCORRECT: To attend the meeting.

4. A noun or verb with attached phrases or dependent clauses

INCORRECT: The responsible person who had come early, made coffee, and turned on all the machines.

Three Ways to Correct Fragments

1. Change the fragment to an independent clause.

~~When~~ The boss was in the office.

2. Combine the fragment with another sentence.

When the boss was in the office~~.,~~ She was usually in a meeting.

3. Add an independent clause to the fragment.

The boss had come early that day to attend the meeting.
Running into the office at 9:15, *I thanked Marco.*
Marco was the responsible person who had come early, made coffee, and turned on all the machines.

EXERCISE 20

As you read this paragraph, find and correct the eight fragments, using all three correction strategies. The first one has been done for you.

Scientists have developed computers. ~~T~~hat can match the best chess players in the world. Garry Kasparov, who was the top-ranked chess player in the world for 19 years. In 1997, in a six-game match. Kasparov was narrowly defeated by "Deep Blue," IBM's chess-playing computer. Kasparov remarked after the match that the challenge for a human playing a computer is that the computer never gets tired. Five and a half years after his tournament with Deep Blue. Kasparov faced "Deep Junior." Had been programmed by Israeli scientists. This match ended in a tie, 3 to 3. Deep Junior, while not as fast as Deep Blue, played more like a human being. At times giving up pieces to gain an advantage in position on the board. The most recently developed chess-playing computer is "Deep Fritz." Programmed by German scientists. Deep Fritz is said to be superior to both Deep Blue and Deep Junior. Undoubtedly, in the future even better chess-playing computers.

15. Verbs

To express your ideas clearly in English, you need to understand English verbs. Using English verbs requires knowing tenses, active and passive forms, modal verbs, and phrasal verbs.

15a. Verb Tenses

The 12 English verb tenses fall into three time frames—past, present, and future. The third person singular form of the regular verb *clean* is shown in active voice and passive voice in the following chart. Note that the passive is not used in every one of the twelve tenses.

	Tense	Active Voice	Passive Voice
Present Time Frame	*simple present*	cleans	is cleaned
	present progressive	is cleaning	is being cleaned
	present perfect	has cleaned	has been cleaned
	present perfect progressive	has been cleaning	- - -
Past Time Frame	*simple past*	cleaned	was cleaned
	past progressive	was cleaning	was being cleaned
	past perfect	had cleaned	had been cleaned
	past perfect progressive	had been cleaning	- - -
Future Time Frame	*simple future*	will/is going to clean	will/is going to be cleaned
	future progressive	will be cleaning	- - -
	future perfect	will have cleaned	will have been cleaned
	future perfect progressive	will have been cleaning	- - -

Remember that English has many irregular verbs. Use a dictionary or a handbook to find out if a verb is irregular and to learn its past tense and past participle.

EXERCISE 21

The passage on page 305 contains active verbs in the past, present, and future time frames. Find and correct three verb tense errors in each paragraph. When corrected, the passage should contain all the verb tenses. The first error has been corrected for you.

My house stands on a small hill, about a quarter mile from my nearest
neighbor's house. It ~~was~~ ^{is} a small wood-frame structure, and it has withstood
some very powerful storms. I take very good care of my house. I have painted it
outside and inside every three years since I move in. Right now I replace the
front porch, which has become rotten with age.

My grandfather built this house 50 years ago. At the time he built it, he and
my grandmother had only one child, but they were planning to have a large
family. My grandmother give birth to my father, her second child, after they
were moving into the house. In subsequent years, she and my grandfather
have had five more children, and they raised them all in this house.

By the time summer is coming this year, my wife and I will have been living
in this house ten years. In the next few weeks, we will be planting our
vegetable garden. We will already finish preparing the soil several days earlier.
If we will be lucky, we will harvest a lot of fruits and vegetables this summer.

15b. Modal Verbs

Modals are auxiliaries (helping verbs) that allow you to add various meanings,
such as possibility, probability, or necessity, to verbs. Some modals, such as *may*
and *can*, have more than one meaning. Most modals have a present form and a
past form, and many have progressive forms as well. In some cases, there are
differences in meaning between the present and the past forms.

Modal	Present and Future Form and Meaning(s)	Past Form and Meaning(s)
may	POSSIBILITY Ping **may attend/may be attending** college now. Ping **may attend** college next year.	PAST POSSIBILITY Ping's older sister **may have attended/may have been attending** college in 2002.
	PERMISSION Students **may use** a dictionary during the test.	
	REQUEST **May** I **see** your ticket?	

(Continued)

Modal	Present and Future Form and Meaning(s)	Past Form and Meaning(s)
might	POSSIBILITY Ping **might attend/might be attending** college now. Ping **might attend** college next year.	PAST POSSIBILITY Ping's older sister **might have attended/might have been attending** college in 2002.
must	PROBABILITY OR INFERENCE (NEAR 100% CERTAINTY) The woman is wearing a white coat. She **must be** a doctor. She **must be working** now.	PAST PROBABILITY (NEAR 100% CERTAINTY) Louisa is a doctor. She **must have studied/must have been studying** very hard in school.
	STRONG NECESSITY Your application is due today, so you **must turn** it **in.**	Note: Use *had to* for past necessity.
have to, have got to	NECESSITY She **has to/has got to** turn in the application today.	PAST NECESSITY She **had to** turn in the application yesterday. Note: **Have got to** has no past form.
had better	STRONG RECOMMENDATION You **had better take** your medicine so that you will get well.	Note: Use *should have* + past participle for the past.
should, ought to	RECOMMENDATION OR ADVISABILITY You **should do/should be doing/ought to do/ought to be doing** your homework now.	PAST ADVISABILITY You **should have done/should have been doing** your homework yesterday, but you didn't/weren't, so you will lose points.
	EXPECTATION There are dark gray clouds overhead, so it **should start/ought to start** to rain rain any minute.	PAST EXPECTATION The letter **should have arrived** yesterday, but it didn't. Note: **Ought to** is not common in the past.

Modal	Present and Future Form and Meaning(s)	Past Form and Meaning(s)
be supposed to	EXPECTATION The teacher **is supposed to be** in class now.	PAST EXPECTATION The teacher **was supposed to be** in class ten minutes ago.
be able to	ABILITY My daughter **is able to read** now.	PAST ABILITY My daughter **was able to read** at age five.
can	ABILITY My daughter **can read** now. POSSIBILITY IN GENERAL STATEMENTS It **can rain** here in June. PERMISSION Students **can use** a dictionary during the test. REQUEST **Can** I **see** your ticket?	PAST ABILITY My daughter **could read** at age five. Note: Use *could* only for past abilities that lasted for a period of time. For a short-term ability in the past, use *was able to* (I was not the fastest runner in the race, but on that day I *was able to* beat the other runners.).
could	POSSIBILITY If the neighbors' house is dark, they **could be sleeping**. The letter I am waiting for **could arrive** tomorrow. REQUEST **Could** I **see** your ticket? SUGGESTION You **could fly** to New York if you don't have time to go by train.	PAST POSSIBILITY If the neighbors' house was dark, they **could have been sleeping**. Note: In the past negative, *could* expresses near certainty. *The letter could not have arrived yesterday* = It is (almost) impossible that the letter arrived yesterday.
would	REQUEST **Would** you **show** me your ticket? I **would like** a drink of water.	
	UNREAL CONDITIONAL I **would buy** the car if I had money.	PAST UNREAL CONDITIONAL I **would have bought** the car if I had had money.

15c. Verb Form Problems

Verbs have three parts: the **base** (*clean*), the **present participle** (*-ing* form, *cleaning*), and the **past participle** (*-ed* form, *cleaned*). These three parts combine with endings (*-s* and *-ed*) and auxiliaries (*is, has,* etc.) to make all possible verbs.

Base Form

Use the **base form** in the simple present and simple future tenses (*clean, will clean, is/are going to clean*), in present modal verbs (*may clean*), and in the infinitive (*to clean*).

Present Participle

Use the **present participle** or *-ing* **form** in the progressive tenses in the active voice (*is cleaning, has been cleaning, was cleaning, had been cleaning, will be cleaning, will have been cleaning*) and in progressive modal verbs (*may be cleaning*).

Past Participle

Use the *-ed* **form** in the perfect tenses in the active voice (*has cleaned, had cleaned, will have cleaned*), in all tenses in the passive voice (*is cleaned,* etc.), and in past modal verbs (*may have cleaned*) and passive modals (*may have been cleaned*).

Some Common Verb Form Errors

Error 1 **The base form is not used in a modal verb.**

It might ~~rains~~ tonight. *(rain)*

Error 2 **The base form is not used in an infinitive.**

This is the woman he chose to ~~married~~. *(marry)*

Error 3 **The present participle is not used in a progressive tense.**

Meanwhile, they were ~~enjoy~~ themselves at the party. *(enjoying)*

Error 4 **The past participle is not used in a perfect tense.**

They have ~~develop~~ a new plan. *(developed)*

Error 5 **The past participle is not used in the passive voice.**

A great deal of money was ~~save~~. *(saved)*

EXERCISE 22

As you read this passage, find and correct ten verb form errors which reflect the five problems listed above. The first one has been done for you.

                    may erupt

A volcano ~~may erupts~~ about every 100 years. In between eruptions, a volcano may appear quiet, but actually it is changes constantly. Inside, there is always great pressure as liquid rock, called *magma*, moves upward from deep inside the Earth. This upward pressure causes the volcano to expands outward and upward. As the volcano grows, loose rock falls down its sides.

Before May 1980, Mount St. Helens in Washington State had been quiet for over 100 years. It had been calling "the Fuji of America" because its symmetrical cone resembled the famous volcano in Japan. Its massive eruption on Sunday, May 20, 1980 changed that shape. Mount St. Helens lost 3.7 billion cubic yards of rock. Volcanic ash was send 15 miles into the air, and very hot winds blew in all directions. Two hundred thirty square miles of forest were flatten. Seventy percent of the snow and ice on the mountain melted, causing an enormous landslide of mud, volcanic ash, rocks, and trees to speeding down the mountain at 500 miles per hour. In the eruption, 57 people lost their lives, some as far away as 13 miles from the mountain. Most of them were scientists, loggers, and journalists.

On August 27, 1982, an area of 110,000 acres around the volcano was designated as the Mount St. Helens National Volcanic Monument. Over the years since, visitors to the monument have observe the regrowth of plants and the return of wildlife to the area. Scientists know that, deep within the mountain, changes are continually occur, but no one knows when Mount St. Helens might erupted again.

15d. Phrasal Verbs and Particles

Some verbs combine with prepositions to create new meanings. These prepositions are called **particles**, and the verb + preposition combination is called a **phrasal verb**. Here are some examples.

> I **ran into** a friend. (met)
> We **called off** the picnic because of the rain. (canceled)

Some phrasal verbs can be separated by their objects.

> I **looked up** a word. → I **looked** a word **up**.
> I **turned in** my homework. → I **turned** my homework **in**.

Other phrasal verbs cannot be separated.

> She **looks after** her younger sister.
> The party **turned out** well.

To find out which particles can combine with a verb and what new meanings are created by those combinations, look the verb up in a dictionary.

16. Word Choice

English, like other languages, has a rich and varied vocabulary. Some words are appropriate in formal situations, and some are appropriate in informal situations. Compare the following sentences.

> That **gentleman** spoke with the **police officer**.
> That **dude** spoke with the **cop**.

The choice of formal words (*gentleman* and *police officer*) or informal words (*dude* and *cop*) greatly affects the meaning of a sentence, so you must consider formality and informality when you choose words. Academic and business writing are formal, so you should not use informal language in these types of writing.

A good dictionary can tell you whether a word is formal, informal, or **slang** (an informal word used by a specific group of people, usually young people).

17. Word Families

English has many **word families**, or groups of related words, such as the following.

> love
> lovable
> loveless
> unlovable

A word family shares a common **root** (in the example above, *love*) to which **prefixes** (such as *un-*) and **suffixes** (such as *-able* and *-less*) are added. A prefix, which attaches to the beginning of a word, adds meaning. A suffix, which attaches to the end of a word, tells what part of speech the word is. Word-family members with different suffixes are called **word forms**.

Knowing prefixes and suffixes is important to you as a writer. Prefixes and suffixes expand your vocabulary and help you choose the right word forms for your sentences.

17a. Prefixes

The following chart lists some common **prefixes** and their meanings. Some prefixes have more than one meaning.

Prefix	Meaning	Example
anti-	against	antiwar
com-, con-, co-	with	company, connect, co-pay
contra-	against	contradict
de-	from	deduct
dis-	not, apart	dislike, disconnect
ex-	out from, former	exhale, ex-president
extra-	outside, beyond	extraordinary
il-, im-, ir-	not	illogical, impossible, irrelevant

Prefix	Meaning	Example
in-	not, into	insecure, inhale
inter-	between	international
intra-	within	intramural
mal-	bad, badly	malfunction
mis-	not, wrongly	misunderstand
post-	after	postpone
pre-	before	preview
pro-	forward	progress
re-	again	review
super-	over, above, extra	supervision
trans-	across, over, through	transfer
un-	not	unable
uni-	one, undivided	unified

17b. Suffixes

The following chart lists some common noun, verb, adjective, and adverb **suffixes**.

Noun Suffixes	**-ance, -ence**	appearance, independence
	-er, -ar, -or	worker, burglar, actor
	-ment	employment
	-ness	happiness
	-ship	friendship
	-sion, -tion	invasion, recommendation
	-y, -ity	harmony, electricity
Verb Suffixes	**-ate**	investigate
	-en	brighten
	-ify	beautify
	-ize	modernize
Adjective Suffixes	**-able, -ible**	usable, responsible
	-al	musical
	-ful	delightful
	-ive	defensive
	-less	humorless
	-ious, -ous	serious, generous
Adverb Suffix	**-ly**	responsibly

APPENDIX IB: PUNCTUATION AND CAPITALIZATION

1. Apostrophe

The **apostrophe** has two uses: possessives and contractions.

1a. Possessives

With singular nouns, show possession with the **apostrophe + s**.

> a student's composition
> Aiko's laptop computer
> Klaus's notebook

With plural nouns, show possession with the apostrophe alone.

> all the students' compositions
> the Parks' house

(Note that to refer to two or more members of a family or to a husband and wife, place *the* before the last name, and add *-s* to the last name. For example, *Mr. and Mrs. Park* are referred to as *the Parks*.)

When two or more nouns are joined by *and*, the last noun in the series shows possession.

> Mr. and Mrs. Park's house
> Juana, Leyla, and Fatima's group assignment

In general, do *not* use the apostrophe + *s* to show that a thing possesses another thing. Use a noun modifier or a prepositional phrase instead.

> the house's windows → *the house windows* or *the windows of the house*
> the classroom's computer → *the classroom computer* or *the computer in the classroom*

1b. Contractions

In informal letters and written dialogue, you can contract (shorten) the words *am, has, have, had, is, not, will*, and *would* by omitting letters and using the apostrophe to show the omission. Here are some common contractions.

I am → I'm	we have → we've	did not → didn't
she is → she's	you had → you'd	will not → won't
he has → he's	they would → they'd	

Note that contractions are usually *not* used in formal writing such as college papers, letters of application, or business letters and memos.

2. Capital Letters

Use **capital letters** in the following nine situations.

1. The first word in a sentence or a quotation

   He said, "**D**inner is ready."

2. Proper names of people, places, and things

   Gustave Eiffel designed the **Eiffel Tower** in **Paris**.

3. The names of organizations and people's official titles when used with their names

   The speech was given by **Secretary-General** of the **United Nations Kofi Annan** to the **International Atomic Energy Agency**.

   Do *not* capitalize unless proper names are used.

   The $\overset{p}{P}$rincipal of our $\overset{h}{H}$igh $\overset{s}{S}$chool asked us to support the $\overset{s}{S}$occer $\overset{c}{C}$oach.

4. The names of companies and their products

   Microsoft developed a computer operating system called **Windows**.

5. Days of the week, months, and holidays

   Sunday September 16 will be **Independence Day**.

   Do *not* capitalize the names of the seasons.

   Fashions change every $\overset{s}{S}$pring, $\overset{s}{S}$ummer, $\overset{f}{F}$all, and $\overset{w}{W}$inter.

6. Countries, nationalities, races, and languages

   The **Kurds** in **Iraq**, **Iran**, **Syria**, **Turkey**, and other countries speak **Kurdish**.

7. The names of school classes

   I took **Sociology** 101, **Speech** 150, and **Math** 155.

   Do *not* capitalize the names of school subjects.

   I learned a lot about $\overset{s}{S}$ociology, $\overset{p}{P}$ublic $\overset{s}{S}$peaking, and $\overset{c}{C}$alculus.

8. The titles of books, magazines, essays, short stories, movies, television programs, songs, etc.

   In my English class, we studied Gothic works: We read Edgar Allen Poe's short story "**The Tell-Tale Heart**" and Bram Stoker's novel *Dracula*, and we watched the movie *Frankenstein* and an episode of the TV series *Mystery*.

9. The names of relatives only if they are not preceded by a possessive adjective such as *my*

> This photograph, which was taken by Grandpa, shows Grandma with my mother and her sister.

Exercise 1

As you read this paragraph, supply the 27 missing capital letters. The first one has been done for you.

O
~~o~~n october 29, 1923, a military leader named Mustafa Kemal ended the ottoman Empire that had ruled Turkey for 600 years and established the republic of turkey. During his 15-year presidency, Mustafa Kemal Ataturk, as he was called, introduced major political, legal, and social reforms in Turkey. He separated political and religious leadership and introduced democracy. He abolished religious laws and oversaw the writing of new legal codes based on european models which gave women equal rights. Ataturk even changed the calendar and the language. Roman letters replaced arabic script, and turkish words replaced borrowed arabic, persian, and french vocabulary. education played a major role in implementing ataturk's reforms and in bringing about his modernization of turkey. Ataturk unified the educational system and promoted the teaching of science so that turkish students would have the necessary skills to contribute to the country's economy. In *ataturk: The biography of the founder of modern turkey*, turkish writer andrew mango states that Ataturk was "a statesman of supreme realism." The turkish people call him *Ataturk*, that is, *father of the turks*, because the Turkish parliament voted to give him that title in 1938.

3. Colon

The colon has the following uses:

1. To introduce an explanation of the statement that precedes the colon

> For an adult, learning a second language is difficult: The adult learner has to learn numerous rules of grammar, multiple meanings of thousands of words, and complex social rules that affect use of the language in different situations.

2. To introduce a list that explains the noun or noun phrase that precedes the colon

> When I travel, I always carry the following items: a small pillow, a lightweight umbrella, and a tiny first aid kit.
>
> To prepare to write an essay, follow these essential steps: brainstorm, determine the main point you want to make, select two or three supporting points, and make an outline.

Do *not* use a colon after a verb or a preposition.

> INCORRECT: My goals include: getting a Bachelor's degree and finding an administrative position in the airline industry.
>
> CORRECT: My goals include getting a Bachelor's degree and finding an administrative position in the airline industry.
>
> INCORRECT: In my personal library, I have several classics such as: *Moby-Dick* by Herman Melville, *Dream of the Red Chamber* by Tsao Hsueh-Chin, and *One Hundred Years of Solitude* by Gabriel García Márquez.
>
> CORRECT: In my personal library, I have several classics: *Moby-Dick* by Herman Melville, *Dream of the Red Chamber* by Tsao Hsueh-Chin, and *One Hundred Years of Solitude* by Gabriel García Márquez.

4. Comma

Use a **comma** in the following seven situations.

1. To separate items in a list (see Parallel Structure, page 283)

   > The development of written language, the printing press, and the computer greatly increased human knowledge.

2. To separate independent clauses in compound sentences (see Coordination, page 282, and Sentence Types, page 298)

   > Colleges and universities encourage the development of knowledge, and libraries encourage the sharing of knowledge.

3. After a dependent clause at the beginning of a sentence or a dependent clause of comparison, contrast, or surprising result at the end of a sentence (see Adverb Clauses, page 270, and Sentence Types, page 298)

   > Until public libraries were created, only the wealthy had access to books.

4. After a long prepositional phrase or a participial phrase (reduced adverb clause) at the beginning of a sentence

   > With nearly 128 million items on approximately 530 miles of bookshelves, the Library of Congress is the biggest library in the world. Adding 10,000 new items to its collections every day, the Library of Congress has an enormous task to catalogue its holdings.

5. Before and after a non-restrictive adjective clause or reduced adjective clause (see Adjective Clauses, page 261)

   > The Library of Alexandria, (which was) the most important library in the ancient world, was destroyed by fire.

6. Before and after a word or phrase that interrupts the flow of a sentence

   > The Egyptian government, with the help of UNESCO, plans to build a new library on the site of the ancient Alexandrian library.

7. Before or after a quotation (see Quotation Marks, page 317)

> Thomas Carlyle said, "The greatest university of all is a collection of books."

Exercise 2

As you read this paragraph, supply the 10 missing commas. The first one has been done for you.

Between about A.D. 250 and 900, the Maya of southern Mexico and Central America developed astronomy, mathematics three calendars, and a writing system. The Maya writing system consisted of about 800 symbols. These symbols stood for sounds, words, or entire sentences. After the Maya ruins were discovered in the nineteenth century scholars spent 100 years trying to decipher the writing system and now most of it can be read and understood. While very few Maya books have survived a good number of texts on buildings, stone monuments, small ornaments and ceramic vessels have been found. These texts or inscriptions have some interesting features. Inscriptions on stone monuments contain many dates referring to events in the lives of Maya leaders. The Maya who seem to have been keenly interested in time and dates took pains to record the dates of their leaders' births, marriages, and battles in great detail. Maya writing on small objects has another interesting feature: The text often names the object it is on, and it may even state the purpose of the object. For example, the text on cups often contains the word *cup* and sometimes says *chocolate*, indicating that the Maya used cups for a chocolate drink. Another aspect of all Maya writing is that it accompanies pictures. Sometimes a picture of a person shows words near the mouth, indicating speech. For example, a painting on an eighth-century vase shows a scribe teaching mathematics and saying "Seven, eight, nine, twelve, thirteen, eleven." Maya writing can teach us a lot about who the Maya were and what kind of civilization they developed 1,100 to 1,750 years ago.

5. Dash

The **dash** is an informal punctuation mark that is used for emphasis in place of the colon or the comma in these two situations.

1. Use a dash to introduce a list that explains the noun phrase before the dash.

> The store sells some unusual gadgets—backscratchers, foot warmers, and caps that have small umbrellas attached to them.

2. Use a dash before and after an interrupting phrase or clause.

> At the end of the movie—and this was my favorite part—a huge dinosaur-like monster destroyed the enemy's city.

Because the dash is informal, avoid using it in academic writing.

6. Parentheses

Use **parentheses** to enclose supporting information that is less important than the rest of the information in a sentence.

> The longest suspension bridge in the world is the Akashi Kayo Bridge in Japan (6,570 feet), and the second longest is the Storebaelt Bridge in Denmark (5,328 feet).

Whenever possible, avoid using parentheses and place supporting information directly into sentences.

7. Period

The **period** is perhaps your most important punctuation mark. When you use a period at the end of a group of words, you send a signal to readers: You tell them that this group of words is a sentence, that is, a complete thought (see Sentence Types, page 298, and Logical Connectors, page 299).

> Every sentence needs a period.

Periods are also used in some abbreviations.

> Dr.   Mrs.   A.M.
> Mr.   Ms.   P.M.

Many abbreviations (names referred to by their initials) do not include periods.

> AIDS   IBM   the UK
> the BBC   the UN   GM

Note that the abbreviations of states in the United States do not include periods.

> Raleigh, NC   Los Angeles, CA

8. Quotation Marks

Quotation marks have three uses: to show the actual words that someone said or wrote (direct speech); to show that there is something unusual about a word or phrase; to identify a title of a short story, essay, article, poem, or any other part of a book.

8a. Direct Speech

To show the actual words of a speaker or writer, follow these rules.

RULE 1 If a quotation is less than one sentence, don't place a comma before it or start it with a capital letter.

> My mother always said her parents were "as different as night and day."

RULE 2 Place a comma before a quoted sentence, and begin the sentence with a capital letter. If the end of the quotation is the end of the sentence, place a period *inside* the quotation marks.

> My grandmother always said, "Into every life a little rain must fall."

RULE 3 When a sentence continues beyond a quotation, place a comma *inside* the quotation marks.

"Always look on the bright side," my grandfather would reply.

RULE 4 When a reporting phrase like *he said* interrupts a quoted sentence, place a comma at the end of the first part of the quoted sentence and at the end of the reporting phrase.

"I don't know why," Grandma would say, "the children have to make so much noise."

RULE 5 When showing a quotation that is more than one sentence long, do not close the quotation marks until the end of the person's speech.

Grandpa would reply, "They are having a good time. Let them be. Let's go out on the back porch."

RULE 6 When writing dialogue, start a new paragraph every time the speaker changes.

"I'm afraid they'll break something or get hurt," Grandma fretted.
"No, they won't," Grandpa said as he ushered her out the back door.

RULE 7 If a quotation is not introduced with a phrase like *Menander said* but with a full sentence, place a colon before the quotation.

Menander, a playwright of ancient Greece, made the following statement: "The character of a man is known from his conversations."

8b. Quotation Marks that Signal Special Uses of Words

Use quotation marks to indicate that there is something special or unusual about a word or phrase, as in these four cases.

1. A word is being defined

   "Collaboration" means the act of working with others to achieve what you all want.

2. A foreign word is used

   The Cantonese word "ho-ho" means great happiness and good fortune.

3. A new word that has been invented to describe a new situation or a familiar word that is being used in a new way

   The company has developed a robotic window washer that they have decided to call a "washatron."
   In the "language" of driving, a turn signal is your request to other drivers that they allow you time to change lanes or turn.

4. A word that is not appropriate in a certain context, such as an idiom or a slang word or phrase that is used in an academic paper

> A political party is an institution that makes its own rules. Winning is everything, and parties will "fight tooth and nail" for electoral victories.
>
> When two individuals sign a legal contract, they are bound by the terms of the contract, and they cannot "weasel out" without facing legal consequences.

8c. Quotation Marks in Titles

Use quotation marks around the name of a short text that is part of a longer work, such as a story, essay, article, or poem. Underline the name of a book, newspaper, or magazine (or use italics if you are writing on a computer).

9. Semicolon

A **semicolon** can replace a period between two sentences that you want the reader to see as closely connected.

> The instructor described his plan for the course; the students listened attentively.

You can use a semicolon in place of a period with transitions.

> My friend thought that a course in computer animation would be fun and easy; however, he soon discovered that animation programs are very complex.

Appendix 1C: Citation and Summarizing

1. Citation

Giving a **citation** means identifying the source of your information. Whenever you use outside sources—whether you are quoting or paraphrasing a single sentence or summarizing an entire book—you need to identify the source of your information and give credit to the author. You do this with **in-text** and **end-of-text citations** and **text references**.

1a. In-text and End-of-text Citations

You will need to use **in-text** and **end-of-text** citations together. Look at this example.

IN-TEXT CITATION

> Cory Meacham wrote, "Tigers are a wonder. It doesn't matter what language we use to explain that" (223). A tiger can weigh up to 800 pounds (363 kilograms), and yet move through forest or tall grass almost soundlessly. The tiger's stripes, while very noticeable in open areas, make the animal almost invisible in dense vegetation. When hunting, tigers will seek out the largest prey they can find as they need to consume about 35 pounds (16 kilograms) of meat per day. Tigers hunt and live alone, marking and defending their own territories, yet they communicate with one another over long distances, making some sounds so low that they are inaudible to humans.

END-OF-TEXT CITATION

Meacham, Cory. *How the Tiger Lost Its Stripes: An Exploration into the Endangerment of a Species.* New York: Harcourt, 1997.

The in-text citation (**223**) is the page number from the source. Place it in the sentence that contains the quote or paraphrase. The end-of-text citation is the line that identifies the author, title, place of publication, publisher, and date of publication. Place this line at the end of a paper.

The citations above are in MLA style. There are two main styles for citations, MLA (Modern Language Association) and APA (American Psychological Association). MLA style is used in business, literature, history, and related subjects. APA style is used in science.

The MLA and APA styles are briefly described below. For more details about these styles, refer to an English handbook or the *MLA Handbook for Writers of Research Papers* and the *Publication Manual of the American Psychological Association.*

Do not mix citation styles. Ask your teacher which style you should use in an assignment, and use only that one style.

1a.1. In-text Citations An in-text citation in your paper alerts readers that the information in a sentence is from an outside source, and it directs them to your end-of-text citations. Use in-text citations wherever you include words, ideas, or facts from an outside source in your writing.

MLA style in-text citations. Write page numbers in parentheses at the end of the sentence in which the information from the source appears. If you don't mention the author in the sentence, include his or her name with the page numbers.

DIRECT QUOTATION
Cory Meacham writes, "Tigers, though they do not purr, make a delightful array of endearing noises" (250).

PARAPHRASE
Cory Meacham writes that tigers produce a great variety of wonderful sounds, but they do not purr (250).
Tigers produce a great variety of wonderful sounds, but they do not purr (Meacham, 250).

APA style in-text citations. Write the year of publication in parentheses after the author's name in the sentence in which the information from the source appears. If you don't mention the author in the sentence, include his or her name in the parentheses and place the citation at the end of the sentence.

DIRECT QUOTATION
Cory Meacham (1997) writes, "Tigers, though they do not purr, make a delightful array of endearing noises."

PARAPHRASE
Cory Meacham (1997) writes that tigers produce a great variety of sounds, but they do not purr.
Tigers produce a great variety of sounds, but they do not purr (Meacham, 1997).

1a.2. End-of-Text Citations   Your in-text citations must match your end-of-text citations, or list of works (also known as a bibliography). That is, for every in-text citation in your writing, you must include a complete reference to a book, magazine, or Web site in your end-of-text citations. In addition, your end-of text citations will probably include some sources which you do not cite in in-text citations. That is because you must include in your end-of-text citations any source which you have summarized in your writing or which you have used to get background information about the topic you are discussing.

Each style (MLA or APA) distinguishes between books, periodicals (magazines), and online sources in various ways. Look at the following examples.

MLA style end-of-text citations

MLA BOOK CITATION
Matthiessen, Peter. *Tigers in the Snow*. New York: North Point, 2000.

MLA PERIODICAL CITATION
Brooke, Michael. "Birds in Decline around the Globe." *New Scientist* 13 March 2004: 14–15.

MLA ONLINE CITATION

"Welcome to CITES." *The Convention on International Trade in Endangered Species of Wild Flora and Fauna.* 2 July 2004. 6 July 2004. <http://www.cites.org/>.

If the Web site does not list an author, begin the citation with the title of the Web page.

Form and dating of MLA end-of-text citations

- If you are typing, **underline** or **italicize** the titles of books, periodicals, and Web sites. (The MLA recommends underlining, but says either way is acceptable.) If you are handwriting, **underline** titles. Whether you use underlining or italics, be consistent.

- Put **quotation marks** around titles of parts of books, articles from periodicals, or individual Web pages on a Web site.

- Put **periods** after authors' names, after titles, after dates in Web site citations, and at the end of citations.

- Internet citations have two **dates**. The first is the date when the site was created or updated. The second is the date you accessed it.

APA style end-of-text citations

APA BOOK CITATION

Matthiessen, P. (2000). *Tigers in the snow.* New York: North Point.

APA PERIODICAL CITATION

Brooke, Michael. (2004, March 13). Birds in decline around the globe. *New Scientist,* 181(2438), 14–15.

APA ONLINE CITATION

Welcome to CITES. (2004, 2 July). *The Convention on International Trade in Endangered Species of Wild Flora and Fauna.* Retrieved July 6, 2004, from http://www.cites.org/

Form and dating of APA end-of-text citations

- **Italicize** titles of books, periodicals, and Web sites. If you handwrite your paper, **underline** the titles.

- In titles, use capital letters *only* for the first word or the first word after a colon. Do *not* use *any* quotation marks.

- Put **periods** after dates of book or periodical publication or Web site creation/updating, after titles, and at the end of citations, except after a URL.

- Put **dates** after the authors' names, or, if there is no author's name, after the title. In online citations, put *Retrieved* and the date of access followed by *from* and the URL, or Internet address, at the end of the citation.

1b. Text References

In your text, you can refer to sources two ways: You can use *according to* or a reporting verb like *say* or *write*.

According to John Smith, many animal species are endangered.

John Smith *says/writes* that many animal species are endangered.

Reporting verbs. Reporting verbs, which are shown in the chart that follows, vary in meaning. For example, the verbs *say* or *write* express a neutral attitude. In contrast, verbs like *argue, assert, claim, contend,* and *maintain* indicate that there are opposing opinions and that there may be a strong challenge to the opinion expressed in the text reference.

John Smith *contends* that many animal species are endangered. However, he does not offer solid scientific evidence to support this view.

Here are the common reporting verbs. Check your dictionary to learn about the differences in their meanings.

Reporting Verbs			
Neutral Verbs		**Verbs That Indicate Persuasion**	
discuss	report	argue	maintain
explain	say	assert	recommend
observe	state	claim	remind*
present	tell*	contend	suggest
point out	write	encourage*	urge*
relate			

Note the following rules about reporting verbs.

1. Verbs differ in terms of what patterns may follow them. Most of the verbs in the chart are followed by a noun clause:

   ┌------------------------- NOUN CLAUSE -------------------------┐
   John Smith *explains* that the world's fish supplies are dwindling.

   The verbs in the chart above that are followed by an asterisk (*) require an indirect object.

           I. O.
   John Smith *tells* <u>readers</u> that the world's fish supplies are dwindling.

           I. O.
   John Smith *urges* <u>readers</u> to avoid buying fish species that are endangered.

   To learn what sentence patterns may be used with a particular verb, check your dictionary.

2. In text references, reporting verbs are used in either the present or the past tense with little difference in meaning. However, if you use a past tense reporting verb, you must make sure that any verbs that follow it agree in tense. (For more information about verb tense in noun clauses, see Appendix IA, section 10a.)

Adding the source. In addition to naming the author, you may want to include the title of the source (book, periodical, or Web site) or part of the source (chapter, article, or individual Web page) that your excerpt is from. Look at the following examples.

David Malakoff (2004), author of "New Tools Reveal Treasures at Ocean Hot Spots," reports that

In "New Tools Reveal Treasures at Ocean Hot Spots," David Malakoff (2004) reports that

According to David Malakoff (2004) in "New Tools Reveal Treasures at Ocean Hot Spots" in *Science*,

} zones in the sea that are very rich in marine life have been found.

Malakoff, D. (2004, May 21). New tools reveal treasures at ocean hot spots. *Science*, 304 (5674), 1104–1105.

Note that in text references, you must underline or italicize titles of books, periodicals, and Web sites. Put titles of chapters, articles, and individual Web pages in quotation marks.

EXERCISE 1

The items in this exercise are statements that summarize readings. Each statement is followed by an end-of-text citation in APA style. On a piece of paper, rewrite each statement, adding (1) the author's name (or authors' names); (2) an APA style in-text citation; and (3) the title of the publication (book, periodical, or Web site) or the title of the article, chapter, or Web page. For each item, choose a reporting verb and one of the sentence patterns presented above. See the example below. Vary your sentences.

1. SUMMARY STATEMENT: Biological diversity refers to the genetic characteristics of species, the variety of species and habitats in a given area, the relationships between species and their habitats, and the relationships among species.

   END-OF-TEXT CITATION
   Botkin, D. B., & Keller, E. A. (2003). Biological diversity. In *Environmental science: Earth as a living planet*. Hoboken, NJ: Wiley 109–129.

   TEXT REFERENCE
   In Environmental Science: Earth as a Living Planet, Botkin and Keller (2003) explain that biological diversity refers to the genetic characteristics of species, the variety of species and habitats in a given area, the relationships between species and their habitats, and the relationships among species.

2. SUMMARY STATEMENT: The world may not be able to feed its growing population in the future.

END-OF-TEXT CITATION
Brown, L. (2004, April). Three billion more. *NOVA: World in the Balance.* Retrieved July 8, 2004, from http://www.pbs.org/wgbh/nova/worldbalance/voic-brow.html

3. SUMMARY STATEMENT: Public policies vary in their goals and their views of private property rights.

END-OF-TEXT CITATION
Field, B. C. (2000). Public policy for natural resources. In *Natural resources economics.* (Ch. 7). New York: McGraw-Hill.

4. SUMMARY STATEMENT: Meat production is harmful to the environment in a number of ways, and meat consumption is not good for human health.

END-OF-TEXT CITATION
Halweil, B. (2004, July and August). The humble hamburger. *World Watch,* 17(4), 2.

5. SUMMARY STATEMENT: Scientists, activists, and world leaders say that although awareness of the human impact on the natural environment has increased in the last decade, the rate of environmental destruction has increased overall.

END-OF-TEXT CITATION
Klesius, M. (2002, September). The state of the planet. *National Geographic,* 202(3), 102–116.

6. SUMMARY STATEMENT: "Bioenergy" refers to the production of fuels such as ethanol and methanol from plant materials.

END-OF-TEXT CITATION
U.S. Department of Energy. (2004, July 6). Bioenergy topics. Retrieved July 9, 2004, from http://www.eere.energy.gov/RE/bioenergy.html

7. SUMMARY STATEMENT: Through use of pollution control measures, recycling, and public transportation, cities can become healthier for people and less harmful to the natural environment.

END-OF-TEXT CITATION
Walsh, T. (1995, April 17). Sustainable resources for cities. *Nation's Cities Weekly,* 18(16), 6.

2. Summarizing

Finding and presenting the main and supporting ideas of a whole article or section of a text is called **summarizing**. In general, summaries contain broad concepts and explain relationships between ideas but include very few facts or statistics. They can vary in length from one sentence to a paragraph or more. If you are writing a paper for school and want to include a summary of an article in it, you should keep the summary short—probably no more than two or three sentences. But if you have an assignment to write a summary of an article or a section of a textbook, you will need to write a longer, more complete summary. A complete summary of a section from a textbook might be a paragraph in which each sentence summarizes a paragraph in the original text. Follow these five steps to write a summary of any length.

STEP 1. **Read carefully.** Read the selection once to get a general idea of what it is about and to determine what the author's purpose is. Ask yourself if the author is trying to persuade or inform and what the main message is. You do not have to understand all the vocabulary in the reading in order to summarize it, but you do need to know what an unfamiliar word means if it relates to a main or supporting idea in the text.

STEP 2. **Locate the main and supporting points.** Read the text again, and underline the words, phrases, clauses, and sentences that contain the main and supporting points.

Different kinds of writing have different types of organization. Academic writing is highly organized, so if you are summarizing an excerpt from a textbook or an academic journal, you will probably find the main and supporting points easily: The main idea will be stated near the beginning, and most of the supporting points will be in the topic sentences of body paragraphs. A summary statement may be included near the end.

If, however, you are summarizing an article from a newspaper, a popular magazine, or the Internet, you will see that the organization is looser. The main idea may appear anywhere in the article, and the paragraphs may be very short and may lack topic sentences. In such writing, look for signals that tell you what the writer wants to emphasize, such as a carefully developed description or explanation, an attention-getting quotation, a short one-sentence paragraph after a longer paragraph, or transition signals such as *major, main, largest,* and *above all.*

In the following article, words, phrases, clauses, and sentences containing the main and supporting ideas have been underlined.

The Rain Forest in Your Cup

1   If you drank coffee this morning, you are most likely responsible for clearing a patch of <u>rain forest</u> about the size of your coffee mug. That's the amount of forest, in Latin America at least, that is <u>cleared for firewood to dry the beans required for a cup of coffee</u>. And if you drink a cup every morning, that adds up to a lot of forest: Each year in Latin America, about 65 square kilometers (16,000 acres) are cut to fuel coffee drying, according to the Mesoamerican Development Institute. This loss of forest is occurring despite the fact that in recent years coffee growers have adopted new production methods which are better for the environment.

2   All coffee beans—whether they are grown with new environment-friendly or with conventional methods—still need to be dried after the berries are picked. And currently that's being done with tons of firewood and diesel fuel.

3 "<u>The largest threat to forests right now</u> is not shade-coffee plantations being cleared and converted to plantations," <u>said Raul Raudales, an energy engineer</u> who has been working to develop forest-friendly technologies. "The biggest impact on forests <u>is the use of firewood to dry the coffee</u>." Coffee is the second largest traded commodity worldwide. So the amount of forest cleared to dry millions of coffee berries each year is large.

4 <u>Raudales and his team have developed an efficient alternative</u> to the massive blast-furnace dryers that are used to dry coffee all over the world. His company, Solar Trade, builds <u>a solar coffee dryer which uses</u> a high-tech heating chamber kept hot by <u>solar heaters and</u> super-efficient fans to dry the coffee beans. On rainy days or at night, the dryers get their heat from burning the <u>husks of previously dried coffee berries</u>.

5 Right now there are three solar dryers in operation, two in Costa Rica and one in Nicaragua. There is already some demand in Europe for the solar-dried coffee. "We call it 'Café Solar,'" said Richard Trubey, the company's vice president for marketing. "We are promoting the benefits of preserving the forest by not burning it to dry coffee."

6 The design for the conventional industrial dryers that are in widespread use hasn't changed in the last 80 years. <u>The old-style dryers heat the coffee with firewood and diesel fuel</u>. Large horsepower fans blow the hot air through the wet coffee beans, requiring large amounts of electricity.

7 "So the energy consumption each year at a facility that handles 10,000 sacks of coffee—which is small, there are many others that produce 20 times that—costs about $20,000 for electricity and firewood," said Raudales. "For the solar dryer, those costs are about $1,700." <u>In many parts of Latin America, electricity prices have been rising rapidly in the past decade</u>, increasing by about 20 percent a year.

8 Solar Trade estimates that the efficiency savings would easily cover a company's cost of changing to solar within seven to eight years. "<u>It makes sense for</u> these <u>companies to change right now</u>, whether they have newer or older equipment, simply <u>because the conventional systems require a tremendous amount of energy and money to operate</u>," said Trubey. (WRI Features)

Adapted from Runyan, C. (2004, January). The rain forest in your cup. *World Resources Institute.* Retrieved July 6, 2004, from http://pubs.wri.org/pubs_content_text.cfm?ContentID=2368

STEP 3. Paraphrase. Once you have underlined the main idea and the supporting points, you can paraphrase what you have marked. (For more information about how to paraphrase, see pages 222–223). Look at the paraphrases below.

> . . . <u>rain forest</u> . . . <u>is cleared for firewood to dry the beans required for a cup of coffee</u>.
>
> *People are cutting down rain forests to get firewood to dry coffee beans.*

The largest threat to forests right now . . . said Raul Raudales, an energy engineer . . . is the use of firewood to dry the coffee.

Energy engineer Raul Raudales says cutting firewood causes the most damage to rain forests.

Raudales and his team have developed an efficient alternative . . . a solar coffee dryer which uses . . . solar heaters and . . . husks of previously dried coffee berries.

Raul Raudales and his partners have created a solar-powered coffee dryer that runs on sunlight and the skins of previously dried berries.

The old-style dryers heat the coffee with firewood and diesel fuel.

The traditional dryers burn firewood and diesel fuel to dry coffee.

In many parts of Latin America electricity prices have been rising rapidly in the past decade . . . .

Much of Latin America has experienced rising energy costs over the last ten years.

It makes sense for . . . companies to change right now . . . because the conventional systems require a tremendous amount of energy and money to operate . . . .

Due to the very large amount of energy and money required by conventional coffee-drying methods, solar coffee dryers offer a sensible alternative to companies right now.

STEP 4. **Write a paragraph.** When you have finished paraphrasing, combine the paraphrases in a paragraph. Include a text reference (the author's name, the in-text citation, and, if you wish, the name of the article or publication) in the first sentence. If your summary will be more than three sentences long, begin with a topic sentence that introduces the general idea of the reading, similar to the sentences you wrote in Exercise 1. If you find that there are information gaps in your paragraph, reread the text, looking for information to paraphrase in order to fill in the gaps. After you have finished writing, check your paragraph for cohesion, and revise if necessary. Be sure to include an end-of-text citation.

Curtis Runyan (2004) reports in WRI Features that people are cutting down rain forests to get firewood to dry coffee beans. He quotes energy engineer Raul Raudales, who says that harvesting trees for firewood causes more damage to rain forests than any other aspect of coffee production. Raudales and his partners have created a solar-powered coffee dryer that runs on sunlight and the skins of previously dried berries. The traditional dryers burn firewood and diesel fuel to dry coffee. Due to the rising energy prices in much of Latin America and the very large amount of energy required by conventional coffee-drying methods, solar coffee dryers offer a sensible alternative right now.

Adapted from Runyan, C. (2004, January). The rain forest in your cup. *World Resources Institute.* Retrieved July 6, 2004, from http://pubs.wri.org/pubs_content_text.cfm?ContentID=2368

EXERCISE 2

A. Summarize the following two readings. The first one is from a college textbook and the second one is an editorial (an argumentative essay written for a newspaper). Follow the four summarizing steps listed above and include in-text and end-of-text citations. Use the APA style.

1. **The Ecological Capital of Brazil**
By Daniel Botkin and Edward Keller

1   In 1950, the city of Curitiba in Brazil had 300,000 inhabitants; but, by 1990 the population had grown to 2.3 million . . . making it the tenth largest city in Brazil. . . . The growth of Curitiba resulted primarily from migration of rural people displaced by mechanization of agriculture. The newcomers lived in squatter huts at the edge of the city in conditions of great poverty, poor sanitation, and frequent flooding caused by conversion of rivers and streams into artificial canals. By 1970, Curitiba was well on the way to becoming an example of environmental degradation and social decay. The story of how Curitiba turned itself from an urban disaster into a model of planning and sustainability by 1995 illustrates that cities can be designed in harmony with people and the environment.[1, 2]

2   Much of the credit for the transformation of Curitiba goes to its three-time mayor, Jaime Lerner, who believed a workable transportation system was the key to making Curitiba an integrated city where people could live as well as work. Rather than a more expensive underground rail system, Lerner spearheaded development of a bus system with five major axes, each containing lanes dedicated to express buses . . . with others carrying local traffic and high-speed automobile traffic. Forty-nine blocks of the historic center of Curitiba were reserved for pedestrians. Tubular bus stations were built in which passengers paid fares before boarding, an arrangement that avoids long delays caused by collecting fares after boarding. Circular routes and smaller feeder routes between the major axes maintain vital connections between the central city and outlying areas. As a result, more than 1.3 million passengers ride buses each day. Although Curitiba has the second highest per capita number of cars in Brazil, it uses 30 percent less gas than eight comparable Brazilian cities, and its air pollution is among the lowest in the country.[2, 3]

3   To solve its serious garbage problem, Curitiba required each household to sort recyclables from garbage. As a result, two-thirds of the garbage, more than 100 tons a day, is recycled, with 70 percent of the population participating. Where streets are too narrow to allow access by garbage trucks, residents are encouraged to bring garbage bags to the trucks. They are reimbursed with bus tokens, surplus food, or school notebooks.

---

[1]Dobbs, F. 1995. Dobbs, F. *Curitiba: City of the future?* Video. World Bank.

[2]Rabinovitch, J. 1997. *Integrated transportation and land use channel Curitiba's growth.* Washington, D.C.: World Resources Institute.

[3]Hunt, J. 1994 (April). Curitiba. *Metropolis Magazine.* (1994, April).

4   Through a low-cost housing program, 40,000 new homes were built, many placed so that residents have easy access to job sites. The city also embarked on a program to increase the amount of green space. Artificial drainage channels were replaced with natural drainage, reducing the need for expensive flood control. Some areas, including those around the river basins, were set aside for parks. In 1970, Curitiba had only 0.5 m² of green area per capita; by 1990, the area had increased to 50 m² for each inhabitant. The accomplishments of Curitiba have led some to call it the "ecological capital of Brazil" and to hope that it is also the "city of the future."[2, 4]

---

[4]Rabinovitch, J. & Leitman, J. (1996, March). Urban planning in Curitiba. *Scientific American*, pp. 45–53.

Botkin, D. B., & Keller, E. A. (2003). The ecological capital of Brazil. In *Environmental science: Earth as a living planet* (pp. 576–577). Hoboken, NJ: Wiley.

2.   **The Death of the World's Coral Reefs**
                              By Joshua Reichert

1   Bigger than anything ever built, Australia's Great Barrier Reef is about 92,000 square miles in size. Like all reefs, it's the product of trillions of tiny animals, no bigger than ants, building the reefs as they secrete limestone.

2   Generations of new corals grow on top of the skeletons of previous generations, building up the reefs at the rate of about 1 inch per year. Coral colonies can live for thousands of years, and at some Pacific atolls, the skeletons of dead coral stretch nearly a mile below the living reef.

3   One would think that creatures capable of such architectural feats would be impervious to human activity.

4   Yet, one quarter of the world's reefs have already been lost, and those remaining are under stress from pollution, sedimentation, destructive fishing practices, and global climate change.

5   Reefs have existed on Earth for millions of years, but unless strong action is taken to protect them, up to 70 percent of the world's shallow reefs could be gone in the next few decades.

6   The world's reefs are being threatened in a variety of ways. Each year, new coral diseases are identified which many scientists believe are linked to human activity.

7   Sediment, pesticides, and pollution from human activities damage coral reefs when transported by rivers into coastal waters. Excessive nutrients in seawater, caused by wastewater discharges from sources that include hotels and resorts, agriculture, golf courses, and sewage treatment plants, promote algal growth on coral, blocking sunlight and stunting coral growth.

8   In some parts of the world, destructive fishing practices, including the uses of sodium cyanide and explosives, are seriously damaging coral communities and the fish that live in them.

9   The biggest threat to the world's coral reefs, however, is global warming.

10   Reefs need the right balance of sunlight, temperature, nutrients, and salinity to survive. Most shallow water reefs exist within a narrow temperature range.

11 Increases of more than 3 degrees can have a devastating effect on these tiny organisms, causing them to expel the symbiotic microalgae that provide them with food. The corals turn white and eventually die—a process called bleaching.

12 Over the next century, the Earth's temperature is expected to rise by as much as 10.4 degrees Fahrenheit. This is more of an increase than has occurred since the last Ice Age. Many scientists believe that the resulting rise in ocean temperature will be fatal to many reefs.

13 Why should we care?

14 For one, because reefs harbor at least one quarter of all marine life. About 10 percent of the world's fisheries come from reefs, and much of this feeds protein-starved people in underdeveloped countries. Because they harbor so much biodiversity, reefs, like tropical rain forests, also offer excellent prospects for new medicines and natural compounds that can benefit humanity.

15 For example, Australian scientists have developed a highly effective sunscreen from substances that corals use to protect themselves from ultraviolet light.

16 The beauty of coral reefs draws millions of tourists each year, generating revenue for the countries where they are located, many of them impoverished.

17 Finally, reefs provide a natural seawall that protects many coastal populations from tides, storm surges, and hurricanes.

18 What can be done to save the world's coral reefs?

19 First, we must curb global warming. As the world's largest emitter of greenhouse gases, the United States must exercise leadership on this issue. . . .

20 Second, because the United States is the number one importer of coral-reef fish, Americans must ensure that tropical fish are collected in ecologically sound and sustainable ways.

21 Although the United States and many other countries forbid using cyanide and explosives to stun fish, these methods are still widely practiced in the South Pacific and Southeast Asia.

22 In 1997 the [U.S.] Senate passed a resolution to discourage these methods of collection, but stronger action, coordinated with other nations, is needed.

23 Like many of the planet's living creations, reefs can recover if given some encouragement. But unless action is taken soon, the next generation may never have the chance to experience firsthand one of the world's most marvelous feats of nature.

Reichert, J. (2001, July 20). The death of the world's coral reefs [Editorial]. *The San Francisco Chronicle*, p. A25.

STEP 5. **Follow up.** Now with a partner or small group, compare the parts of each article you identified as the main and supporting points, and tell how you found the main and supporting arguments in each reading. Finally, read your summaries to each other. If you do not agree on the main and supporting points, discuss this question with other classmates and your teacher.

Peer Review Form

Chapter 1—*Possessions*   **Descriptive Paragraph**

Writer: _____   Reader: _____

Read a classmate's paragraph and answer each of these questions.

1. Did the writer use correct paragraph form as shown on p. 12?   ❑ Yes   ❑ No

2. Does the paragraph have a topic sentence?   ❑ Yes   ❑ No

3. Does the paragraph contain enough information to support the topic sentence?   ❑ Yes   ❑ No

4. Does the paragraph include sensory details about how the possession looks, feels, or sounds?   ❑ Yes   ❑ No

   Write the sentence that contains the best sensory information.

   _____

   _____

5. Do you think the writer used adjectives and noun modifiers effectively?   ❑ Yes   ❑ No

   Write the phrase that shows the best use of adjectives and noun modifiers.

   _____

PEER REVIEW FORM
Chapter 2—*Changes*   **Narrative Paragraph**

Writer: _____   Reader: _____

Read a classmate's paragraph and answer each of these questions.

1. What is the main point of the narration? Write it here. _____

   _____

   _____

   Is the main point expressed clearly at the beginning of the paragraph?   ❑ Yes   ❑ No

2. Did the writer include background information?   ❑ Yes   ❑ No

   If so, what questions does it answer? _____

   _____

3. Look at the writer's use of specific details and explanations. Did the writer
   include information about sight, sound, smell, touch, or taste in the paper? ❑ Yes   ❑ No

   Is there any point that you would like the writer to explain or describe in
   greater detail?   ❑ Yes   ❑ No

   If yes, write some focused questions to help the writer. _____

   _____

4. Are all the details in the paragraph linked to the main point?   ❑ Yes   ❑ No

   If not, what details should be omitted? _____

   _____

5. Did the writer use dialogue?   ❑ Yes   ❑ No

   If yes, does the dialogue give you information about the characters or the main
   point of the story?   ❑ Yes   ❑ No

   Explain. _____

   _____

6. Did the writer use time signals and correct verb tense to guide you through
   the narrative?   ❑ Yes   ❑ No

   Write two of the time signals (words, phrases, or clauses) that helped you follow the narration.

   _____

7. Does the paragraph have a concluding sentence?   ❑ Yes   ❑ No

PEER REVIEW FORM

Chapter 3—*Memory*   **Expository Paragraph**

Writer: _____   Reader: _____

Read a classmate's paragraph and answer each of these questions.

1. Does the paragraph have three levels?   ❏ Yes   ❏ No

2. Is the main idea stated in the topic sentence?   ❏ Yes   ❏ No

   Write the controlling idea of the topic sentence. _____

   _____

3. Does the paragraph contain supporting points that are clearly presented
   in sentences?   ❏ Yes   ❏ No

   How many supporting points are there? _____

4. Did the writer use transitions when necessary to mark the supporting points?   ❏ Yes   ❏ No

   If so, write down two transitions the writer used. _____

5. Did the writer use examples to develop the supporting points?   ❏ Yes   ❏ No

   Are the examples specific enough?   ❏ Yes   ❏ No

   If you would like more detailed examples, write questions to guide the writer. _____

   _____

   _____

6. Does the paragraph contain sentences with subordinating conjunctions?   ❏ Yes   ❏ No

   If yes, write down two subordinating conjunctions the writer used. _____

   _____

7. Does the paragraph have a concluding sentence?   ❏ Yes   ❏ No

PEER REVIEW FORM

Chapter 4—*Culture, Identity, and Homeland*   **Simple Division Essay**

Writer: _____   Reader: _____

Read a classmate's essay and answer each of these questions.

1. What is the writer's thesis? Write it here. _____

   _____

   Does the thesis statement make clear that the writer will analyze the topic
   by logical division?   ❏ Yes   ❏ No

   Does the thesis reveal the basis of division (time, place, aspects, etc.)?   ❏ Yes   ❏ No

   What is the basis of division? _____

2. Do the thesis statement and the topic sentences of the body paragraphs clearly
   name the parts of the topic?   ❏ Yes   ❏ No

   If not, explain. _____

   _____

3. Does the essay have cohesion?   ❏ Yes   ❏ No

   If so, what repeated words, synonyms, or transition words did the writer use to link the thesis
   statement to the topic sentences of the body paragraphs? _____

   _____

4. Do any of the body paragraphs need more development (examples or explanation)? ❏ Yes   ❏ No

   If yes, which one(s)? _____

   If you have any questions that will help the writer expand the body paragraphs, write them here.

   _____

   _____

   _____

5. Did the writer use adjective clauses to include additional information in the
   sentences?   ❏ Yes   ❏ No

   If not, can you suggest which sentence(s) the writer could add an adjective clause to? Write the first
   three words of that sentence or those sentences. _____

   _____

PEER REVIEW FORM

Chapter 5—*Full Pockets, Empty Pockets*　　　　　　　　**Cause-and-Effect Essay**

Writer: _____　　　　Reader: _____

Read a classmate's essay and answer each of these questions.

1. What is the writer's thesis? _____

_____

_____

　　Does the thesis make clear whether the essay will focus on causes or effects?　❏ Yes　❏ No

2. What introduction strategy or strategies (general statement, background, anecdote) did the writer use? _____

　　Do you think this strategy or these strategies are effective in this essay?　❏ Yes　❏ No

　　Why or why not? _____

_____

3. Do the topic sentences of the body paragraphs clearly state the supporting points?　❏ Yes　❏ No

　　How many supporting points are there? _____

4. Are the supporting points organized according to time order or order of importance?　❏ Yes　❏ No

　　If no, do you think the writer should use time order or order of importance?　❏ Yes　❏ No

　　If yes, explain. _____

_____

5. Are the body paragraphs sufficiently developed?　❏ Yes　❏ No

　　If no, write some questions that will help the writer expand the body paragraphs.

_____

_____

6. Which sentence(s), in your view, show the best use of cause-and-effect signals? _____

_____

_____

7. What strategy or strategies (summary, suggestion, prediction, opinion) did the writer use in the conclusion? _____

　　Does the conclusion give you the sense that the essay is complete?　❏ Yes　❏ No

　　Why or why not? _____

_____

PEER REVIEW FORM

Chapter 6—*Marriage and Family*   **Comparison/Contrast Essay**

Writer: _____   Reader: _____

Read a classmate's essay and answer each of these questions.

1. What two things is the writer comparing? _____
_____

2. Does the paper discuss differences only, similarities only, or both similarities and differences?
_____

   If it addresses both, which did the writer emphasize, and how do you know? _____
_____

3. What kind of organization does the essay have (side-by-side or point-by point)?
_____

4. Are the points of comparison named in the thesis statement?   ❏ Yes   ❏ No

   What are the points of comparison? _____
_____

5. Does the essay have balanced development? That is, are the two things being compared
   equally well-developed, and are the points of comparison equally well-developed?   ❏ Yes   ❏ No

   If you would like to see more development in some part of the essay, write some questions to guide
   the writer. _____
_____
_____

6. Did the writer use comparison/contrast signals effectively?   ❏ Yes   ❏ No

   Write the first three words of a sentence that contains a good use of comparison/contrast signals.
_____

7. Does the essay have cohesion?   ❏ Yes   ❏ No

   Check (✓) the strategies the writer used to link the thesis statement to the topic sentences of the
   body paragraphs.

   _____ repeated words   _____ similar sentence beginnings

   _____ transitions   _____ correlative conjunctions (not only . . . but also)

   _____ word forms

PEER REVIEW FORM

Chapter 7—*Teamwork*   **Classification**

Writer: _____   Reader: _____

Read a classmate's essay and answer each of these questions.

1. Does the thesis statement identify the class, basis of classification, and categories?   ❏ Yes   ❏ No

   What is the basis of classification? _____

2. Does the thesis contain any qualifiers?   ❏ Yes   ❏ No

   If so, what are they? _____

3. Does the essay have one body paragraph for every category?   ❏ Yes   ❏ No

4. Check (✓) the development strategies the writer used in the body paragraphs.

   _____ description   _____ cause and effect

   _____ narration   _____ comparison/contrast

   _____ example   _____ classification

   _____ logical division   _____ process

5. Are the body paragraphs developed in a balanced way?   ❏ Yes   ❏ No

   If not, which body paragraph should be developed more? _____

6. Are the body paragraphs cohesive?   ❏ Yes   ❏ No

   If not, where would you recommend that the writer add signals of cohesion (repeated words and phrases, synonyms, word forms, logical connectors, time phrases, and pronouns and possessive adjectives)? _____

   _____

7. What is the overall point of view of the essay (first, second, or third person and singular or plural)?

   _____

   Is there a problem with the point of view in the essay?   ❏ Yes   ❏ No

   If yes, explain. _____

   _____

8. Did the writer use any direct quotations or paraphrases from outside sources?   ❏ Yes   ❏ No

   If yes, do the quotes or paraphrases effectively support the points the writer is trying to make in the essay?   ❏ Yes   ❏ No

Peer Review Form

Chapter 8—*The Science of Everyday Life*   **Definition Paragraph or Essay**

Writer: _____   Reader: _____

Read a classmate's paragraph or essay and answer each of these questions.

1. Is there a one-sentence definition near the beginning of the paper?   ❏ Yes   ❏ No

   If so, what kind of definition is it (synonym, negative statement, comparison, or classification)?

   _____

2. Check (✔) the development strategies the writer used in the body of the paragraph or essay to develop the definition.

   _____ origin of the word   _____ logical division or classification

   _____ negation   _____ cause and effect

   _____ description   _____ comparison/contrast

   _____ narration   _____ process

   _____ example

   Would you have chosen the same strategies?   ❏ Yes   ❏ No

   If no, explain _____

   _____

3. Do you think the organization of the definition is effective?   ❏ Yes   ❏ No

   Does the most essential information come first?   ❏ Yes   ❏ No

   Would you have organized the paper differently?   ❏ Yes   ❏ No

   If yes, explain. _____

   _____

4. Is the paragraph or essay written cohesively?   ❏ Yes   ❏ No

   If no, where do you think the cohesion should be improved? _____

   _____

5. Is there any redundancy in the paper?   ❏ Yes   ❏ No

   If yes, write the first three words of the sentence(s) that contains redundant words or phrases.

   _____

6. Did the writer cite any outside sources in the paper?   ❏ Yes   ❏ No

   If yes, do you think that the use of sources is effective?   ❏ Yes   ❏ No

   Explain. _____

   _____

Peer Review Form

Chapter 9—*From School to Work*   **Argumentative Essay**

Writer: _____   Reader: _____

Read a classmate's essay and answer each of these questions.

1. Does the introduction engage your interest in the topic?   ❏ Yes   ❏ No

   Would you have used a different introduction strategy (general statement, background, anecdote, definition, quotation, turnabout)? _____

   _____

2. Does the introduction define and limit the topic?   ❏ Yes   ❏ No

   If not, what would you like it to define, or how would you like the topic to be limited? _____

   _____

3. How many supporting arguments did the writer include? _____

   Did the writer use transitions to link the supporting arguments and provide cohesion?   ❏ Yes   ❏ No

4. Are the supporting arguments developed in a balanced way?   ❏ Yes   ❏ No

   Check (✓) the development strategies the writer used.

   _____ the ideas of authorities   _____ examples

   _____ facts   _____ cause and effect reasoning

   _____ explanation   _____ comparison

   In your opinion, which body paragraph contains the most persuasive or the best developed supporting argument? _____

5. Did the writer include an opposing point of view?   ❏ Yes   ❏ No

   If yes, in what part of the essay does the opposing view appear? _____

   Did the writer respond to the opposing view effectively?   ❏ Yes   ❏ No

   If you would have responded to the opposing view differently, explain. _____

   _____

6. Did the writer use any qualifiers in the essay?   ❏ Yes   ❏ No

   Do you think the use of qualifiers is effective?   ❏ Yes   ❏ No

   Explain. _____

   _____

7. Did the writer use outside sources?   ❏ Yes   ❏ No

   If yes, did the writer include both in-text and end-of-text citations?   ❏ Yes   ❏ No

INDEX

adjective clauses, 95–96, 261–266
adjectives, 21, 267
  as nouns, 106
  participial, 107, 268–269
adverb (adverbial) clauses, 42–43, 270–275
adverb (adverbial) phrases, 42
adverbs, 275–277
  of manner, 30
  of time, 42
agreement of subjects and verbs, 264, 299–301
anecdotes in essay introductions, 117
another, 294–295
antonyms, 107
APA (American Psychological Association), 189, 320–322
apostrophe, 312
articles, 277–280
audience, 2
authority, 237

background
  in essay introductions, 117
  in narration, 34–35
balanced development in comparison/contrast essays, 155
basis of classification, 173–174
basis of division, 81–82
brainstorming, 9

capital letters, 313–314
categories, 19, 55, 59–60, 173–174
cause and effect, 109
  clusters, 113
  vocabulary of, 126–131
citations, 177, 189, 220–221, 320–324
classification, 173–174
  in definitions, 207
cohesion, 91
  and pronouns, 215
  and transitions, 121, 156–157
  in essays, 91, 156–158
  in body paragraphs, 185
colon, 314–315
comma, 315–316
  with adjective clauses, 263–264
comparison, 144
  in definitions, 207
comparatives, 280–281
comparison/contrast, 144
  vocabulary of, 161–162

compound nouns, 171
concession, 253–254
conclusions
  for essays, 123–124
  for paragraphs, 41, 72
conditionals, 274–275
contractions, 312
contrast, 144
controlling ideas, 63, 88–89
  in comparison/contrast essays, 152–153
coordinating conjunctions, 22
  of cause and effect, 128–129, 130
coordination, 282–285
correlative conjunctions, 158, 285

dash, 316
definition, 206–210
  in argumentative essays, 241
details, 6
development in essays, 93–94
dialogue
  in narration, 40–41
drawing conclusions, 6

ellipses in quotations, 190
ellipsis, 286
  and redundancy, 217
end-of-text citations, 320, 321–322
essays
  argumentative, 241–256
  cause and effect, 109–125
  classification, 173–189
  cohesion in, 91, 121, 156–158
  comparison/contrast, 144–160
  conclusions, 123–124
  definition, 206, 213–214
  expanding paragraphs to, 85–88
  introductions, 116–117, 150–151, 249
    logical division, 87–95
examples
  in three-level paragraphs, 55–56, 67
  in essays, 93
explanation in essays, 93–94
expository writing, 55

first draft, 11
focusing, 9–10
for example, 69